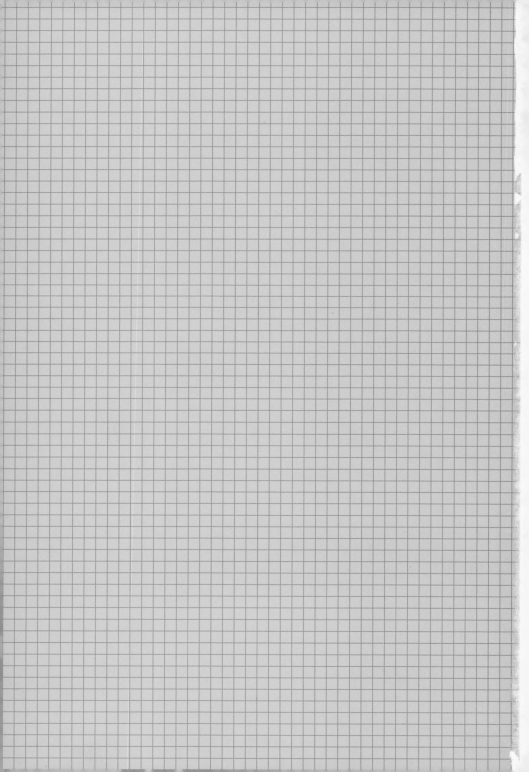

DOLLARS AND SEX

HOW ECONOMICS INFLUENCES SEX AND LOVE

DR. MARINA ADSHADE

Baker College of Clinton Twp Library

CHRONICLE BOOKS

SAN FRANCISCO

Library of Congress Cataloging-in-Publication Data:
Adshade, Marina.
   Dollars and sex : how economics influences sex and love / by Marina Adshade.
       p. cm.
   Includes bibliographical references.
   ISBN 978-1-4521-0922-0
1. Interpersonal relations—Economic aspects. 2. Sex—Economic aspects.
3. Mate selection—Economic aspects. I. Title.

   HM1106.A334 2013
   306.7—dc23

                          2012031593

Manufactured in China

Designed by Allison Weiner
Cover illustration by Arthur Mount
Typesetting by DC Typography

10 9 8 7 6 5 4 3 2 1

Chronicle Books LLC
680 Second Street
San Francisco, California 94107
www.chroniclebooks.com

CONTENTS

INTRODUCTION

HAVE YOU EVER WONDERED if national well-being is higher in countries in which men have larger penises than in those in which men are less well-endowed? Or, more to the point, does it surprise you to learn that upon discovering the "Global Penile Length Distribution Map" that an economist started looking around for an economic question that the data might answer?

Economics is called the dismal science, but it didn't earn that moniker because economists failed to predict the most recent global recession or, for that matter, pretty much every recession in history. It is because erstwhile economist-cum–parish priest Thomas Malthus, at the end of the eighteenth century, predicted that as long as British peasant women couldn't keep their knees together there was no hope for society to prosper.

When it comes to sex, Malthus, admittedly, was a bit of a downer. But not all economists take such a dismal view of what is one of life's sweetest pleasures. In the past ten years, in particular, there has been a frenzy of research activity as academics have eagerly used economic theory and data in exploration of matters of the heart—and other body parts.

The resulting body of literature is a collection of theories and evidence that would give anyone, frankly, a hard-on for economics.

Which was exactly the reaction I was looking for when four years ago it occurred to me that talking about sex and love could be a terrific way to get my university students excited about the prospect of learning economics.

Over time I came to realize that what started out as a fun collection of topics designed to help my students understand the way that markets operate was evolving into a completely novel way for them to understand their place on the market for sex and love. They began to appreciate the way in which economics influences their mating behavior and to apply the concepts we covered in class to their own lives.

It wasn't just my students' perspective that was changing. Once I started exploring ways to apply economic reasoning to issues of sex and love, I came to realize how much clarity viewing the world through an economist's lens affords me when thinking about more intimate matters in my own life.

Let me give you a brief, personal, example.

I had never really thought that online dating sites were a good place for me to look for a mate (for reasons that I will talk about later). But then I started to think about the difference between thick and thin markets. Markets that are thin have few participants, making it difficult for buyers and sellers to settle on a price at which they both want to trade. Markets that are thick, however, have many participants, meaning that it is possible to settle on a price at which both buyer and seller are willing to trade.

Online dating sites really are thick markets. If I interpret the "price" at which I am willing to trade, as both buyer and seller on this market, in terms of meeting a man who is the best possible match for me, while at the same time I am the best possible match for him, then it actually makes sense for me to search online for a relationship. It's not because it is easier (in many ways it is not) but because in a thicker market it should be possible for me to find a man with whom to have a higher-quality relationship.

That is my theory, at least; I have yet to test it.

I argue that almost every option, every decision, and every outcome in matters of sex and love is better understood by thinking within an economic framework. In fact, I would go further than that and say that without taking into consideration economic forces, our understanding of the world around us is incomplete. That is as true when we are trying to decide if we believe the government should subsidize access to birth control as it is when we are trying to decide if we believe that the government should bail out big business. It is as true when we are assessing the costs of being personally promiscuous as it is when assessing the costs of spending one more year of our lives in school. And it is as true when we are choosing whether or not we want to risk having sex outside of our marriage as it is when we are choosing whether or not we want to risk putting our savings into the stock market.

Dollars and Sex is a collection of different styles of stories that illustrates the way in which economic theory can complete our understanding of sexual relationships in today's world. Some are short stories, scattered throughout the book, that illustrate how economic forces can influence an individual's sexual behavior (all are true, to some degree, with the names changed to protect the sometimes less-than-innocent). Some are stories told with data. Statistics have the power to reveal the choices of, literally, thousands of men and women in a way that satisfies the economic desire to find measurable relationships between particular situations and the decisions that people in those situations make. Finally, there are the stories that give us a framework for understanding the decisions we all make at some points in our lives. Those are the stories told by the economic theories that are used to model the markets for sex and love.

The book is organized in three acts, each representing a different stage of our lives, with each act broken down into three chapters.

In act I, I consider the lives of those who are young, wild, and free. Revolutions are often started for economic reasons, and the Sexual Revolution was no different; the liberalization of sexual values over the second half of the twentieth century is an economic story in which individuals have weighed the cost of premarital sex against the benefits and decided that the answer to the question "Should I have sex tonight?" is "Why not?" One group that has embraced this liberalized view of sexuality with enthusiasm is college students, but their market for sex and love is not necessarily in equilibrium. Now that female students outnumber male students, there is more casual sex on college campuses and traditional dating has gone the way of the dinosaurs. Speaking of the end of traditional dating, the final chapter in act I is about the online market for sex and love; on behalf of the economics profession, I would like to take this opportunity to thank you for participating in this massive data-collection exercise that has helped us understand how men and women everywhere search for love.

Most of us eventually reach a stage of our lives when we feel that the person who has been leaving a toothbrush at our place for months really should stay a little longer, which brings us to act II. In marriage, as in life, we don't always get what we want, but hopefully we have set our reservation value for a mate high enough and have sufficient opportunities to exploit the gains from trade within marriage, that we get what we need (romantic, I know; wait until you see my idea for economic wedding vows!). Marriage is not always the union between one man and one woman; there are alternatives to that arrangement, and economic factors have played a big role in influencing which arrangements are legally, and socially, acceptable. The final chapter in act II is about the way in which couples decide whose turn it is to be on top. Okay, that is a bit of an oversimplification, but we will talk about bargaining within marriage because, as everyone who has been married knows, the negotiations don't stop just because the marriage contract has been signed.

Inevitably, we reach act III. In this stage of our lives, our children are growing up and having sex lives of their own. Some school systems take a multidisciplinary approach to sex education; after reading the first chapter in act III, I think you will agree that economics should be included on the list of classes in which sexual behavior is discussed. I will also tell you an economic story about the people who weigh the costs of extramarital sex against the benefits and decide, sometimes with and sometimes without the knowledge of their partner, that the answer to the question "Should I have sex outside my marriage?" is "Why not?"—even if they regret that decision later. And finally, as the sun sets over the horizon, we will talk about the fastest-growing market for sex and love—the market in which men and women are hooking up, and sometimes settling down, in the second half of their lives.

Here are a few things to keep in mind as you read through *Dollars and Sex*.

The first is that empirical evidence, the stories that are told to us by the data, and economic theories are not intended to describe the behavior of everyone in society but rather the behavior of people on average. Human behavior is complex, and ultimately the choices we all make are a function of our individual preferences. As an example, the evidence suggests that, on average, women have strong preferences to date men who share their ethnic background. You might read that evidence and think that it isn't true because that is not your preference. That response is inevitable because, in reality, there is a distribution of preferences between those women who would never date outside of their ethnicity and those women who would never date within it. What this observation means is that the midpoint on this distribution lies closer to the side in which women prefer to date within their ethnicity than to the side in which women prefer to date outside their ethnicity. That is the average preference, and while it may not be true for you, it can still help you understand the behavior of others.

This brings me to my second point, and that is that none of the evidence in this book comes from public opinion polls. Economists are interested in the choices individuals actually make, not the choices individuals say they would make when given options. We put our faith in a concept called *revealed preference* to tell people's stories; we observe the decisions that they make and infer their preferences from that information. So, for example, we don't ask women how they feel about dating men who are of different ethnicities from themselves. If we did, most women, for obvious reasons, would feel compelled to say that they have no same-race preference. Instead we use data collected from online dating sites or speed-dating events to see the type of men that women choose to meet. The observation that women more often than not express interest in meeting men of their same ethnicity reveals to us that this is the preference of the average woman.

The third point is that our discussion here will focus exclusively on how people actually behave rather than on how people *should* behave. I want to make it clear from the beginning that I have no interest in talking about "good" and "bad" or "right" and "wrong" behavior, either from the perspective of the individual or from that of the society at large. It is not that I don't think that those conversations are important, but, as an economist, it is not my job to judge people based on their behavior.

Oh, and before we begin, you probably want to know the answer to the question I posed at the beginning of this introduction. The answer is yes and no—when it comes to penis size and economic well-being, all the action is in the tails of the distribution, so to speak. Countries in which the average penis size is small tend to be worse off. As penises get bigger, however, national incomes increase but only up until a certain point, after which bigger penises are associated with smaller national incomes. Countries in which penises are large, on average, tend to be worse off, although not necessarily on every dimension (clearly). I like to call this relationship the Boner Curve. I wouldn't put too much stock in these results, though as far as (economic) models go; it is pretty easy to get this one to give you what you are looking for.[1]

---

1 These results are based on a paper written by a courageous doctoral student at the University of Helsinki, Tatu Westling.

CHAPTER 1
LOVE THE ONE YOU'RE WITH

▨▨▨▨▨ **CASANOVA USED LEMONS AS CONTRACEPTIVES**

It's 2003, and this is what the keynote speaker, an eminent macroeconomist from the University of Pennsylvania, has just said: "Casanova used lemons as contraceptives." The lunch crowd, a group of attentive economists, is now wide-eyed. While 95 percent of the room (the men) wonder "How the hell does that work?" the other 5 percent of the room (the women) think "Ouch!" I, a member of the latter group, note for future reference the effect of weird sexual facts on audience engagement.

Casanova's seductive behavior aside, the speaker is making a very good point: The liberalization of sexual values during the twentieth century is an economic story. In this case, the Penn economist is arguing that new technologies, in the form of effective contraceptives, have shaken the great cost-benefit analysis of, well, coitus. The analysis, conducted by millions of women and men each day, goes like this: "Should I have sex tonight, or not?"

This new "technology," along with changes in education and equality, has completely transformed the sexual landscape. If you doubt that it is economic factors that have been at play in the transition to a more promiscuous society, consider the following evidence:

- In 1900, only 6 percent of unmarried 19-year-old women were sexually active compared with 75 percent of unmarried 19-year-old women a century later.
- Contraceptive technology has become increasingly effective at preventing pregnancy over the last half century, and yet the number of births to unmarried women has increased from 5 percent to 41 percent over the same period.
- Despite this trend toward a greater number of births outside of marriage, 66 percent of Americans still believe that out-of-wedlock births are bad for society.
- Premarital sex is strongly tied to family income; girls who live in the poorest households are 50 percent more likely to be sexually active than are girls in the richest households.
- Premarital sex may have become the norm, but it has not become completely destigmatized; only 48 percent of women and 55 percent of men under the age of 35 think that premarital sex is not morally wrong.
- Attitudes toward teen pregnancy are tied to family income; 68 percent of girls in higher-income households report that they would be "very upset" by a pregnancy compared with 46 percent of girls in lower-income households.
- Marriage is increasingly a privilege enjoyed by the rich; in the 1960s, almost equal shares of people with college degrees and people with only a high school education were married (76 percent and 72 percent). Today the marriage rate of less-educated people has fallen to 48 percent while that of college-educated people has stayed relatively high at 64 percent.
- According to the Pew Research Center, young adults in the 19-to-29-year-old age range, more than any other generation, don't see the point of marriage, with 44 percent reporting that the institution is obsolete and with only 30 percent agreeing with the statement "Having a successful marriage is one of the most important things in life."

To illustrate how these behaviors and beliefs have come together to transform our sexual landscape, let me begin with a tale of a woman who has lived her life in three parts.

This is the story of Jane who, at the age of 17, ran away from home. Up to that point, Jane had been a good student in an all-girls boarding school. It was not really the type of school that a student leaves to work as a hotel chambermaid and live in a seedy building in an underprivileged neighborhood. But while every other girl in her class went off to university (in search of husbands and degrees), Jane chose another path.

In the year that Jane lived this way, she spent her time with female companions whose perspective on life was very different from hers. Unlike her, they had grown up in poverty. Some were sex workers, having entered the trade in their early teens, following the path of their sex-worker mothers. A few had migrated from different parts of the country to be near their boyfriends, who were incarcerated locally. Others had fallen off the precipice at a very early age and had never been able to climb their way back up.

As it turns out, Jane's friends (even the ones who were not sex workers) were extremely promiscuous; they had sexual relations with a variety of men, some of whom treated them well and others who did not. Their promiscuity was not the result of a lack of moral fortitude. The economic forces at work made it so their answer to "Should I have sex with him tonight?" was almost always "Why not?"

What are those economic forces?

Well, first of all, education. Starting in the early 1980s and up to the present, workers hoping to be economically successful have needed a college education. This has been true not only because educated workers' earnings are climbing, but also because the wages of workers with lowest education levels are falling. In fact, Jane's one year in the ghetto was near the beginning of a thirty-year decline in real earnings for those with a high school education or less, a decline that would turn the gap between educated and noneducated worker's wages from a narrow crack to a yawning fissure.

While these women may have not known that their earning opportunities were becoming increasingly limited due to their lack of education, there was a second economic factor that they were painfully aware of: The marriage prospects of underprivileged women had become bleak. Incarceration rates were on the rise and, in fact, no less than three of Jane's friends had boyfriends who were in prison. Even without a criminal record, the lifetime earning prospects for low-income men were insufficient to make sustaining a family possible. In a time in which more successful men started to seek out wives who would make equal contributions to the household income, higher-income men were out of reach as a possible marriage partner for uneducated and underemployed women.

So, while most women might have feared that promiscuity would affect their lifetime earnings and their prospects for marriage, Jane's new friends figured they had little to look forward to, regardless of their sexual histories. They lived in a culture of despair where a mistimed pregnancy or "fast" reputation made very little difference to their standard of living—then and into the future.

And so, the answer to "Should I sleep with him tonight?" was fated. "Yes, why not?" They really had nothing to lose.

Part two of Jane's story begins with a particularly frightening confrontation with a local pimp who had been trying to recruit her. This was about the same time Jane realized that her decision to diverge from the traditional path might have serious repercussions. So, Jane grabbed her purse (and nothing else) and headed to the airport where a kind airline representative took pity on her, handed her a ticket, and allowed her to fly across the country to a sister who gave her both shelter and a second chance.

We will return to the details of that stage of Jane's life in chapter 6, but right now I want to skip to the third part of Jane's life. This is the stage of her life in which she finds herself, coincidentally, sitting in the same lunchtime seminar as I am, wondering how lemons make good contraceptives.

The days of waking up to find her roommate's latest conquest passed out on the living room floor are far behind Jane. While she is now unmarried, divorced in fact, and is parenting a young child with another baby on the way, she is also educated and independent, having recently started a PhD program at a prestigious university.[2] The same Jane who had once found herself flailing alongside disenfranchised and promiscuous women was now marching with a generation of highly educated, and (as it turns out) fairly promiscuous twenty-somethings, women on the way up the economic ladder.

Jane's new academic friends are among those who have benefited from the growing wage gap, earning far more than educated women, or men, did in the past. Not only are they part of a new generation of highly educated women, they are part of the first generation of women who are more educated, on average, than are men. Finding a husband who is as—or more—educated has become more difficult as all women now compete for relatively few educated men.

Jane's new friends, always on the prowl for the perfect (i.e., educated and high-income) male, are also quite promiscuous. They are perhaps not as promiscuous as the women in the first stage of Jane's life, but they are far more promiscuous than previous generations of women. Their promiscuity is not the result of a lack of moral fortitude, again, but rather because in the great cost-benefit analysis, there are few compelling reasons to say no.

The reason for this decision is simple: there are few ill effects of promiscuity for these women. Jane's female peers know how to avoid pregnancy and disease, and they've got the bargaining power within their relationships to insist that protection is consistently applied. Should the promiscuity result in a mistimed pregnancy, well, they have the both means to care for the child alone or to terminate the pregnancy.

Most important though, these women do not face the shame and persecution their mothers and grandmothers would have experienced had they given birth outside of marriage, and, as a result, they face none of those costs.

---

2 Once, while I was working as a research assistant (coincidentally for the same eminent economist who is now giving the Casanova talk), I had the opportunity to look to the U.S. Census to see how many woman had both given birth as a single parent and completed a PhD. You can probably guess the answer—not one.

WHY WE'VE HAD TO WAIT FOR MALE BIRTH CONTROL

Scientists may argue that it is harder to control a billion sperm than it is to control a single egg, but there is an economic reason for why male birth control (MBC) has taken so long to arrive, and it can be described with two words: supply and demand.

The cost of an unplanned pregnancy for a man is much lower than it is for a woman, even when we ignore biological costs. A mistimed pregnancy often leads to underinvestment in a woman's education and wage penalties that can reduce her lifetime income. Some men may have a similar experience, but a career disruption for a man who unexpectedly becomes a father is generally much less costly than for a woman.

Over time, two things have happened that have increased the demand, and the price men would be willing to pay, for protection from accidental pregnancy.

The first is that men who, postconception, would rather opt out of the family plan altogether, are having a harder time doing so as governments have become more effective at forcing men to assume a portion of the economic costs of having a child.

The second is that women are working more and couples are desiring fewer children. Not only does time in the workforce by women increase the overall demand for birth control, but it also puts women in a better position to negotiate away the responsibility for birth control to their husbands.

Will men actually use MBC? A couple of studies have pretended to answer this question, but there is a big difference between asking men to respond to the question "Would you use MBC if it were available?" and asking them

"Would you be willing to pay $300 every three months to have drugs injected into your balls?" So I would say the jury is still out on that question.

The drug companies seem to now be investing in MBC, so they must feel there is sufficient evidence of demand. Cynical me wonders if these same drug companies are really hoping to make a return on their investment through the sales of sexually transmitted disease (STD) treatments. This could be a winning strategy, since it is likely that MBC will reduce women's ability to insist upon condom use during sex. If that is the case, then there are profits to be made on both ends of the market, so to speak.

This, coincidentally, brings us back to Casanova and his lemons.

A BRIEF HISTORY OF BIRTH CONTROL TECHNOLOGY

It is a common misconception that birthrates within marriage began to fall only when the birth control pill became available in the 1960s. In truth, birthrates began to fall right after the onset of the Industrial Revolution over two hundred years ago as couples chose to have fewer children in response to higher wages for skilled workers (we will return to this later). Oral contraceptives may have made it easier for women to control the timing of their births, but women have found ways to control their fertility for centuries.

In the United States, for example, the average woman in 1800 had given birth to seven babies by the time she turned 40. That number fell every decade in the nineteenth century and right up until the end of the 1930s, when the average woman had given birth to only two children. So, thirty years before the pill was available on the market, birthrates had already fallen to today's low level.

Throughout most of human history, the only way to have sex and avoid pregnancy was coitus interruptus—a.k.a. withdrawal. Marrying later in life also helped to reduce a woman's childbearing years (in a time in which extramarital childbearing was virtually unheard of) and was actively promoted by Thomas Malthus, whom I mention in the Introduction. High rates of spinsterhood also helped to lower average birthrates (and, in fact, the main contributor to the increase in children during the baby boom was not families that had four or five children, but rather the increase in women who had just one child rather than none at all). Anal sex and nonejaculation were also used to control fertility but apparently were techniques more commonly used by sex workers.

Condom use appears to go back three thousand years, but the first really useful technology to control pregnancy was the cervical cap, introduced around 1838. As we have already heard, Casanova (who lived from 1725 to 1798) had a similar idea, using lemons as a barrier, but that didn't appear to catch on to any degree (perhaps because only a man as charming as Casanova could convince a woman to insert half of a lemon into her vagina).

In the 1850s, Charles Goodyear learned how to vulcanize rubber, making possible the production of condoms that were more comfortable, fairly inexpensive, and effective at preventing pregnancy. At roughly $34 per dozen (measured relative to today's real wages), they were still expensive for frequent usage by the average worker; they were so expensive, in fact, that it was common for men to wash and reuse them.

Diaphragms became available in 1882, followed by the intrauterine device (IUD) in 1909. Latex condoms were produced in 1912, making them, thankfully, disposable and much cheaper.

▨▨▨▨ SO, THE PILL IS RESPONSIBLE FOR INCREASED PROMISCUITY, RIGHT?

It seems that ever since women could predictably control their fertility, more and more women have been deciding that the benefits of having premarital sex outweigh the costs. It would be easy to argue that the availability of contraceptives, particularly the availability of the birth control pill, is directly responsible for this change in behavior if there weren't a confounding factor: if women are simply having more sex now because it is less risky to do so, then why have out-of-marriage pregnancies increased over the same period when contraceptives have been improving?

Improvements in birth control technology are a decrease in the "cost" of promiscuity in the *probabilistic sense*. In economic thinking, the cost of premarital sex is determined by the probability that a woman will become pregnant and/or contract a disease multiplied by the costs associated with pregnancy and/or disease. So any factor that decreases either the costs or the risk will decrease the *expected costs* of premarital sex.

For example, imagine that it is 1930 and there is an 85 percent chance that a woman will become pregnant while repeatedly having unprotected sex with a man who is not her husband. Also imagine that if this woman becomes pregnant she loses the opportunity to marry a man with a good income (since she now carries the stigma of having borne an illegitimate child), and that as a result of this lost opportunity, she misses out on $50,000 in future income that she would have gained had she not become pregnant and married a man with a good income instead. Her cost of premarital sex without protection, then, is:

PROBABILITY OF PREGNANCY		FORGONE INCOME FROM MARRIAGE		EXPECTED COST OF PROMISCUITY
0.85	**X**	**$50,000**	**=**	**$42,500**

Now instead imagine that latex condoms are available and she is able to convince her partner to use one when they have sex. If the chance of becoming pregnant is 45 percent with a latex condom, which was actually the failure rate of condoms in 1934 (reported by Kopp), then now the expected cost of premarital sex is:

$$0.45 \times \$50,000 = \$22,500$$

Giving her the option of sex with a condom has reduced the cost of premarital sex by $20,000.

Any economist will tell you that the quantity demanded of a good or service will increase when the price falls, which is why a standard demand curve is downward sloping when drawn on a graph with quantity on the horizontal axis and price on the vertical axis. So, it isn't that surprising that when contraceptives became more effective at reducing pregnancy and disease, more women (and men, of course) chose to have sex before marriage. And, of course, some of these women will still become pregnant because even with contraceptives the risk of pregnancy has not dropped to zero. In fact, statistically speaking, 45 percent of sexually active women will become pregnant.

Despite improvements in contraceptive technology, the number of pregnancies to women who are not married has not fallen; it has increased dramatically, which suggests that there has to be more to this promiscuity story than individual women making rational choices to have premarital sex based on the efficiency of contraceptive technology.

To understand what has happened, consider a very simple model in which there are two distinct groups of unmarried people who are reluctant to participate in premarital sex in a society in which sex outside of marriage is very much frowned upon. The people in the first group avoid premarital sex because they are worried about unplanned pregnancy but not because of the stigmatization of premarital sex. In the second group, the people avoid premarital sex because they are worried about the stigmatization of premarital sex but not about an unplanned pregnancy. Of course, in reality, everyone will worry a little bit about both pregnancy and stigmatization, but this distinction into groups will make clearer the following explanation as to how attitudes have changed.

Now let's introduce effective birth control to these two groups of previously celibate people. Premarital sex is still stigmatized, but now a small number of people, those who care only about the risk of pregnancy, will decide to become more adventurous. They form a small group of relatively promiscuous people. Over time, others begin to join this group. They do this not because of the reduced risk of pregnancy but because the behavior of the group has changed what society sees as socially acceptable. The people in the first group join because the pregnancy risk has fallen, and the people in the second group join because the act of premarital sex is now less stigmatized.

So, everyone is having more sex outside of marriage because it has become less risky and more socially acceptable. Where there is always a chance of pregnancy when a man and a woman have sex, an increase in the number of sexual "events" between unmarried couples is bound to increase the number of births outside of marriage. Add to that the fact that birth control effectiveness has decreased births within marriage, then the rise in the *share* of births to unmarried woman is not only unsurprising—it was a mathematical inevitability.

According to Jeremy Greenwood and Nezih Guner, whose research this whole section is based on, the availability of the birth control pill has played only a small role in the increase in premarital sex. They estimate that less than 1 percentage point of the 75 percent of unmarried teenagers having sex in 2002 is the result of the availably of the birth control pill. They argue that we shouldn't take this to mean that contraceptive technologies are unimportant, but rather that the pill is only one of several effective birth control options, all of which have contributed to the social change that has led to an increase in promiscuity.

▨▨▨ YOU PROBABLY KNOW THE BENEFITS OF SEX, BUT WHAT ARE THE COSTS?

In Jane's story, we met two distinct groups of women. The women in the first group, those who had little education or hope of a bright economic future, were promiscuous because the costs of promiscuity for them were not high. The women in the second group, those who were both well educated and economically independent, were promiscuous not because the cost was low, in fact the cost was quite high, but because they could afford these costs.

These specific costs that I am talking about don't include the daily wear and tear that raising children alone imposes on a woman; those costs are significant but vary from individual to individual. The costs I am

HOW THE SEX MARKET PRICES RISK

On the market where sex is explicitly bought and sold, economists have observed that when the risk of sexually transmitted disease is high, the price paid for sex without a condom is very low. That observation seems counterintuitive; after all, wouldn't sex workers need to be compensated for exposing themselves to a high risk of infection? But there is a straightforward economic explanation as to why we observe this particular relationship between risk and price on the sex market.

Imagine a buyer on the sex market who has the option of buying unprotected sex from two different sellers. He knows with absolute certainty that the first seller is free of STDs and that unprotected sex with that seller bears no risk of infection. He also knows that the second seller is not free of STDs and that if he has unprotected sex with that seller, he will become infected. Whom do you think he will pay more to have the privilege of having sex without a condom? Obviously, it is the seller who exposes him to no risk. In fact, what rational person would be willing to pay for the privilege of being infected with a disease?

As strange as it might seem, when a buyer is negotiating the price for unprotected a sex in a market where infection rates are high, he gets a discount price on that service to compensate him for taking the additional risk—despite the fact that he is the one arguing against protection.

On the supply side, it seems like an increase in rates of infection should increase the compensation sellers would need to encourage them to supply sex without a condom. That is true for a seller who is free of infection; in fact, that seller probably cannot be compensated to take the risk and so will only sell sex with a condom. For sellers who are already infected, though, they will be willing to supply condom-less sex and at a low price, since there is no cost to them; they are already infected.

Buyers on the sex market should remember the old adage: you get what you pay for. Or perhaps it would be more suitable on the sex market to say you get what you could have avoided for the price of a condom.

---

talking about are very specific—they are costs incurred by women and men who fail to complete their education and/or are unable to invest as much in their careers as they might have had they not had a mistimed pregnancy. These costs are important to our story, as they have evolved over the past fifty years as promiscuity has become more common.

The first important economic factor is the increasing importance of university education. According to the U.S. Department of the Census, the share of 18- to 24-year-olds enrolled in postsecondary degree programs increased from 24 percent in 1973 to 41 percent in 2009. Much of that increase in enrollment was due to the increased university attendance of women; between 1999 and 2009, the number of full-time female students increased by 63 percent compared to an increase of only 32 percent for full-time male students. This more rapid enrollment of women wasn't just because women were catching up to men: since 1988, women have made up the majority of postsecondary students. In the past forty years, the share of university students who are female has doubled from 30 percent to 60 percent, and by 2010, 36 percent of women between the ages of 25 and 29 had completed a bachelor's degree compared with only 28 percent of men.

This steady rise in university enrollment has had some important consequences for those who are not able to take that step. The first consequence is that as a greater proportion of the population becomes university educated, individuals who do not have a postsecondary education have become increasingly marginalized and, to a certain degree, stigmatized. The stigma of not having an education extends into the workplace as employers progressively have come to expect workers to have a university education, even for jobs that could be productively filled by high school–educated workers. The result is that workers without a postsecondary education are shelved in low-paying, and extremely low-skilled, jobs.

Low-skilled jobs have what economists call a very flat earnings profile—the wages low-skilled workers are paid increase very little as workers gain years of experience. Because of this, low-skilled workers are not penalized for workforce interruptions (such as taking time out of the workforce to care for small children) in the same way as high-skilled workers. High-skilled workers, who see their pay increase as they gain years of experience, both lose their current income and see a decrease in future income when they take time out of the workforce to care for their children.

The second consequence for workers on the low end of the growing educational divide is that the gap between the wages paid to skilled and unskilled workers has increased substantially over time. Firms are investing more in technologies that complement the talents of educated workers at the expense of technologies used by less-educated workers. This means that not only are the wages of educated workers increasing but also the wages of low-skilled workers are falling. In fact, by some estimates, the wage of an average worker with less than a high school education fell by 30 percent for men and 16 percent for women between the mid-1970s and the late 1990s.

Given that education has become so important both for finding employment and for earning a living wage, you might be tempted to think that young women and men would carefully avoid any circumstances that might prevent them from staying in school—circumstances like having a baby. If that were the case, premarital sex and promiscuity among adolescents and young adults should have fallen as education has become increasingly important. The reason it hasn't is that for many young people there is no hope of ever continuing in school regardless of the choices they make. This is true, of course, because postsecondary education is not freely available to everyone.

We will return to this relationship between promiscuity and education in more detail in chapter 7, when we talk about the sexual behavior of teenagers. Suffice it to say for the time being that a young adult's willingness to be promiscuous is tied to the cost of tuition in college—when tuition fees are high, youth tend to engage in riskier sexual behavior. This observation explains, in part, why the teen pregnancy rate is so much higher in the United States than it is other developed nations with more affordable postsecondary education.

Of course, tuition is not the only reason why some students can reasonably expect never to go to college, and for those youth, those who don't anticipate a bright future, the costs of promiscuity are significantly lower than for other students who do look forward to a good education and a higher income.

One of the reasons women have abstained from sex in the past was fear that having a sexual history would send a bad signal to any potential future husband. It said: *This woman will not be a faithful wife.* Premarital sex has become the social norm, perhaps, but marriage prospects still play a role in the sexual choices made by unmarried woman and men.

▨▨▨ WOMEN (OR MEN) WITH CHILDREN NEED NOT APPLY

Ten minutes on a dating site should be sufficient to convince anyone that having had a child before marriage will limit a lonely single's options on the marriage market. I have seen more than one online dating profile in which the prospective lover had written something along the lines of "What part of 'No WOMEN WITH CHILDREN' don't you people understand?"

I don't read many women's online dating profiles, so I don't know if women are as upfront as men are in stating their preferences for a childless partner, but I do know that many women, especially younger women, will not date a man if he has had a child. Being a father suggests to women that a man has fewer resources and time than otherwise unencumbered suitors.

HOW "LOVING THE ONE YOU'RE WITH" MAY NOT MAKE YOU HAPPY

Throughout this discussion, we have just assumed that there are some benefits to promiscuity; after all, if there weren't, the risk would not be worth taking. If there is a benefit to promiscuity, though, then it is worth asking if people with more sexual partners are happier than those with less. Economists David Blanchflower and Andrew Oswald have the answer to this question. They asked sixteen thousand Americans how happy they were (on a scale of one to three) and found that promiscuity, in general, does not make for happier people.

Don't get me wrong; sex makes people happy, and the more sex people have, the happier they are. Sex particularly makes women happy—happier, in fact, than any other activity. More-educated people are made happier by sex than less-educated people. Younger people are happier in general but are not made any happier by sex than are older people. Being lesbian or gay doesn't make you any more or less happy than anyone else, but it does mean having slightly more sexual partners.

The point is that while more sex makes people happier, having more sexual partners does not. The happiest people are those with just one sexual partner and, in fact, the more sexual partners they have had in the last twelve months, the less happiness people reported.

Of course, we don't really know what this happiness measure is capturing. For example, people who are unhappily married are more likely to cheat and, as a result, have more sexual partners. They aren't necessarily unhappy because they are promiscuous, but they may be promiscuous because they are unhappy. People who have had a series of failed committed relationships in one year would look promiscuous, but who could blame them for being unhappy?

The real test of whether or not having one additional sexual partner makes people happy is that people make that choice, frequently. We called this evidence *revealed preference*, because by choosing to have one additional sexual partner, for example, a person has revealed that they prefer to pay the expected costs for that experience over other possible choices they might have made.

That isn't to say they won't regret later having made that decision; it just means that facing disappointment was a risk they were willing to take.

As a friend once said to me, "Why would I date a man who is off buying his children snowsuits when he could be spending that money on me?" (Honestly, I don't make this stuff up.)

If a child is the result of a causal fling, rather than a committed relationship, even potential partners who otherwise wouldn't have minded having those children in their lives think otherwise. The problem for women is that having had a child both before marriage and outside of the context of a serious relationship suggests to potential future husbands that a woman is promiscuous. For men who have children with whom they are not involved, it suggests to future wives that they are both promiscuous and unwilling to live up to their obligations.

People might reasonably avoid promiscuity for fear that it will later affect their marriage prospects. Given that, a reasonable explanation for the increase in promiscuity is that people feel they are less likely to ever marry regardless of their behavior, or at least if they do marry it will be so late in their life that a few years of promiscuous behavior in their youth will seem less important.

As I said in the introduction, the general feeling among the current generation of youth is that marriage is not necessary to ensure future happiness. According to the Pew Center for Research, among 19- to 29-year-olds who had no children and had never been married, only 66 percent say they want to marry at some point in their lives. Most of these young men and women are likely to marry at some point in their lifetimes; the share of the population that marries at some point in their lives has stayed fairly stable over the decades at around 90 percent. But over the past fifty years, the marriage rate (the share of the population that is married at any one point in time) has fallen for everyone.

No one group has been affected more by the decline in marriage rates than the group of men and women who are both low skilled and, as a result, low paid. If we go back to our previous example that I used to illustrate the economic costs of promiscuity, and assume that our fictional woman would have had only a 48 percent chance of marrying, even without a mistimed pregnancy, then really the expected cost of promiscuity for her is something like this:

PROBABILITY OF PREGNANCY		PROBABILITY OF MARRIAGE		FORGONE INCOME FROM MARRIAGE		EXPECTED COST OF PROMISCUITY
0.45	X	**0.48**	X	**$50,000**	=	**$10,800**

Even without an improvement in the effectiveness of contraceptives, her cost for premarital sex has fallen by more than half, making it even less likely that she will choose to wait to have sex in the hopes of marrying a man with a good income.

Of course, this is a simplified view, but many other factors that we might consider will only increase the incentives men and women have to be promiscuous. For example, knowing that they will not marry until they are in their late 20s or early 30s makes it more likely that men and women will have not only one premarital sexual partner but several before they meet the person they will eventually wed. The ease with which couples can now divorce has reduced the need to find a partner who has the characteristics we would look for in a faithful mate, such as virginity, because the credible threat of ending the relationship makes it easier to enforce fidelity. More independent decision making by young adults has effectively eliminated the chance that the families will force them to marry their sexual partners against their wishes, freeing us to have sex with people whom we hope will make good sexual partners but know would make lousy spouses.

Just the fact that young adults are expected to live away from their parents for a period before they marry, if they are spending time in post-secondary education for example, increases promiscuity in that it reduces parental supervision and some of the shame associated with having premarital sex.

All of these economic factors, and no doubt others, have contributed to a change in social norms that have freed many to engage in riskier sexual behavior. But while promiscuity among heterosexuals is increasing, it seems that one community is actually experiencing a decrease in promiscuity: gay men.

▨▨▨ SAME-SEX ATTRACTION, A LOVE STORY

In light of new changes to marriage laws in many countries and in response to greater societal acceptance of same-sex relationships, it seems that gay men are opting less for casual sex and instead having committed relationships.

In 1996, a U.S. Gallup poll found that 68 percent of respondents indicated that they were opposed to laws that would allow same-sex couples to be married with the same rights as in opposite-sex marriages. Just fifteen years later, many people have changed their opinion on same-sex marriage; only 44 percent of respondents indicated that they were opposed to legalizing same-sex marriage. Likewise, tolerance toward same-sex preferences, in general, has been on the rise. For example, the percentage of people who believe that sexual relations between two adults of the same gender are not wrong at all has increased from 15 percent in 1991 to 43 percent in 2010.

In the United States, the acceptability of same-sex relationships varies not only from person to person but also from state to state. We will talk more about who does, and does not, support same-sex marriage in chapter 6. However, for now those state-by-state variations in same-sex marriage laws and in tolerance toward same-sex relationships create a possibility for economists to test the following hypothesis: in states where people are more tolerant and/or have no ban on same-sex marriage, members of the gay community engage in less promiscuous behavior. Thankfully for us, testing this hypothesis this is just what Andrew Francis and Hugo Mialon have done.

They prove the hypothesis by testing to see if states in which the public is less tolerant of same-sex relationships have more places in which gay men might meet for anonymous sex (parks, beaches, restrooms, and other public grounds that have been identified by a gay men's travel magazine). They find that a 20-percentage-point rise in tolerance decreases the average number of such meeting places in a state by about four places. If that doesn't convince you that promiscuity has decreased, a similar increase in tolerance (20 percentage points) is also associated with a decrease in HIV of one per hundred thousand of the population. They find the imposition of a same-sex marriage ban increases the HIV rate by between three and five new HIV cases per hundred thousand.

This result may seem counterintuitive; after all, I have just argued that the destigmatization of premarital sex has increased promiscuity among heterosexuals. So why should the destigmatization of sex between people of the same gender decrease promiscuity within that community? It is because an increase in tolerance changes both the way that currently openly gay men behave and encourages other men who had previously been fearful of revealing their sexual orientation to come out of the closet, so to speak.

For men who already have a gay lifestyle, increased tolerance makes it possible to have committed relationships without incurring the costs that intolerance imposes (including, incidentally, being paid a lower wage because of their sexual orientation). Alternatively, for men who have chosen to either have no sex life or to act as heterosexual men, increased tolerance makes it possible for them to be openly gay without incurring the costs intolerance imposes (including, incidentally, not being able to marry and have a family).

So promiscuity in the gay community falls when the stigma attached to same-sex preference declines, both because men who would otherwise have been promiscuous are more likely to be in a relationship and because men who are less promiscuous by nature (for example, men who are more family oriented) are willing to join that community.

FINAL WORDS

I know this methodology seems to impose too much rational behavior on an event that often begins with a man and a woman meeting in a bar and ends with some poor hungover individual stumbling home in her high heels in the blinding morning sun. I am not suggesting that all individuals do this promiscuity math every time they have sex, or ever, for that matter. In economics, all that matters is that people behave *as if* they are solving a cost-benefit problem—they may not calculate the expected cost of promiscuity, for example, but when economic factors change costs, men and women respond by making different decisions than they might have otherwise.

This economic approach helps us understand not only why we have experienced a liberalization of sexual values over the twentieth century, but also how the growing gap in incomes between the rich and the poor has led to high rates of unintended pregnancies among poorer women. It is because those women behave as if they have estimated the low probability of finding a husband who can afford a wife and family, or the

DOES PROMISCUITY MAKE NATIONS RICH?

There is a huge amount of variation in the level of promiscuity among nations. According to evolutionary biologist David Schmitt, for example, the most promiscuous nation in his forty-eight-nation study, Finland, is more than two and a half times as promiscuous as the least promiscuous nation, Taiwan. As an economist, I can't help but wonder if some of the variation in promiscuity among nations is related to variations in national income.

Social psychologist Roy Baumeister finds that countries with greater gender equality are also those with more promiscuity, measured in terms of greater number of sexual partners, more one-night stands, lower age at first sex, and a more liberal attitude toward sex before marriage. And since there is a strong correlation between gender equality and national income (it is the wealthiest nations in the world that allow women the greatest independence), this evidence substantiates my view that the wealthiest nations are the most promiscuous.

Why might there be a correlation between national wealth and promiscuity? It might simply be the case that promiscuity is a luxury that is affordable to more people in richer nations. After all, in poor living conditions, you likely have other things to occupy you rather than seeking multiple sexual partners.

This probably isn't the right approach because within all nations there are both rich and poor individuals. If the argument held that promiscuity was the result of high incomes, we would expect high-income individuals to be more promiscuous than low-income individuals within the same nation. This is generally not the case.

In my mind, the answer to this question comes down to what makes a nation wealthy in the first place, and one of the reasons for this is that they have legal institutions and social norms that promote innovative activity.

For example, a few national qualities that encourage economic growth are openness to new ideas, trust, and a willingness to accept risk. It is possible that these same cultural characteristics that have allowed nations to become wealthy are the same ones that encourage promiscuity. After all, what can be more trusting, and more risky, than sex with a stranger? It is probably not high levels of national income that lead to high levels of promiscuity, but rather other characteristics of a free society that lead to both high income and high promiscuity.

---

probability that they will be able to go to college and have a rewarding career, and they have found that the benefits of casual, risky sex exceeded the expected costs.

Taking into consideration economic factors such as income and education also prevents us from lapsing into a mistaken belief that access to contraceptive technologies is entirely responsible for promiscuous behavior today. Birth control may have historically played a role in stimulating the social change that brought us to where we are in terms of sexual freedoms today, particularly for women, but viewing current behavior as a function of access to birth control technology alone paints an incomplete picture. This is especially important because while birth control technology is unlikely to become any more efficient, economy factors are constantly changing—especially as governments adopt, and abandon, programs that influence the distribution of income and access to higher education.

Speaking of higher education, we are about to delve into the realm of the hammered and horizontal academics. Student behavior has been influenced by increased access to contraceptives and changing social norms, just like that of everyone else. Because they are investing in education, they are subject to even greater pressure to avoid a costly mistimed pregnancy, or any other event that will make it difficult for them to finish school. Do these concerns reduce their promiscuity? Of course not! In fact, if any one knows about promiscuity, it is college students . . . or at least that is what they like to tell me.

CHAPTER 2
HOOKING UP IN COLLEGE

**░░░░░ MY STUDENTS THINK THAT THEIR GENERATION
INVENTED PREMARITAL SEX**

This is not an exaggeration. And even students whom I can convince otherwise continue to argue that even if they aren't the first generation to have sex before marriage, they are certainly getting more action than anyone else. When I show them evidence that university students have sex less frequently, on average, than do people their age who are not students, they protest vociferously. Their proof? Well, of course everyone knows that university students have more sex.

I sometimes worry that this is why my students are in college.

There are two possible explanations for their skewed perception. The first is that the students in my sex and love class are not representative of students in general; they are having far more sex than anyone else on campus. Maybe that is true, but, to be honest with you, they already give me too much information, and so I would rather not know if this is the case. The second, more defensible, explanation is that my class is overpopulated with male students.[3] And right now, more than ever before, university campuses are great places for young men who are looking for sex.

---

3 Only about 42 percent of Canadian university students are male, but for some reason, male students have made up 66 percent of the students in my Economics of Sex and Love class.

Let me tell you a story that illustrates how economics helps us understand how the market for sex operates on university campuses.

It's a Thursday night and, as anyone who works on a university campus will tell you, Thursday is the new Friday (which, if you ask me, is why the fifth year of college is the new fourth year). A group of female friends is hanging out at an off-campus bar that is packed wall-to-wall with well-lubricated students out for the night. This bar allows students too young to drink legally to come in, but it doesn't serve them alcohol, so the women in our group (some of whom are below legal drinking age and some of whom are not) started drinking hours ago on the front porch of the house they share. They are very drunk and dancing mostly with each other because in this bar, as on campus, there are far more women than men.

The women in the group are all friends, but they differ in what they are looking for when they go out on a Thursday night. Some will use their own drunken state as an excuse to hook up with anyone who is willing. Others will ignore the guys who come by looking for action, interested only in hanging out with their friends. The remainder will enjoy the male attention, not because they are looking to hook up, but because they are looking for a relationship that will last more than one night.

Sarah, our main character in this story, is in this final group of women who are looking for a relationship. It isn't that she doesn't like casual sex; it is just that she has learned the hard way that the events of a night that starts with a group of friends drinking can have life-altering consequences.

Her lesson started a year ago, one night at the beginning of her first term on campus, in this same bar where she was happily drinking and having a good time with her new college friends. She had been on her way to the bathroom when a man she was passing grabbed her by the arm and dragged her back to the bar, proclaiming that she looked like she could use another shot. She was so drunk, and he was so good-looking, that all she could do was to laugh in response. After a few drinks, he suggested they go back to her residence to hang out, and to her that seemed like a pretty good idea. After a brief period of actual hanging out, she found herself in her dorm room doing what she believed everyone else on campus was also doing—having random sex with a virtual stranger. Later she remembered having asked if he had a condom and that he had told her just to relax, so that is what she did. She blacked out shortly after, only vaguely remembering the next day that she had woken up at one point to see him pulling on his jeans by the door, complaining that he had left his credit card in the bar.

The next morning she realized, brain hammering on the top of her skull, that not only did she not know his name, but that she had never even seen him before on campus. She tried to laugh the whole episode off and, despite not remembering the sex, told her friends that that he was athletic and attractive—so she must have had a good time. Secretly she was flattered that an older, and more experienced, man had chosen her out of all the hot girls in the bar that night and congratulated herself for her quick integration to college life.

The day of her first midterm, Sarah woke up feeling as if she had run a marathon the day before. She had prepared all weekend for the test and so, unlike her dorm mates, had forgone the all-night study session in favor of a good night's sleep. Apparently, the sleep hadn't paid off—she was still exhausted. Drinking a coffee she had grabbed from the cafeteria and sitting outside on a bench in the sun, it suddenly dawned on Sarah that she was not just tired, something else was wrong. She had a few hours before the exam, so she grabbed her crib sheets in order to study while she headed over to the medical clinic and waited to see the nurse. Within an hour, she knew that she had a problem. Later, she would recall that, at that moment, she felt more sorry for the nurse who had the unfortunate job of telling her that she was pregnant than she did for herself.

Being three weeks pregnant at midterm meant four difficult weeks of missed assignments and failed exams while waiting to have an abortion. She didn't have a medical certificate to explain her poor performance, not because she couldn't get one but because she was too ashamed to ask, and so her professors were unsympathetic. The term ended not with final exams and partying with friends, as she had thought it would, but with a medical procedure and a feeling that she had let herself down.

So here Sarah is again, same bar and same friends, out on a Thursday night. While her friends are starting their second year of college, Sarah is getting a second chance at her first, thanks to the help of a sympathetic dean. She is not about to make the same mistake again and, as I have already said, is out tonight looking for more than one night of drunken sex. But because Sarah still wants to have sex, but with fewer risks, she would really like to have a boyfriend whom she could trust to consistently use protection.

The problem she now faces is that on her campus there are far more women than men. That fact is not only making it hard for her to find a man; it is making it impossible to find one who is willing enter a relationship with a woman who is cautious about having sex. If she meets a man tonight, for example, she knows that not having sex with him in the first few hours after they meet will likely rule out any possibility that he will want to date her in the future. After all, he has to assume little of the risk of a casual sexual experience and, because the market for single men is so competitive on her campus, there are other women who are willing to take the risk—especially tonight, since they are having a hard time seeing the risk through their beer goggles.

What Sarah would know if she was listening carefully in her Economics of Sex and Love class is that an excess of women on the college sex market has driven down the price of sex, making it, essentially, a buyer's market. She would also know that there is a strong correlation between binge drinking and student promiscuity leading to pregnancy. But this last point, I suspect, she doesn't need me to tell her.

A BUYER'S MARKET FOR PROMISCUOUS MALE STUDENTS

Another misperception that my students seem to hold dear is the idea that men like having sex more than do women. I would never try to convince you that is the case, mostly because I just don't believe it myself. So how can I describe a market for casual sex where the desires of men are driving down the price as a buyer's market? It isn't because men want sex and women need to be compensated to be encouraged to have sex with them, that is, women are sellers; it is because men have a greater preference for multiple sexual partners than do women and women prefer to be assured that the sex they are having is not a one-time experience. Within this context then, the "price" that is being driven down is the level of assurance that a woman requires from the man she is having sex with that he will treat her well—whatever that means to the individual woman.

If you doubt that men have a greater desire for multiple partners, I propose that you undertake the following study. Go and ask your friends, coworkers, and random people you meet on the street the following question: Ideally, how many sexual partners would you like to have over the next two years? I can tell you now that the men will report a desire to have far more partners than will the women. When these studies have been conducted in the past, women, on average, report that they would like only one sexual partner while men report that on average they would like to have eight. When asked if they would like to have sex with multiple partners at the same time, 42 percent of male respondents in a nationally representative survey said that they would, compared with only 8 percent of female respondents.[4]

Statistically, women do not appear to share men's love of variety in sexual partners. This is a topic we will return to in chapter 8, when we talk about infidelity in marriage.

You could also ask this question instead: what is the minimum amount of time you would need to know someone before you had sex with him or her? I am going to guess that few women will say five minutes, but when these questions have been asked in surveys in the past, many men had no trouble with that time frame. Women, on the other hand, often said that ideally they would know a man for six months. In the same nationally representative survey I just mentioned, 31 percent of men reported finding the idea of having sex with a stranger appealing, compared with only 8 percent of women.

---

4 Results tabulated by Donald Cox.

RANDOM SEX WITH STRANGERS

It is men's desire for variety in sexual partners, and their willingness to engage in anonymous sex, that has fueled the world sex trade. But the reason a market for sex exists in the first place is that, in general, women have to be paid to have sex with a stranger. Men don't have to be paid to have sex with strangers and, even if they did, most women would be unlikely to pay for their services.

This fact explains why the sex market for female buyers is almost nonexistent.

The best study that I know of that examines the willingness of men and women to engage in sex with strangers was done on university campuses in the late 1970s and again in the early 1980s. This evidence may seem outdated, but in fact the timing was perfect; the sexual revolution was in full swing, and yet lovers were still blissfully unaware that right around the corner was a new disease, AIDS, that was about to change the way we think about casual sex.

During the course of the study, moderately attractive men/women walked up to a woman/man on a university campus and said, "I have been noticing you around campus, I find you very attractive. Would you . . . " and then offered the unknowing participant one of three options: "have dinner with me tonight?"; "come to my apartment tonight?"; or "go to bed with me tonight?" Both the target men and women must have found the person attractive since more than 50 percent of each group said yes to dinner (56 percent of women and 50 percent of men). The interesting result, though, is that as the offers became more sexual the men increased, while the women decreased, their willingness to participate. Remarkably, 50 percent more men were willing to have sex with the random stranger than were willing to have dinner with her. And even those who said no (only 25 percent of the sample) expressed regret at having to do so.

None of the women in the sample agreed to have sex with the handsome random stranger. Not one.

It isn't true that no women like sex with strangers—just as it isn't true that all men do—but there aren't enough to make female brothels, for example, profitable business ventures. After all, if women turn down offers of free sex, why should anyone think that they'd be willing to pay for it?

The outnumbering of women to men on university campuses not only makes it difficult for women to find partners from a simply numerical perspective (fewer men means each individual woman has a lower probability of finding an available man), but it is also changing the nature of male-female relationships as men have acquired greater sex-market power.

Using data collected from a large number of U.S. students from a variety of different colleges, sociologists Mark Regnerus and Jeremy Uecker find that in colleges where the ratio of women to men is high (women greatly outnumber men), women have more negative attitudes toward dating and sexual relationships than in those in which the ratio of women to men is low.

Comparing campuses where women outnumber men to those where men outnumber women allows the authors come to the following conclusions. They find that women who have never had a college boyfriend have a 69 percent chance of being a virgin when only 47 percent of all students are female, compared with only a 54 percent chance of being a virgin when 60 percent of all students are female. When there are fewer men available on campus, women who have never been in a committed relationship are more likely to have had sex at least once compared to when there are more men available.

The gap between those who have been sexually active and those who have not is no smaller for women who report having had at least one college boyfriend. These women have a 45 percent chance being a virgin on a campus in which men outnumber women but only a 30 percent chance of being a virgin on campuses in which women outnumber men.

Even women with a current boyfriend seem to have a better chance at postponing sex when there are fewer women on campus relative to men; those women have a 17 percent chance of being a virgin when there are more women than men on campus and a 30 percent chance when there are more men than women.

This evidence demonstrates that when there are fewer men than women, individual women lose some of their ability to negotiate at what point a couple has their first sexual experience together.

Given this evidence, you won't be surprised to hear that casual sex is also more frequent when women outnumber men on a campus. For example, women who have had a boyfriend in the past but are currently single have a 27 percent chance of having had sex in the last month on a high-sex-ratio campus compared with only a 20 percent chance on a low-sex-ratio campus; single women are more sexually active when men are relatively scarce than they are when men are relatively abundant.

Traditional dating is far less common when fewer men are available. This isn't really surprising, of course, as there are simply fewer men to date, but the data suggests that there is far less traditional dating than the mere shortage of men would suggest. In fact, a 1 percent decrease in the proportion of female students increases the probability that a woman will have had six or more traditional dates by an incredible 3.3 percent.

This evidence supports the idea that when women are abundant, there is far less traditional dating and far more "hooking up." Beyond that, the same authors report in their recently published book that a number of the women who they interviewed were participating in sexual acts they disliked or were having sex more often than would have been their choice.

That says to me that a woman's ability to bargain with her sexual partner over both the timing and nature of sex acts has been eroded on university campuses in the face of increased competition for men among relatively abundant women.

BOTTOMS UP

The behavior of Sarah and her friends in the bar that night wasn't just about male-female bargaining over sexual relationships. Part of the promiscuity on campuses everywhere has to do with binge drinking. How much is an empirical question that we can answer, thanks to research that has been published by economist Jeffrey DeSimone. Using data collected from 136 U.S. postsecondary institutions, DeSimone finds that binge drinking is a major contributing factor to risky sexual behavior on university campuses.

According to his research, in the month preceding the survey, 46 percent of students reported that they had binge drank at least once, and 60 percent reported that they had sex in the preceding three months, with 12 percent claiming that they had multiple sexual partners. Many students admitted to not being cautious when having sex; 65 percent of those who had sex in the last month say they didn't use a condom. And, just in case you think my story of Sarah is an exaggeration, 10 percent reported that they had previously become pregnant or had impregnated someone else at least once.

What is one of the main determinants of how sexually active a student is? Alcohol consumption. The (almost) half of the student population who are binge drinkers are far more likely to be having risky sex than the non-binge-drinking half. For example, relative to the non-binge-drinking students, binge drinkers are 25 percent more likely to be sexually active, 20 percent more likely to have had sex without a condom, and 94 percent more likely to have had sex with multiple partners (not necessarily at the same time, just in case you were wondering).

Binge drinking increases student promiscuity, as we have seen, but what increases the binge drinking? Sarah and her friends binge drank

USING SEX TO PAY YOUR WAY
THROUGH COLLEGE

Many years ago, when I was an undergraduate student, I frequented a local bar with my friends that we liked because it had cheap Long Island iced tea. It also happened to have strippers, which none of us paid much attention to. (We really were there just for the cheap drinks.) That all ended one afternoon when one of the guys in our group looked up in horror as a girl stepped onto the stage; he slunk into his chair and whispered, "That's my lab partner!"

Paying your way through school in the sex trades is probably more common than you think; prostitution, stripping, pimping, answering phones at escort agencies, and being drivers/security for sex workers are just a few jobs that students will do to help pay their way through school.

Researchers at Leeds University confirm this view. They spent a year interviewing three hundred British lap dancers and found that one in four have completed a university degree and one in three are engaged in some form of education (including 6 percent who are lap dancing their way through a postgraduate degree). Another, by the Berlin Studies Centre, reports on interviews with 3,200 students that found that 4 percent had used sex to pay for their education. Furthermore, 33 percent of students in Berlin, 29 percent of students in Paris, and 18.5 percent of students in Kiev would consider using sex to pay for school.

Websites in the United States that cater to matching both men and women with men who are looking to be "sugar daddies" offer special programs for students, including upgraded accounts if prospective escorts use a student e-mail account as their contact. One such site in New York claims that 35 percent of its eight hundred thousand escorts are university students paying their way through school on their backs.

If promiscuity has risks that can seriously affect a student's lifetime income and marriage prospects, participating in the sex trades adds a whole new dimension that, probably, explains why sex work pays so much more than other unskilled jobs that students might consider.

---

at home before heading to the bar because age-of-majority laws prohibit many university students from drinking in bars and encourage them to drink excessively at home before heading out for the night. In fact, since July 2008, 135 chancellors and presidents of colleges and universities in the United States have signed a petition asking the government to lower the minimum drinking age because they believe that a minimum age of 21 has led to dangerous behavior among underage students who drink covertly to avoid punishment.

There is another, economic, factor that has contributed to excessive drinking: alcohol prices. Alcohol prices not only influence how people consume, but also how they behave when they are under the influence.

DOLLAR DRINKS AND RISKY SEX

In December 2007, the city of Halifax, Nova Scotia, decided that it had had just about enough rowdiness from the students and imposed a citywide minimum drink price, bringing an end to popular dollar drink nights in the bars. The law was intended to reduce partying (and fighting) when students poured out onto the streets after the bars closed. But economic research suggests that laws that increase the price of drinks can also reduce risky sexual behavior. I wonder, though, does it really reduce risky sexual behavior of college students in particular?

SEXY PROFESSORS IN A HORMONALLY CHARGED CLASSROOM

Female and male professors alike won't be surprised, mostly because they were all students once too, that while students may look like they are hanging on to their every word they are also judging how hot (or not) their professor is. In fact, a popular online professor-rating website lets students rate their professor's hotness, along with assessments of fairness and teaching ability.

Using data from this website, Canadian economists Anindya Sen and Frances Woolley find that male professors who are hot are financially rewarded, while female professors who are hot are not.

Woolley and Sen consider the productivity and hotness ratings of economics professors in Ontario and find that male professors who are rated as "hot" on the Rate My Professor website are paid more than those who are not. Interestingly, this hotness premium only appears once men are beyond the middle of their career; there is no hotness wage premium for young male professors. This suggests that this "beauty" premium is not paid for what we traditionally think of as hotness, but rather other qualities like confidence, assertiveness, and creativity.

Female professors, regardless of where they are in their career, are paid no more or less for being attractive— apparently students don't rate their 50-year-old female professors as "hot" because she is confident or assertive.

Academics is a profession in which physical appearance matters little and exuding sexuality, particularly for a woman, can actually undermine a career. Female professors often have to strive to find a balance between looking presentable and not looking like too much effort has been made on their appearance.

Research by social psychologists Stefanie Johnson, Kenneth Podratz, Robert Dipboye, and Ellie Gibbons backs up this assertion. They find that attractive women are considered unsuitable employees in occupations that are considered masculine and in which appearance is unimportant. The study finds no negative effect for men; attractive men are always perceived to be more suitable for jobs, including the ones that are considered to be feminine.

If students judge a more attractive woman as less suitable to be a professor, then women who are rated as being "hot" have more to worry about than their students' daydreaming. Given how important student evaluations are to promotion in universities, they should be worried about their jobs.

In order for an increase in drink prices to reduce risky sexual behavior, all of the following must be true:

❶ The sexual behavior of some people is riskier when they have been drinking.

❷ Higher drink prices cause some people to drink less.

❸ Those same people who drink less when prices increase are the same people who engage in alcohol-induced risky sex.

The first point we have already established: as far as students are concerned, it appears that drinking increases not only promiscuity but also sex without a condom and unplanned pregnancies. (I haven't forgotten about disease, by the way; we will get to that shortly.)

The second point requires an economic interpretation. If people reduce their alcohol consumption when prices go up, then economists would say demand for alcohol is *price elastic*. Not everyone's demand for alcohol is price elastic though. For example, people with a high income probably don't change their consumption just because drinks are a buck more than they had been in the past. Elasticity not only depends upon income but also on the alternatives drinkers have to buying drinks in the bars, and in this case there is an almost perfect substitute to drinking in a bar—to go to the store, buy some cheaper alcohol, and load up on cheap drinks at home before heading out for the night.

If students have enough income so that they don't really care about the price of a bar drink or if they simply substitute the cheaper alternative of drinking at home, an increase in the price of bar drinks won't decrease drunkenness. And if an increase in drink prices doesn't decrease drunkenness, then there is no reason to expect that the same increase will decrease rowdiness or risky sex.

The final point is that the same people who reduce their alcohol consumption would need to be the same ones engaging in risky sex. As I have already said, my students certainly believe that they are getting more action than anyone else. Regardless of whether or not that is true, students, particularly those on campuses with a high female-to-male ratio, are having sex.

So the real questions are: do students drink less when prices are higher and how does their change in alcohol consumption affect their sexual behavior?

Recent research by Canadian economists Anindya Sen and May Luong seeks the answer to these questions by testing to see if there is a relationship between beer prices and the rate of sexually transmitted diseases. They find that a 1 percent increase in the price of beer lowers gonorrhea and chlamydia rates by about 0.8 percent. So it would appear that in Canada, higher beer prices do reduce risky sexual behavior.

A second study by Harrell Chesson, Paul Harrison, and William Kassler using U.S. data also finds striking evidence that people respond to increases in alcohol prices by reducing both their consumption of alcohol and their risky sexual behavior. Taking advantage of state-by-state differences in taxes on alcohol, they find that a $1 increase in the liquor tax reduces gonorrhea rates by 2 percent and that a tax increase of just $0.20 per six-pack reduces gonorrhea rates by 9 percent and syphilis rates by 33 percent.

To put these results into context, the authors' calculations suggest that an increase in beer taxes of just $0.20 per six-pack in the United States would annually reduce new HIV cases by 3,400, cases of infertility caused by pelvic inflammatory disease by 8,900, and new cases of cervical cancer by 700.

Finally a third study, by Bisakha Sen, finds that an increase in beer taxes has no effect on births to adolescent mothers, but that a 100 percent increase in beer taxes reduces teen abortion rates by about 7 to 10 percent—suggesting a small but still significant reduction in the number of unwanted pregnancies.

When talking specifically about college student behavior, however, there is a reason to be a bit skeptical that an increase in drink prices would change student sexuality as dramatically as in the general population. The reason goes back to what I said earlier about income and price elasticity: the percent change in demand for drinks when the price increases by 1 percent.

Students may not have high incomes, but they tend to consume like people who earn much more than they actually do. The reason why they spend more is that university students expect to earn more in the future than they do in the present and, as a result, they consume more today relative to other people with similar current income levels; they essentially eat (and sometimes drink) part of their future income, today. This makes me think that students don't reduce their alcohol consumption by as much as other people in their income group when the drink prices increase.

If students don't reduce their drinking in bars, or if they just drink at home before heading out, then it is unlikely that higher drink prices have much of an effect on their sexual behavior.

SEXUALLY STIMULATED MEN ARE IMPATIENT TO CONSUME

Several studies by marketing professors have found that men who are sexually stimulated by pictures of scantily clad women, the type of pictures that surround us every day, are not only impatient to consume but more willing to accept unfair offers.

One such study by researchers Bram Van den Bergh, Siegfried Dewitte, and Luk Warlop asked participants to choose between receiving €15 today or some other amount one week in the future. The monetary amount chosen in the future then gave researchers a measure of how impatient the participant was to consume. Someone who is very impatient, for example, would want far more than €15 in one week's time—maybe even €30. Someone else who is more patient would need very little more to encourage him or her to wait—perhaps close to €0 more.

Students in general are impatient to consume because they expect to have higher incomes in the future and are, therefore, less concerned about saving today. It is this fact that explains why students are less likely to respond to an increase in alcohol prices the same way as other people with similar incomes.

In this study the male participants, after being exposed to different types of visual stimuli, were asked to choose how much money they would need to be given to encourage them to postpone consumption to one month in the future. The authors found that men who were exposed to images of women posed provocatively (in swimsuits and lingerie) were significantly more impatient to consume than those who were exposed to visually appealing, but nonerotic, landscapes—in other words, they were more likely to behave impulsively when aroused.

A second study by the same authors found that, using an experiment in which men could choose to accept or reject an offer to split $10, men who were exposed to erotic images were far more willing to accept unfair offers. This was particularly true for men who were deemed high testosterone. This suggests that men who are aroused are far less concerned with whether or not the price they are paying for a good is fair than a man who is not aroused.

So do men, at least, drink less in a bar when the drink prices are higher? If attractive women surround them, they probably care very little what the drinks cost.

Last year in one of the buildings where I teach, I saw a poster that was recruiting students to participate in an on-campus psychology study. The poster's heading posed the question: "Why do you drink?" Below this heading, someone—presumably a student and not a faculty member—had written, "So I can get laid."

This story raises a third possibility, and that is that students don't get drunk and make poor choices because they are drunk, but rather that students get drunk so that they can make poor choices. If this is the case, then the question is not how elastic is the demand for drinks, but rather how elastic is the demand for sex in response to an increase in drink prices. Given how much people are willing to pay for sex on the market (i.e., the market where sex is explicitly bought and sold), it is unlikely that a few dollars for a drink will do much to reduce the demand for random sex for those who want, and can afford, it.

▰▰▰ SEX FOR THE PRICE OF A JÄGERBOMB

I like to play the following game with my students: I give them a scenario in which two people are having a sexual relationship, and they tell me whether or not the individuals are involved in prostitution. I start with the obvious: one party gives the other party money in exchange for sex. Of course, they all feel that that is prostitution. I then move on to more subtle cases: a woman has sex with her landlord instead of paying him rent. Most students, male and female, feel that is also prostitution. A woman has sex with a man in exchange for being taken to New York for the weekend. Fewer students agree that is prostitution, with a growing divide between male and female students. The game always ends with: a man buys a woman drinks all night in a bar, and she has sex with him because she feels obliged to do so.

Well, at this scenario my class protests loudly. The female students look horrified and say "No!" When I ask them why, they tell me that the woman is not contractually bound to have sex and could walk away if she wanted. I remind them that in each of the scenarios the woman could do the same, but this does not sway them in their belief that this behavior is not in any way prostitution.

What I find interesting, though, is the response of my male students. They are largely undecided, and before they are willing to answer, they generally have one question: how expensive were the drinks?

The results of a recent experiment conducted by psychologists Susan Basow and Alexandra Minieri is consistent with the observation from my simple classroom exercise that female students feel less obligated to have sex following a date than male students feel they ought to be. The most interesting result in this research, if you ask me, is that while the female participants in the study may not feel that paying for an expensive dinner entitles a man to sex, they do feel that his entitlement increases with the price of the date. If this is the case, then this explains why my male students want to know how much the man had laid out for the drinks before deciding how obliged the woman was to having sex with him.

In this experiment, university students were asked to read a vignette in which a man (John) and woman (Kate) go out on a date. In the story, the man returns to the woman's apartment at the end of the night and has sex with her despite the fact that she has clearly rejected his sexual advances.

After reading the story, the students participating in the study were asked to respond to a series of statements, including "Kate should have expected John to insist on sexual intercourse" and "John should have expected Kate to desire sexual intercourse." The responses to these statements were indicated on a scale of 1 to 6, where 1 indicated strong disagreement and 6 indicated strong agreement.

In order to tell if the price of the date mattered to whether or not Kate should have felt obliged to have sex with John, and if John was right to have expected sex from her, the students were split into four groups. In two of these groups, the date was expensive and either paid for by John or split between Kate and John. In the other two, the date was cheap and again either paid for by John or split between the two.

The average response by male participants to the question that asked if Kate should have expected to have sex with John when he paid for the expensive date was 3.21 (where 6 denotes strong agreement), while the average response for female participants to the same question was only 1.85. Not surprisingly, men feel more strongly than women that Kate should have expected John to want sex when he has paid for a pricey date.

The response to the question as to whether or not John should have felt entitled to sex, however, was closer for males and female students: 2.93 for male participants and 2.15 for female participants. When John paid for the expensive date, the men in the study clearly thought that Kate should have felt that she owed John access to sex at the end of the night, and both the men and women in the study, to varying degrees, felt that he was right to have expected it.

The economic implications of this research become interesting when we consider how these results change with the price of the date, specifically when the date is cheap, and John and Kate split the bill. The average

IN THE HEAT OF THE MOMENT, BAD IDEAS SEEM LIKE GOOD IDEAS

In most experiments, participants are asked to make decisions while sitting in a laboratory. It isn't at all clear that the decisions people make in that environment are the same decisions they would make in a state of sexual arousal. Economists Dan Ariely and George Loewenstein are, as far as I know, the only scholars in my field who have asked participants (all male students) to masturbate while reporting on their decision making. As odd as that may sound, they found that the students made very different choices in a heightened sexual state than they did when they were not aroused.

For example, they asked participants whether or not they would take a date for a fancy dinner in order to encourage her to have sex with them. Just over half of the non-masturbating (and presumably nonaroused) participants said that they would pay more compared with 70 percent of the masturbating participants. When asked if they would tell their date that they loved her in order to get her to have sex with them, the share who said yes increased from 30 percent (nonaroused) to 50 percent (aroused). Sixty-three percent of masturbating participants would encourage their date to drink in the hope that it would increase the chance that he would get to have sex with her compared with 46 percent of the nonaroused. Twenty-six percent of the aroused participants said that they would be willing to slip her a drug and 45 percent of the same said they would persist with having sex after their date had said no. Finally, and this is not surprising, masturbating participants felt significantly less inclined to use protection against pregnancy or disease than did nonaroused participants.

The fact that people make different decisions when they are aroused than they would have otherwise explains, in part, why students (and everyone else) make choices that even they themselves might consider poor ones in a nonaroused state. Economics depends on individual players making rational decisions that weigh the costs against the benefits. In the heat of the moment, however, the costs are discounted (because they are in the future) and the benefits heightened (because they are immediate).

Rationality, as I have already said, doesn't necessarily rule out the possibility of regret.

---

response by male students to the question that asked if Kate should have expected to have sex with John when they split the bill for the cheap date was 2.27 (down from 3.21 with the expensive date) and for female students was 1.37 (down from 1.85 with the expensive date).

The results for the question as to whether or not John should have felt entitled to sex when the date was cheap and the price shared fell to 2.20 for male participants (down from 2.93) and to 1.53 for female participants (down from 2.15).

What this evidence tells us is that even if female students, on average, don't feel Kate was obliged to have sex with John, or that he was right to expect it, they certainly seem to think that her obligation and his expectations are directly tied to how much John spent on their date together. So, the difference between male and female students' expectations about sex is not whether or not men are entitled to have sex after paying for a date; the difference is in how much the man has to pay before he is entitled.

That brings us back to where we started.

To say that it is a buyer's market for men on university campuses implies that on the campus market for sex the supply exceeds the demand. If that is true, then the price of sex should be falling. As I said earlier, the use of the word "price" does not imply that men need to compensate women to have sex with them; it could simply imply that they don't need to invest in a relationship in order to get laid. I also said that on campuses with more men than women, female students went on far more traditional dates than on campuses with more women than men. If a date is costly for a man, either in terms of his time or his money, then it isn't that surprising that in a buyer's market there is less traditional dating. It is entirely possible that both men and women in such markets revise down their expectations of how much a man should have to pay to sufficiently oblige a woman to have sex with him.

It might also be true that raising the price of drinks in student bars could actually increase promiscuity if it means that women feel a greater obligation to have sex with a man who has not only been buying her drinks but has been buying her expensive drinks.

At the beginning of this chapter, I told you that I have a hard time convincing my students that, on average, they have sex less frequently than people their own age who are not in school. Given how much promiscuity there is on university campuses this may seem just as unlikely to you as it does to them, but the surprising fact is that this is true.

The explanation for this is simple: people who have multiple one-night stands have sex less frequently, on average, than those in committed relationships. The DeSimone research I mentioned earlier finds that students who had had sex with more than one person over the past three months had sex less frequently than those who only had one sexual partner. In fact, those who had sex more than twenty times in the last month were much more likely to have had only one sexual partner than they were to have had multiple sexual partners.

If women outnumber men in college, and if sex markets are essentially closed (students have sex only with other students and nonstudents sex only with nonstudents), then in the population of people aged 19 to

25 who are not students, there must be more men than women. We have already shown that when men outnumber women there is more traditional dating, which would explain why nonstudents have sex more frequently than do those operating on the college market; it is because they are more likely to be in a relationship than their college counterparts.

▨▨▨▨ FINAL WORDS

Poor Sarah! It is too bad she didn't see this evidence before her disastrous first term. Maybe then she would have understood that while she was freely making her own sexual decisions, she was also subject to market forces that were beyond her control. This is good information for students, parents, colleges, and governments to have if they want to make informed decisions around promiscuity on college campuses.

For example, parents who worry that promiscuity will impose a high cost in the long run on their college-aged children would be well advised to look for schools in which male students outnumber female students. That argument probably seems counterintuitive to those parents whose daughters are college bound, but when seen within the economic environment, it makes sense to avoid putting your daughter in a position in which she needs to compete with many other women on the market for college dates.

Likewise, colleges that worry that the cost of student promiscuity imposes too high a cost on the institution—for example, when it leads to high rates of student attrition—might consider if they are giving preferential admission to female applicants. If they are, then eliminating that bias should raise the "price" of sex on their campus (measured in terms of the investment needed to secure a sexual relationship) by making male partners less scarce. Raising the price of promiscuity should reduce the overall level of casual sexual relationships on campus.

Again, the economic approach yields counterintuitive advice; it recommends that in order to lower the rate of casual sex and raise the rate of traditional dating on campus colleges, they should encourage the enrollment of more students who are naturally inclined to be promiscuous, that is, men.

My final example of how useful this information is for those who want to make informed decisions stems from the recognition that the college sex market is not an entirely free market in the sense that it is subject to the outside influence of government policy. Governments have the power to influence college sex markets through laws that control the distribution and taxation of alcohol. You might very well feel that governments have no business in the bedrooms of the nation. However, if specific alcohol policies (like having a legal drinking age of 21) are leading to binge drinking and, as a result, higher rates of promiscuity on college campuses, then changing those policies is not, in the market sense, interfering in the sex lives of the individual. On the contrary, it is removing an existing market distortion that has already shifted the equilibrium away from the one that would be found in free market.

Again, applying the statistical tools used by economists leads us to a counterintuitive recommendation—alcohol prohibitions that encourage binge drinking should be removed if governments feel that promiscuity imposes too high a cost on students and society.

Eventually, almost everyone decides it is time to search for a longer-term relationship (and the possibility of more frequent sex!). When that happens, many people will consider using the Internet to find themselves a mate. And for that, I thank them. Online dating has provided economists with a virtual treasure trove of data with which to untangle the desires of the human heart. It is a little voyeuristic, I admit, but you might just see a little bit of yourself in the next chapter, in which we will take an economic view of love in the era of cyberspace.

CHAPTER 3
LOVE IN CYBERSPACE

▨▨▨▨ HOW ONLINE DATING DIFFERS FROM BUYING SWEETS

It would be a lie for me to tell you that I have been single so long that it is starting to get embarrassing—it *started* to be embarrassing a long time ago, and now it is just plain awkward. This seems like the type of information you might want to hide on a first date, like an eating disorder or the fact that you used to smoke a lot of pot. But just like a job interview, prospective mates want to know what experience you bring to the "position." And while few people are looking for a new partner who has had a string of lovers in the past six months, you have to admit that a (very) long period without dating makes one look like the car that has been sitting in the lot all year-round—probably a lemon.

Personally, I need to come up with an excuse for this protracted period without a partner. My friends tell me that mine ("I've been too busy") is not very convincing and that I need to come up with a more creative explanation, something more appealing that prospective buyers will believe, like "I've just been loving the single life!"

Of course, I could just tell them the truth: that my rational mind has a problem with looking for love online and since that is where almost everyone else in my age group is looking, I am little out of luck.

It is not that I am judgmental of online love seekers; I am not, and I know that many people are finding love online. My problem is this: When rational decision makers are faced with a large number of options, they like to simplify. How do they do that? They use a process of elimination.

Let me use an analogy to illustrate why, for me personally, this is a problem.

Looking for a mate on an online dating site is like looking for a sweet in a pastry shop. In both cases, I wouldn't know exactly what I was looking for at the beginning of the search, and so I would simplify the decision-making process by eliminating some of the possibilities. When there is a large variety of treats, or potential partners, I wouldn't just eliminate individual possibilities, because that would be very time-consuming, but rather larger categories of possibilities. The difference between the two situations is that in the pastry shop, the categories of treats I have eliminated don't disappear altogether—they stay in the case in front of me, making it impossible to ignore how delicious they must be.

For example, I would never just walk into a pastry shop and declare, "I will have a chocolate-raspberry macaron!" Instead, I might look around and decide that I don't really want a cookie because I can easily make those at home and so eliminate cookies as a possible treat. Then I might think that I really like chocolate-covered caramels, but I already had chocolate this week. And so I'd take chocolates off the list of possible treats as well. I would continue to eliminate categories of treats until all I was left with, say, are éclairs and fruit tarts.

If on that particular day neither éclairs nor fruit tarts appeal to me, however, I wouldn't just leave the shop feeling sad that while everyone else seems to find treats, I am going home empty-handed. No, I would take another look around and decide that what I really want, after all, is a chocolate-raspberry macaron, despite previously disavowing both cookies and chocolate, and I'd go home happy with my treat selection.

Decision making on online dating sites proceeds along the same lines, but the problem of choice is far more insidious. Online people are rejected as possible partners without ever having been seen—not because of who they are but because they have characteristics that fall into a broader category that was eliminated in order to make the search less time consuming.

If shopping for treats worked the same way as online dating sites, before I even started to consider my options I would have already filtered out the cookies by refining my search (literally, by using the site's search filter) to "Things I can't make at home." And I would have screened for "Treats I haven't had recently." So, both macarons and chocolates would appear to be unavailable. At the end of the screening process, I would be left with a couple of choices, éclairs and tarts, that didn't really interest me that day. What would I do then? Probably walk away with a sense of resignation about my treat-free existence, believing that no pastry shop out there produces the perfect treat for me.

When I consider the men in my life whom I have really loved, and there have been a couple, I honestly believe that they never would have survived a filtered search on an online dating site. They would have been too young or had too little education. They would have been the wrong religion or not nearly tall enough. Or they would have been underemployed or lived too far away.

Just as important, I doubt I would have survived their searches either.

My guess is that, after a little reflection, you would agree that many of the people in your life who have made you happy—including possibly the person you are with right now—wouldn't pass muster based on a "must have" list that was searchable online. This is because online searches encourage us to find qualities that are easy to measure: age, height, education, race, income, etc. The quality of a relationship, however, is more about experiential qualities than it is about empirical qualities, and those are much harder to quantify and to search for online. This is why many online dating sites are now trying to capture experiential qualities by using search algorithms, but even those sites still allow searchers to screen out potential matches who fail to meet their quantitative criteria.

From an economics perspective, limited searches take "thick" markets and turn them into "thin" markets. The fact that online dating markets are

SLF—SINGLE LIBERAL FEMALE—
SEEKS SLM FOR ROMANCE

The characteristic that married individuals have most in common with their partners, other than religious beliefs, is their political beliefs. If finding a marriage partner that shared their political beliefs were important, though, then singles would only search within the dating pool of those with their same beliefs, in the same way they might search within the pool of those who have the same level of education.

A recent paper by political scientists Casey Klofstad, Rose McDermott, and Peter Hatemi finds that most online daters choose not to advertise their political beliefs to potential mates, and that among the subset of people that were willing to explicitly state their political preference, the vast majority (more that 67 percent) stated their political beliefs as being "middle of the road," "some other viewpoint," or "no answer."

Some specific groups of daters were willing to state their beliefs. Age mattered; older daters were more likely to state a political belief than were younger daters. Education mattered; college-educated daters were 15 percentage points more likely to state a political belief than were those with only high school.

Income mattered, but perhaps not the way you might expect. A single earning between $75,000 and $100,000 was 7 percentage points more likely to report political beliefs that were "middle of the road" than one who earned between $25,000 and $35,000.

The problem here is that the only way researchers can really determine preferences in dating is not to observe stated preferences on daters' profiles but to observe the choices that daters make while operating on that market.

When psychologists Andrew Fiore, Lindsay Shaw Taylor, Gerald Mendelsohn, and Coye Cheshire examine the messaging behavior of online daters, they find that just because a dater stated a preference to find a mate of their same religion, that does not necessarily mean that was who they looked for when they searched.

For example, approximately 50 percent of older women indicated that same religion mattered, but less than 30 percent actually contacted men who fit that description. If researchers had considered only stated preferences, they might have concluded that the majority of older women were searching for a mate within the pool of single men of their same religion, but that is not the case.

In fact, men and woman of all ages exhibit a willingness to date outside of their religion, despite the observation that people frequently marry those who share their religious beliefs.

---

thick should imply, in theory at least, that not only is it easier to find love on that market compared with a more traditional dating market but also that the relationships that form there are of a higher quality.

When we limit our searches, for example, when we only contact people who share our ethnicity, we create artificially thin dating markets—markets where there are few buyers and sellers—and it is difficult to settle on a price at which everyone is willing to trade. Not only do thin markets clear slowly, if at all, but also the matches that form on those markets are likely to be of lower quality.

Personally, I would like to limit my searches to "Men who feel soft and smell good when I roll over in the morning," but even if I could, I suspect that when I filtered for "Men who are not hurt when I find their blunders hilarious," there would be no one left on the list for me to consider.

And this, pretty much, explains why I am still single after all these years.

ONLINE DATING AS A JOURNEY OF SELF-DISCOVERY

My consternation about this process aside, as mate seekers we do limit our searches when faced with a large number of choices on any market. While this behavior may confound the search for a perfect mate, the beauty of it—from an economist's perspective—is that these searches generate extraordinary data that can be used to understand an individual's preferences for a mate.

They give economists an opportunity to observe the market for sex and love in action and help us understand how buyers and sellers on that market ultimately engage in trade (i.e., settle with a partner).

Before online dating sites started making this data available to researchers, reliable data on how relationships form was extremely difficult to obtain. You might think we could just observe existing relationships, but that information doesn't come close to telling us what we need to know because what we observe to be a "couple" is really the outcome of a dating market that has already closed. The reason why this is a problem is that in this particular market the "equilibrium" (i.e., the couple we can observe) is as much a function of the preferences of the other players on the market (the people we don't end up with) as it is a function of the preferences of the two people who have formed the couple.

Let me give an example of what it means to say that this market is in equilibrium. Suppose (hypothetically) that I looked at data collected from married couples only and found that women with small breasts are often married to men who are balding. If I were very naive I might jump to the conclusion that this is proof that balding men prefer small-breasted women. Of course, it doesn't prove that at all.

It might be the case, for example, that large-breasted women have a particular preference for men with hair, leaving only balding men available to marry small-breasted women. Or perhaps women don't care whether men have hair or not, and the reason we see this particular matching is that men who are not balding prefer large-breasted women, leaving only small-breasted women for the balding men to marry.

Either way, knowing that small-breasted women are often married to balding men tells us nothing about those individuals' preferences for breast size or hair thickness because at the end of the market for spouses, men and women do not necessarily marry the type of person their initial preferences dictate: they marry the person who is both available and willing to be married to them.

I am not suggesting that they don't prefer their partners to other men/ women, only that they prefer them to the subset of all the men/women who are willing to be with them. Who is available in that particular subset of willing partners is determined largely by the decisions made by everyone else on the market.

The example above may seem silly, but let me give you an example from the real world. According to the 2006 U.S. census, there are far more black men married to white women (6.6 percent) than there are white men married to black women (0.2 percent). We know that this outcome is not the result of a shortage of single black women (black women are significantly more likely to be single than women of any other race; in 2007, only 33 percent of black women were married). So what does this data tell us about the racial preference of men and women who are searching for a spouse?

Absolutely nothing.

To understand racial preferences in dating, we need to look at data collected while markets are in action, and some very clever ways have been found to do just that. For example, economists Raymond Fisman, Sheena Iyengar, Emir Kamenica, and Itamar Simonson arranged speed-dating trials in which men and women (Columbia University graduate students) met with a series of potential partners for short three- to five-minute "dates." Following the trial, participants were given an opportunity to share their contact information (through the organizer) with those whom they would like to meet again for a real date. The point of this experiment was to untangle whose preferences were driving the racial segregation we observe in marriage data.

Based on the evidence in these trials, it appears that the racially segregated marriage market is driven almost exclusively by the same-race preferences of women; men in this trial exhibited far less same-race preference in dating. White women, on average, preferred to date white men, but the preferences of black women to date black men were even stronger.

This evidence tells us that the reason that white women are married to black men more frequently than black women are married to white men is not because white men are not attracted to black women, but because black women prefer to date men of the same race as themselves.

Another dating market study that looks at partner preferences used data generated from an online dating service that included information on member-to-member first contact e-mails (i.e., "Hi, I read your profile and it looks like we have a lot in common," etc.) and found similar results to the Columbia speed-dating trial.

Dan Ariely, Günter Hitsch, and Ali Hortacsu find that even after controlling for all other factors that might contribute to an individual's decision to send a first contact e-mail (age, marital status, income, education, children, etc.), every ethnic group "discriminated" based on race and the same-race preferences of women exceeded those of men.

In fact, to measure just how much ethnicity matters to white women, these particular researchers decided to measure ethnic preference against another male characteristic that women seems to care quite a bit about: a man's income.

To do this, they essentially posed a question that can be answered using the data: If a hypothetical woman cares about her potential mate's income and whether or not he is the same race as she is, what would a specific man's income have to be in order to make a woman initiate contact with him even if he belongs to a different racial group?

In this experiment a hypothetical man earns $62,500 a year and is the same race as the woman. The other hypothetical man earns $X per year and is one of three races differing from the woman's. All other observable characteristics about these two men are identical. The metric that measures how much a woman cares about race over income is how large X has to be in order to encourage the woman to contact the man who is not in her ethnic group.

The results, using the online data, are informative. For a white woman, the experiment predicts that a black man would have to earn $154,000 more than the white man in order for a white woman to prefer to contact him instead of the otherwise identical white man. A Hispanic man would need to earn $77,000 more than the white man, and an Asian man would need a remarkable $247,000 in additional annual income to make her want to contact him.

The results are even stronger for black women. In this case, the experiment predicts that a white man would have to earn $220,000 more than a black man in order for the black woman to prefer to contact him, and a Hispanic man would have to earn $184,000 more.

Alternatively, Asian women appear to have stronger preferences for white men than they do for Asian men—a white man could earn $24,000 less than an otherwise identical Asian man, and an Asian woman would still prefer to contact him.

These income differentials are large, but don't let that fool you into thinking that all women care about is income. In fact, if that were true and income really mattered to women, these numbers would be quite small; it would take very little additional income to entice a woman to date a man of a different race. The fact that the numbers are so large suggests that a man's race is very important relative to his income.

If you are wondering what this experiment tells us about the choices of men, it shows that men care so little about a woman's income that it is completely meaningless as a measure of how men value different female traits. Even though men's online behavior suggests they care less about their partner's race than do women, the income needed to encourage men to make the trade-off between a same- and different-race partner is incalculably large. This doesn't indicate a strong same-race preference though; it just shows that in men's mating preferences a woman's income is irrelevant. To really estimate how much men care about race, you would have to find a different measure that is important to men—like physical beauty.

▨▨▨▨ AN ECONOMIC APPROACH TO THE "MEET" MARKET

This exercise I just described above is a good example of how online dating operates like a market, with individual players trading off characteristics they value in a mate in an attempt to find the best possible match given their own value on the market.

The dating market is like any other market in that it is made up of buyers and sellers, and, just like any other market, it is in equilibrium only after all the prices have adjusted so that buyers and sellers are both willing to trade. In most dating markets, there is no explicit exchange of money; that is not the price that I am talking about. Prices on this market are determined by the forgone alternative opportunities—or as economists like to call them, "opportunity costs"—that people accept when they finally meet a person with whom they choose to have a relationship.

Consider the following as an example: You are searching an online dating site and see the profile of a man/woman who is extremely physically attractive. In fact, if you ranked all people who are currently on your market, he/she would be in the top 10 percent of the distribution in terms of looks. Now, someone this attractive is going to be very "expensive" because everyone on the market will be competing for his/her attention and competition for a limited product always drives up its price. Whether or not you in particular will be successful at attracting this (incredibly hot) person will depend on your own price on the market because, in this market, everyone is both a buyer and a seller.

When the market clears, I can guarantee that the expensive people will end up with other expensive people, the midrange people end up with the other midrange people, and so on through the market until inexpensive people are left to date the other equally inexpensive people.

When men and women end up in relationships with others who are similar to themselves, economists call their behavior *assortative mating*. There is plenty of evidence that, on average, people end up with a partner who is very similar to themselves in terms of education, income, and even physical attributes such as height, weight, and beauty—that says that assortative mating is very common.

BEAUTY IS NOT REALLY IN THE EYES OF THE BEHOLDER

Just to give you an idea of how competitive the online market is in terms of physical beauty, let me introduce a study that was conducted using data from a website that allows users to rate others' level of attractiveness and, if they choose, send them a message in the hopes of initiating a relationship.

Individual users on the site Hot or Not (www.hotornot.com) upload a picture of themselves along with a few lines of text, if they wish to say something. Visitors to the site can rate the level of hotness of members on a 10-point scale based on members' pictures that appear on their screen in a random order. If the visitor comes across someone whom they would like to meet, they can log on and hit a "Meet Me" link indicating their interest in meeting the person in the photo.

Using just ten days of data, the authors of this study (Leonard Lee, George Loewenstein, Dan Ariely, James Hong, and Jim Young) were able to observe the behavior of 16,550 members—75.3 percent male and 24.7 percent female. Each member viewed an average of 144 pictures over the ten-day period, and each of the more than two million observations in the data set is an individual decision to hit the "Meet Me" link. By observing

ARE PROVOCATIVELY DRESSED WOMEN FUELING ECONOMIC GROWTH?

In the 1920s, George Taylor, an economist at the University of Pennsylvania's Wharton School, claimed there was an inverse relationship between the state of the economy and skirt lengths. In good economic times, women shortened their skirts to show off their silk stockings, but when times were bad, they lengthened them to hide the fact that they couldn't afford stockings. So when the economy boomed, skirts were short, and when it lagged, skirts were longer.

There isn't any evidence that this theory held up in the long run, but, recently, marketing researchers Kim Janssens, Mario Pandelaere, Bram Van den Bergh, Kobe Millet, Inge Lens, and Keith Roe found that single men show a much higher preference for status-type goods when they are exposed to a provocatively dressed woman during an experiment than when exposed to a conservatively dressed woman. Men in a committed relationship show none of this preference. The argument for this result is that when a single man is in the presence of an attractive young woman, his preference for products turns to those that can help him secure her as a mate. He assumes, perhaps subconsciously, that the products that will attract her are those that indicate his wealth.

These results raise an interesting question: Has the fact that women's fashion has evolved over time in a way that makes women more conspicuously sexual changed men's preference for products that more conspicuously demonstrate their wealth and status?

The answer to this question is probably no. One of the fundamental principles of economics is that the price of a good is related to its relative scarcity. If scantily clad women are scarce, then their price is high (where here the "price" is the amount a man must spend in order to demonstrate his affluence to a relatively attractive woman). When scantily clad women increase in abundance, however, their price is bound to fall as men no longer need to compete with each other over the relatively scarce good. In fact, as hemlines go up, conspicuous consumption of status goods might fall for precisely this reason.

---

the choices made by users as to whom they would like to meet, researchers were given the opportunity to measure the preference for a mate based on physical attractiveness alone.

Singles compete heavily for very attractive people on dating sites, and this study provides evidence of that; members with the highest "hotness" rating were far more likely to receive requests to meet than were other, less hot, users. For example, increasing a person's attractiveness rating by just 1 point (say from a hotness level of 5 to a hotness level of 6) increased the likelihood that a person viewing that photo wanted to meet by 130 percent. Although male members appear to use a "shotgun" approach (they were 240 percent more likely than female members to click on the "Meet Me" link), you perhaps won't be entirely surprised to learn that men in particular tried to meet women who were far more attractive than they are. Women, on the other hand, appeared to be less concerned about trying to meet men who are more attractive than they are.

On Hot or Not, talk is cheap, literally, since it only requires users to click a free link, but in other environments, pursuing a potential partner is more costly in terms of time and, sometimes, money. Because of those costs, most people prefer to spend as little time searching as possible. The quickest way to find a mate and get off the market is to accurately estimate our own value on the market—we need to price ourselves appropriately. In order to do that, it is useful to know how we stack up against others with whom we are competing on the market.

▨▨▨▨ IN ONLINE DATING, EVERYONE IS ABOVE AVERAGE

People in general are very biased in terms of their own self-assessment; we are all funnier, smarter, kinder, better looking, and better in bed than the average person. For example, when online dating site users are asked to rate their own appearance, less than 1 percent report their appearance as being "below average." That assessment wouldn't be that surprising if many other people then reported themselves as being "average," but only 29 percent of men and 26 percent of women reported that they look "like anyone else walking down the street." The remaining 68 percent of men and 72 percent of women assessed their own attractiveness as being above average.

Looking at the same Hot or Not study I already mentioned, we find even more evidence of our inability to accurately assess our standing on the market. Hot people on that service are very discriminating as to whom they contact, while people with lower hotness ratings initiate contact with far more people—including others who are rated as being much hotter than themselves.

In fact, the less attractive a member (according to the user ratings), the more they initiated contact with other users and the more willing they were to contact women/men who were hotter than themselves, despite the limited probability that those offers to meet would be accepted.

This may seem like wishful thinking on the part of homely lonely hearts, but not only did less-attractive people seek out users who were more attractive than themselves but they simultaneously ignored users who were rated as being equally attractive. On average, people contacted members who never would have contacted them while, at the same time, not contacting members who would have been open to their invitation to meet.

The results might leave you suspecting that if someone expresses an interest in you on a dating site, then you are probably out of their league. I feel obliged to remind you that this is only true in the statistical sense; on average you are probably out of the league of most people who would contact you. It does make me think, however, that there is an online dating equivalent to Groucho Marx's famous line: "Please accept my resignation. I don't want to belong to any club that will accept people like me as a member!"

MONEY CAN BUY YOU LOVE

So, how much do people value physical beauty in online dating? Returning to the metric developed by Ariely, Hitsch, and Hortacsu—the one we discussed when talking about ethnicity—consider a hypothetical woman who can choose between two men: one who is very attractive and one who is not. The first man is in the top 10 percent of all men in terms of appearance (i.e., most people would rate his appearance as at least 9 out of 10) and earns $62,500 a year. The second is in the bottom 10 percent in terms of appearance (i.e., most people would rate his appearance as no more than 1 out of 10) and earns $X per year. How much would X have to be for this woman to prefer a man in the bottom 10 percent, in terms of attractiveness, to a man in the top 10 percent?

The answer is that the seriously unattractive guy would have to earn about $186,000 more than the really hot guy in order for a woman to prefer him. This suggests that compared with income, looks are very important to women.

How much does a man need to be compensated in order to encourage him to date a woman in the bottom of the distribution in terms of appearance? Well, it just isn't possible. Either men care so much about appearance, or so little about income, that it is impossible to financially compensate them sufficiently to encourage them to make that choice.

I said that attractive people are expensive on the market, and this measure tells us *exactly* how expensive they are in terms of how much of a future partner's income a woman would be willing to forgo in order to date a very attractive man. But, there are other trade-offs that people make in dating that are harder to measure in terms of monetary value. For example, some people will sacrifice the opportunity to date an attractive individual in favor of someone who shares religious beliefs. Others will

CAN ECONOMISTS GIVE ONLINE DATERS A SIGNAL THAT CAN IMPROVE THEIR CHANCES AT FINDING LOVE?

Economists are interesting in *signaling*, the ability of one person to credibly convey information to another person in the hope of engaging them in trade. If a signal imposes a cost on the sender, it gives the recipient an indication that the sender's intentions are serious. For example, if a single on an online dating site receives a message from someone who may be "out of their league," the recipient may not respond, feeling that it is a waste of time. Senders, however, have a better sense of their position on the market and so, if they want a response, they will need to send a signal that their intentions are sincere.

In an online dating experiment, Korean economists Soohyung Lee, Muriel Niederle, Hye-Rim Kim, and Woo-Keum Kim find that a small, almost costless signal—the sending of a virtual rose—had large effects in an online dating experiment.

In an online dating party, single men and women could choose to send standardized messages proposing a date to at most ten people. Once the party was over, participants had four days to either accept or reject date proposals. All daters were given two roses each that they could send to signal the sincerity of their interest.

Roses were costly to send only in the sense that not every message could have one attached, so participants had to choose a subset of their matches to receive a rose. Presumably they chose the ones who interested them the most.

Sending roses significantly improved a participant's chance of having a date proposal accepted, with those sending a rose having a 20 percent better chance that their date proposal was accepted than those who did not. This strategy worked best if the sender of the proposal was more desirable than the receiver; with everything else held constant, a sender of a proposal who was ranked as being superior to the receiver increased the probability of having his/her proposal accepted by 50 percent if a rose was attached.

Not all services, particularly free ones, provide users with a signal as explicit as a virtual rose. This leaves senders to find their own ways to signal—sending a personalized message that indicates that the sender has taken the time to read the receiver's profile, for example.

I wonder how many realize, however, that the people they might believe don't need a signal to encourage a response are exactly the same people who are most likely to respond when a signal is given.

---

choose a partner with the same education as themselves at the expense of finding someone who is their ideal height. We observe that men prefer to marry younger women, but some men will forgo the opportunity to find a younger wife if he can find an older woman who is willing to provide him with financial stability (more on this in chapter 9).

Other research, such as that by Abhijit Banerjee, Esther Duflo, Maitreesh Ghatak, and Jeanne Lafortune, shows that in India the preference for people to marry within their own caste is so strong that both men and women are willing to marry someone with fewer years of education in order to make a within-caste marriage possible.

In the final analysis, a person's willingness to sacrifice one quality on their "must have" list over another quality depends on their own personal set of preferences, specifically, how they value one trait relative to another. How much they will ultimately have to sacrifice, on the other hand, will depend on their own value on the market, which depends on the distribution of marketable qualities of those with whom they are competing.

▰▰▰ "I'M NOT WILLING TO SETTLE, AND NEITHER SHOULD YOU"

Try this as an exercise: Give yourself an honest score on a scale of 1 to 10 that represents where you believe you sit in the distribution of physical appearance for your gender and age. For example, if you feel that you are better looking than 70 percent of all men/women your age but not as good looking as anyone in the top 30 percent, then you should give yourself a rating of 7. This is your self-assessment of where you sit on the market.

Now go onto an online dating site and do a search for people the same gender and age as yourself (you will probably have to set up a fake alternative gender profile in order to do this), feeling free to make the market as big as you like, and take a look at the profile pictures of people who are advertising themselves there. My guess is that if you randomly chose ten profile pictures and rated them in order of attractiveness, you would find that your initial self-assessment overstated your position in the distribution in terms of appearance. That is, the people in the pictures that you ranked at your attractiveness level are objectively better looking than you are.

The reason for this discrepancy is not necessarily that you initially overstated yourself in terms of looks (okay, you probably did, but that isn't the point), nor is the reason that only the really good-looking people are operating on online dating sites. The reason is this: everyone can find at least one really good picture. If everyone puts their very best picture on their online dating profile, then anyone trying to estimate the distribution of attractiveness using dating-profile pictures will almost certainly overestimate the average level of attractiveness for people of that gender who are searching on that market.

If this is the case, then when you meet face-to-face with a person from an online setup, or when someone sends you more pictures, you will then be tempted to underestimate their value since you have already overestimated how attractive people are, on average, on the market.

The phenomenon that I am talking about here is what social psychologists call "contrast effects." These effects suggest that when presented with an image that is ranked much higher than the image shown after it, individuals will rank the second image lower than they would have otherwise because of the contrast between the two images. Field studies have shown that men who have been exposed to images of very attractive women will rank average women as less attractive than they would have had they been exposed to a different set of images, like landscapes, or if they'd seen the average woman before they saw the attractive woman.

Said another way, profile pictures on online dating sites are creating "beauty inflation"; they are driving up an individual's perceptions of their own value by skewing perception of beauty distribution overall. And, it isn't only beauty that is inflated but all the other qualities that people enhance when describing themselves online.

Self-reporting has left everyone with the impression that there is an entire online market filled with attractive, educated, high-income individuals just waiting to go for picnics in the park and long walks on the beach. That probably seems wonderful to people who have just started searching. However, in the long run, the perception that everyone is above average prevents the market from clearing as quickly as it might have otherwise because it encourages seekers to overestimate how well they will do on that market.

Given that most of us (including men) are depreciating assets, that is, our value on the dating market falls as we age, the more accurately we determine where we sit on the market at the beginning, the better off we will be in the long run. In fact, it is essential if we hope to exit this market before our value starts to decline.

The economic approach suggests that dating markets in which players start with informed (and honest) estimations of their own value—and think about the value of potential matches in terms of the trade-offs they are willing to accept rather than requiring that they fulfill a list of requirements—are likely to clear more quickly because more people find love sooner.

▰▰▰▰ CAN YOU EVER BE TOO RICH OR TOO THIN?

As much as economists like to describe human behavior in the simplest terms possible, people are, really, very complicated creatures. Finding the perfect mate, as I have already said, is more about experience then about checking off items on a list. And even if the latter is all we do, sometimes it is the combination of traits that matter, not the just the individual traits themselves.

As I have said, physical attractiveness is an important characteristic that women look for in a partner, but women also care about the resources a man brings into the match. Psychologists Simon Chu, Danielle Farr, Luna Muñoz, and John Lycett suggest that while women may prefer a man who is handsome over one who is plain, and a man who is rich over one who is poor, when given a choice, they prefer a handsome man who has lower income over a handsome man who has a higher income.

This seemingly contradictory evidence can be linked to women's preferences to find faithful partners; if a woman can have a handsome man, she would prefer one whom she doesn't have to share with other women, which would be more likely if he also had a high income. The proof is in the numbers. Researchers on this project created online dating profiles for twenty fictional men who varied in terms of physical attractiveness (rated independently on a scale of 1 to 10) and who were assigned an occupational class: high status (doctor, architect), medium status (teacher, social workers), and low status (postman, call-center operator). The dating profiles were shown to women who were then asked which of the men they would prefer for a long-term relationship.

The results suggest that women prefer a man who has a medium income level over a man who has a high income level if he is physically attractive (more than a 7 out of 10). If he is less attractive, though, (between a 4 and a 6), women prefer a man who has a high income level over one who has a medium income level. The strongest results are among women who are less trusting and those who rate themselves as less likely to be successful on the mating market.

So, the general conclusion is that a woman who is afraid that her mate will not be faithful will avoid men whom she believes will attract other women. This could be because she thinks he will cheat, but it could also be that mate guarding is exhausting, and she would rather not incur the cost of being in a relationship with a man who is constantly being pursued by other women.

LOCATION, LOCATION, LOCATION

I have confined my discussion here to people searching on an online dating site, but social networking sites are outpacing traditional dating sites as places where new couples can meet.

For example, an Oxford Internet Institute report by Bernie Hogan, Nai Li, and William Dutton finds that 30 percent of cohabiting couples who met on the Internet since 1997 met on social networking sites compared with 28 percent who met on sites whose specific purpose is to bring people together for romance (i.e., online dating sites). Given that social networking did not become widespread until the beginning of the new millennium, this figure seriously understates how much online dating is happening off dating sites right now.

The value of a social networking site is that it is more experiential than a dating site. You can still get a sense of observable quantitative features on dating sites (age, education, etc.), but you can also do something that is even more important; you can observe the interactions of prospective dates with other people on the site. Among the additional information that these observations give us is how others judge this person. This information helps us to determine a prospective partner's place on the dating market, which is useful when trying to find a mate whose value is equal to our own.

So here's a question: If social networking sites have become the main place to find love on the Internet, then why would anyone pay for an Internet dating service? The free online dating services have put together a pretty convincing case that there are far fewer potential matches on

LESS-ATTRACTIVE PEOPLE HAVE MORE DECEPTIVE ONLINE DATING PROFILES

Several years ago, I was chatting on an online dating site with a man who claimed to have a graduate degree. When I asked him what his degree was, he revealed that in reality he had spent six years in community college, repeatedly starting but failing to complete programs. His comment was, "I could have been a doctor by now!" To which I responded, "Good-bye."

No one likes to be deceived by a person with whom one hopes to one day develop a trusting relationship. It is perhaps for this reason that studies have shown that, unlike this guy, lies on dating profiles are generally quite minor. Men make themselves a little taller (by about an inch) and women make themselves a little thinner (by about eight pounds). But unless you spent a summer working at a local fair guessing people's weight and height, the deceptions are so small, on average, that most people probably wouldn't pick them out on a first date.

A recent study by communications researchers Catalina Toma and Jeffrey Hancock, though, finds that one particular group of online daters is more prone to lying than others—and that is people who are less physically attractive.

This research suggests that less-attractive people are more likely to have chosen a profile picture in which they are significantly more attractive than they are in everyday life and are more likely to lie about objective measures of physical attractiveness such as height and weight.

Interestingly, less-attractive people do not appear to try and compensate for their lack of good looks by elevating their social status; they aren't any more likely than more-attractive people to over-report their income, education, or occupation levels.

This raises a more general issue and that is the underlying assumption that men and women are good at assessing their place on the market in terms of physical attractiveness. It is possible that what really is happening here is that less-attractive people spend longer looking for love online and, given their lack of success, eventually start to tweak their profiles in order to attract a greater response than they had previously. If people "revise" their profile over time in the hope of attracting more attention, then the data will make it appear as if less-attractive people are more deceptive. If this is the case, then the relationship between deception and attractiveness is not a result of people assessing themselves as being less attractive; it is a function of time spent searching on the market.

---

fee-for-service dating sites than on the free sites. This is probably true, but searchers are not looking for a dozen potential mates—they are looking for one actual mate. And the evidence suggests that if you meet someone on an online dating site, that someone is more likely to be willing to meet with you in person if they have paid a fee for the service.

A recent study by psychologist Martin Coleman tests this theory in an online dating simulation where participants "pay" a fee to search online for potential dates after answering a series of questions describing their perfect mate. At the end of the search, they are informed that a match has been found but that he/she does not have all the qualities the participants have been searching for (I think we all can relate to that experience!). At this point in the simulation, the participant is informed that a friend would like to set them up on a blind date with a person who is absolutely perfect in terms of their criteria for a mate. Participants then have to choose how much of a single hour they would be willing to commit to the inferior date from the online service and how much to the superior match that is the blind date.

It turns out that a person's preference to spend time with the person they met online is related to how much they had paid for the online dating service. Those who paid nothing, or very little, for the search were much less willing to choose the online date over the blind date compared with those who paid a higher fee. For example, the length of time men in the study chose to commit to the date that was arranged online was twenty-eight minutes when the cost of the online service was $0 and almost forty-nine minutes when the cost of the service was $50. The length of time women in the study chose to commit to the online date was thirteen minutes when the cost of the service was $0 and twenty-eight minutes when the cost of the service was $50.

▰▰▰ FINAL WORDS

A while back, a friend tried to set me up with a guy she knew. He was in his late 40s, chronically unemployed, and in the midst of a very nasty divorce that involved three children. So I said, "Sure!" (Did I mention that I have been single for a while?) When she told him about gainfully employed, scholarly me, his response was, "No thanks, I am only interested in dating women younger than 25."

Here is a man who would clearly benefit from an economic perspective of markets for sex and love.

These economic dating market stories that I have shared here are not just important for those of use who are still searching for love—they help to explain a whole range of economic and social phenomena of our modern society.

For example, they help us understand, in part, why the gap between the income earned by very rich households and that earned by very poor households has been widening in recent decades. One of several explanations for this phenomenon is that the coordination of dating markets has made it easier for individuals to form couples in which spouses earn at similar levels. Gone are the days in which a highly educated, high-wage-earning man might marry his low-skilled, low-wage-earning high school sweetheart simply because they both come from the same community. A high-wage-earning man is now far more likely to marry a woman who also earns a high income, not just because more women are earning higher incomes (they are, of course) but also because he can now search for a partner on a much larger dating market.

Increased match quality, made possible by searching on a larger market, means being able to find a partner with a similar education level and earning ability. These marriages, between two high-wage-earning individuals, result in households with much higher incomes than those in which high-wage earners marry low-wage earners.

The availability of online dating markets to increase this tendency toward assortative mating has reinforced the existing economic class system and increased the earnings gap between rich and poor households.

A second insight given by an economic approach to dating markets is that inefficiencies in these markets can lead to individuals staying single for much longer than is optimal. If people spend years searching for love because they struggle with determining their own value on the market or get caught up in searching for qualities that are easy to measure (like age, height, education, race, and income), rather than the important experiential qualities, they miss out on enjoying the many economic benefits of marriage earlier in their lives.

We will see what those benefits are in the next chapter, but from a societal perspective when marriage markets do not clear efficiently, the end result can be lower overall fertility rates, a higher percentage of births to unmarried women, and higher expenditure on fertility treatments as men and women delay marriage into their 30s and 40s, or never marry at all.

It is for these reasons that governments in some countries, Singapore for example, have taken over coordinating dating markets by providing free online dating services, real-life opportunities for singles to meet each other, and workshops that teach well-meaning friends how to be good matchmakers.

One final example of the insight this economic approach affords us is explaining why there has been a dramatic decline in marriage rates by black women in the United States. The rise in academic achievement of black women relative to black men and increased incarceration rates of black men (again, topics we will soon discuss) explain two reasons why black husbands are relatively scarce. But those factors only affect the marriage rate of black women, in particular, because of the extremely low rate of interracial marriage. If all singles were indifferent to the race of potential partners, then we might reasonably expect that the marriage rate of black women would be similar to that of white women. The research we have discussed here demonstrating a strong same-race preference in dating enriches our economic understanding of why marriage rates are so low in the population of black women.

Which brings us to marriage. No topic of sex and love has garnered as much attention from economists as the questions surrounding marriage. One thing economics does well is understand change and, like it or not, marriage is changing. Not just the legal definition of marriage, but also what matters to us when we choose a marriage partner and, once the knot is tied, how couples make important decisions. As we are about to see, just because we are off the dating market doesn't mean markets don't play an important role in our sex and love lives.

CHAPTER 4
YOU COMPLETE ME

▰▰▰ **"YOU CAN'T ALWAYS GET WHAT YOU WANT,
BUT IF YOU TRY SOMETIMES, WELL, YOU JUST MIGHT FIND
YOU GET WHAT YOU NEED."**

Mick Jagger may have spent only two years at the London School of Economics in his youth, but he seems to have acquired a good understanding of how at least one market operates—the market for love.

In love, and marriage, you don't always get what you want because your own value on the market limits who you are with when your individual market closes. Market theory suggests that the person you marry is one whose value on the market is equal to your own; otherwise, one of you could have done better by waiting until you found a match with a higher market value. Economic trade theory, on the other hand, argues that the most productive matches are those in which individuals are different enough from each other so as to exploit the gains from trade.

So while you may not get what you want, hopefully the person whose market value is equal to your own is exactly whom you need.

Before we explore how we choose the person we expect to be with for the remainder of our lives, we need to spend a few minutes talking about why it is that people marry, since that is the best way to understand what qualities bring two people together in matrimony.

Just for the record, the observations in this chapter, and in subsequent chapters, apply not only to those unions that are legally sanctioned, but also to any cohabiting relationship in which the couple is committed to a long-term relationship. And while for simplicity I sometimes revert to the traditional terms of husband and wife, bride and groom, much of what I say here is applicable to marriages in which spouses are of the same gender.

▨▨▨ NOT YOUR AVERAGE LOVE STORY

I can't resist starting with my idea for a whole new set of wedding vows that are based on economic theory. These are just an example; couples can fill in the strengths and deficiencies of their own beloved. As you will see later, the vows I have chosen here would have been ideal for the marriage of Jane (whose story we will continue in chapter 6) had she had the foresight at the time that she was writing her own.

Groom: "I, [name of groom], agree to enter into a contract with you, [name of bride], that will govern the terms of our marriage. I accept that while I have met other women whose qualities were such that they surpassed my minimum requirements for a bride, the fact that they found me lacking has led me to choose you, my love, as my wife. What you lack in terms of education and income, you more than compensate for with your youthfulness and attractive appearance, and I vow that this trade-off is sufficient for me to choose you as my bride. I promise to be faithful, even though the low cost of searching and your inevitably declining value might one day encourage me to seek a new wife. I vow to work with you toward the common goal of exploiting the division of labor in the production of household goods so that our household will prosper. I will continue to invest in my human capital to ensure that your future expectations of our household income are met. While it may not be rational, I pledge to invest in our children and my asset portfolio as if I expected us to be together until death do we part."

Bride: "I, [name of bride], agree to enter into a contract with you, [name of groom], that will govern the terms of our marriage. I accept that while I have met other men whose qualities were such that they surpassed my minimum requirements for a groom, the fact that they found me lacking has led me to choose you, my love, as my husband. What you lack in stature and attractiveness, you more that compensate for with your level of education and occupational choice, and I vow that this trade-off is sufficient for me choose you as my husband. I promise that any children born into our marriage will be biologically your own, even as I know that I will be tempted to seek short-term relationships with men who possess a better genetic endowment. I will sacrifice my own human capital for that of our children, in the knowledge that you will bring in sufficient resources for our family to ensure our well-being. While it may not be rational, I will quell my inclination to behave in a risk-averse manner and pledge to invest in our marriage and my asset portfolio as if I expected us to be together until death do we part."

At this point, the bride and groom would exchange rings, and the bride's sister would come to the front to sing a stirring rendition of "Can't Buy Me Love" by the Beatles. Or for those who prefer something more contemporary, Panic at the Disco's "I Write Sins Not Tragedies," with its sage advice for would-be brides and grooms: "Much better to face these things with a sense of poise and rationality."

People marry for a variety of reasons, but from an economic perspective the purpose of marriage boils down to two things: efficient production of household goods and services, and insurance in bad times. I am going to leave the issue of insurance until chapter 6, when we talk about how couples bargain within their marriage and, for now, focus on the qualities that maximize the production of household "goods" and "services," including love, sex, and children.

Many household goods and services can either be produced by one person or purchased on the market, but often they are produced more efficiently (i.e., at a lower cost) when there are two people in the household. Let me give you a few examples:

The first good or service produced within marriage is sex and love. Sex can be purchased on the market, love—not so much. Purchasing sex on the market is very expensive not just in terms of explicit costs, but also in terms of risk of infection, risk of exposure to humiliation and ridicule if the buyer is exposed, risk of arrest if purchasing sex is illegal, and risk of violence. All of these things, plus the sheer inconvenience, make buying sex on the market far less efficient than obtaining sex within marriage. Of course, people can always visit the casual-sex market (i.e., find sex in a bar or online), but that market has many of the same risks as explicit sex-market sex, with the additional concern that as people age, finding sex on the casual-sex market is more of a challenge.

Despite the common perception that married people do not have sex as frequently as their unmarried friends, the evidence from David Blanchflower and Andrew Oswald shows that married people have sex far more frequently than do single people; 76 percent of married people report having sex at least two to three times per month compared with 57 percent of never-married people and 41 percent of those who are divorced, widowed, or separated. In addition, 43 percent of people who are divorced, widowed, or separated and 24 percent of those who never married reported having no sex at all in the previous twelve months—compared with only 6 percent of married people who had no sex in the last year.

You may be tempted to argue that there is a big difference between quality and quantity of sex, and you would be right, but the same research finds that people with only one sexual partner in the previous twelve months were much happier than people who had more sexual partners. Maybe this isn't proof that sex within marriage is better-quality sex, but it is certainly evidence that having more sexual partners does not make people better off in terms of self-reported well-being.

If we consider sex a "service" that marriage provides, then it seems obvious that one of the reasons people marry is because married individuals obtain this service at a lower cost than do unmarried individuals.

The second example of a good or service produced within marriage is biological children. Not all couples want to have their own children, and many who do want them cannot have them, but for heterosexual couples who both want and can have their own biological children, marriage is the most cost-efficient way to make that a reality. There are market alternatives, and for women some nonmarket alternatives, but again those are expensive and inconvenient.

Having children within marriage gives women some assurance that the children's father is committed to providing for them in terms of his time or his resources, or both, and it gives men some assurance that the children he is helping to raise are biologically his own rather than those of another man.

Marriage may not be the only way to have biological children, but it is the most efficient in that couples can produce children cheaply. In fact, for fertile couples who enjoy having sex with each other, the production of biological children is virtually free.

The third, and perhaps most economic, example is the production of goods and services within the home such as food, laundry, and a clean house. The reason these goods and services can be produced more cheaply by a married couple is based on the same reasoning that applies to two countries that are better off when they are trading with each other than they would have been had they both imposed autarky (i.e., completely closed their borders to trade).

People, like countries, differ in what they are good at doing. If one person can undertake a household chore more efficiently than another person can, then there are gains to be made from allowing that person to specialize in doing that particular task while leaving the other person to do other tasks.

Let me give you an example that comes from a couple who I know, Jordan and Alex, who have a 20-month-old baby. Jordan and Alex have two tasks that need to be taken care of every evening: putting their child to bed and cleaning the kitchen. According to what they tell me, Jordan is better at both of these tasks in that Jordan can accomplish both tasks in less time than Alex can.

To be specific, Jordan can clean the kitchen in forty-five minutes, while the same task takes Alex sixty minutes, and Jordan can put their daughter to bed in thirty minutes, while Alex needs sixty to complete that task as well.

Now maybe what this couple should do is designate Alex to watch TV while Jordan spends a total of an hour and fifteen minutes cleaning the kitchen and putting their child to bed. But with this distribution of responsibilities, as a couple they are not exploiting the gains from trade; they can allocate chores in a way that is more efficient for the household.

In order to accomplish this, they need to determine the task at which each person has a *comparative advantage*—the task at which each is relatively efficient. Jordan may be able to complete both tasks more quickly than Alex, but in the amount of time that it takes Jordan to put the baby to bed (thirty minutes), he/she would have been only two-thirds of the way through cleaning the kitchen (which takes forty-five minutes). On the other hand, in the same amount of time that it takes Alex to put the baby to bed (sixty minutes), she/he could have finished cleaning the kitchen.

This means that Jordan has the comparative advantage in putting the baby to bed, and Alex has the comparative advantage in cleaning the kitchen—these are the tasks that each is most efficient at doing relative to the other task that needs to be done.

The best allocation of tasks in this household would be to let Jordan put the child to bed while Alex cleans the kitchen. Given that these are the only two tasks that need to be done in the evening and that Jordan will be finished putting the baby to bed before Alex finishes the kitchen, Jordan could always help Alex finish cleaning the kitchen once their little one is sleeping. If they can further exploit the gains from trade by each doing the kitchen-cleaning task at which they are most efficient, for example, one person empties the dishwasher while the other person cleans countertops, they should be able to finish up quickly and both be relaxing within forty-five minutes of starting their evening chores.

I know that if you are a parent you are currently thinking: "Good luck with that!"

The gains from trade are not always realized in the form of more free time, as they were in this example. Sometimes they are realized in higher quality of household output—the house is cleaner and the children better cared for, for example. What couples do with the gains from trade is a decision they make together, but research suggests that, on average, couples choose to do a little of both—consume more leisure and produce a higher quality of output.

Comparative advantage in marriage doesn't apply just to housework and childrearing. Women have a clear comparative advantage in pregnancy and childbirth because men cannot bear children as cheaply as women can, obviously. As for how individuals in a relationship can exercise their comparative advantages in sex, I am going to leave that one for you figure out for yourself.

Exploiting the gains from trade is not just an important reason for why an individual might want to marry rather than stay single, it also predicts something important about how people choose their future mates; in theory, at least, the most efficient marriages are those in which the two people differ in terms of activities at which they excel.

For example, if an individual who earns a high wage wants to have children who are cared for full-time by a parent, then he/she would be better off marrying someone with the comparative advantage in child care so that she/he can specialize in earning an income while the partner cares for the children during the workday.

This observation explains why traditional marriage evolved into what is called the "male breadwinner model" at around the same time as the Industrial Revolution; it was not because women were naturally endowed as caregivers, but because physical labor was arduous, giving men the comparative advantage in market labor and women the comparative advantage in the care of the home. Household arrangements began to change, and

WHAT IS A HUSBAND WORTH?

New research by Victoria Vernon finds that some married women have thirty-four more minutes a day of (gloriously) free time than their single counterparts, suggesting that they are able to exploit the gains from trade in the production of household goods. But only women in high-income households have this benefit. Married women in low-income households work an extra fifteen to thirty-four minutes each day if they have children and thirty-seven to forty-eight minutes more if they do not.

There is no gain in terms of free time for men who are married, but married men in higher-income households spend an extra thirteen minutes a day working for wages if they don't have children and thirty-five minutes if they do. Men who are in the lower-income bracket work significantly more if they are married: eighty-three minutes more if they have no children and one hour and fifty minutes more if they have children.

The fact of the matter is that even though high-income married women have more free time than do comparable single women, they are also doing more housework than their single counterparts—the increase in leisure time results only from their spending less time in the labor market. In fact, married women with children spend an extra thirty-one to forty-one minutes cleaning, forty-one to fifty minutes cooking, and eight to eleven minutes running errands each day over women who are single.

This doesn't mean that married women are disadvantaged; it means that they are exploiting their comparative advantage in home production while their spouses exploit their comparative advantage in the labor force. The reason for this comparative advantage probably has nothing to do with these women's extraordinary powers of folding laundry; it has to do with fact that men can earn more on the labor market.

You would expect that having a whole other person in the family would save a woman more that thirty-four minutes a day, but one possible explanation for that finding is that the quality of home production is much higher in a married woman's home. A second possible explanation is that some married individuals fail to exploit the gains from trade because they do not understand comparative advantage and instead rely on absolute advantage to allocate tasks; the person who is better at doing a job relative to their spouse does that job, instead of doing the jobs they are better at, and allowing their spouse to do the same.

---

married women with children began to move into the workforce, only after jobs became available that rewarded brains over brawn and the gap between men's and women's market earnings declined.

The efficiency of marriage in which two people bring different talents also explains why, traditionally, it has been more common for older men (who have a comparative advantage in earning) to be married to younger women (who have a comparative advantage in fertility) than it is for older women to be married to younger men. That, however, is changing quickly, and better-educated, high-income women are now, more than ever, marrying younger men.

This also explains why it is that some men in higher-wage countries look for, and can find, spouses in foreign countries where both men and women earn low wages. Those men have an advantage over their foreign wives, in terms of their earning ability, and have no difficulty competing with foreign men for desirable women. The wives on the other hand, at least in perception, are better at keeping a home and raising children than are women in the man's home country.

This is a topic we return to in chapter 6, when we talk about bargaining within marriage because, of course, it is not comparative advantage that has the final say on how couples divide household responsibilities—it only suggests how tasks should be divided if a married couple is collectively interested in doing things with the least amount of effort. If one or both people in a marriage are only interested in minimizing their own effort, then what really matters is who has the power to decide who does all the work and who has all the fun.

▨▨▨▨ SEXLESS IN THE CITY

Singles looking for love flood into large cities for two reasons: the search costs are lower in densely populated areas, and matches are of better quality when the population of potential matches is higher.

The cost of searching for a mate is lower in more densely populated areas simply because singles come into contact with far more people on a daily basis in a city than they do in less-populated areas. People in large cities go to busy coffee shops, restaurants, and bars and meet different people every day—not the same people as they might in similar establishments in a more rural area. You might argue that in urban centers people are less open to speaking to strangers, and that might be true, but the sheer volume of people suggests that search times for a mate should be shorter in densely populated urban areas.

Let me give you a somewhat trivial example of why this is the case. Say you work in an office with five other people. One day you announce to your coworkers that you would like their help in finding love and ask if they have any single friends. In a densely populated urban area, if each of your coworkers suggests one single friend, then you will likely have five potential match opportunities. This is possible because each of your coworkers likely operates on a different social network. In a sparsely populated area, however, it is likely that some of your coworkers operate on the same social network, in which case you may end up with only one or two potential match opportunities since some of your coworkers will have suggested the same person.

Fewer possible matches in less densely populated areas mean that you are less likely to find "the one" with this attempt to turn your coworkers into matchmakers, and since you now have to search far longer, the search for love is more costly. (If the concept of costly searches is unclear, consider the example of a woman who knows that if she doesn't marry in the next few years she will significantly reduce her chances of having children. For her, the "cost" of a longer search is directly measurable by the value of the children she may never have. For others, the cost may be just the time spent being lonely when they could have been part of a pair.)

The second option when there are few match opportunities is to discontinue the search and "settle" for one of the available matches, even if the match is not ideal, because the prospect of continuing to search is too daunting.

This brings us to the second reason why singles move to cities looking for love, and that is that the quality of matches should be higher in urban areas where search costs are lower.

Let's go back to our example where you have asked your coworkers if they have any single friends. Imagine that you have in mind a set of minimum qualities your future mate must possess. This set of requirements is your reservation value for a marriage partner; you will only marry if you can find someone whose value on the market exceeds this level.

If you know that your potential dating pool will consist of only one or two people, as it was in the rural example, you will set your *reservation value* very low because otherwise your search costs could be very high. If you know your potential dating pool will be very large, however, as it was in the urban example, you will set your reservation value at a higher level because you can hope to achieve this level with lower search costs.

When search costs are low, reservation values for a mate tend to be higher because people are willing to search longer in the hope of finding a better-quality match.

This is the same argument that explains why access to the Internet has the potential to increase the quality of marriages—it is because low-cost online searches encourage people to set their reservation value at a higher level.

This implies that because singles in more densely populated areas can search more cheaply for a mate, they increase their odds of finding a higher-quality mate—so it isn't surprising that single people flood into cities looking for love.

One additional consideration is that people who are married, those who are no longer searching for a mate, tend to move out of cities in search of lower property values and places that are more suitable to raise children. This means that cities not only have more single people, but also that single people make up a greater share of the population in the city than they do in rural areas.

So your office friends, from our example, are more likely to have at least one single friend in the city than they are in rural areas where a greater share of the population is married.

Having said that cities are better places to find romance, in general, there is one group of people that traditionally have struggled to find love in an urban market: educated women.

According to Roderick Duncan, the reason there are so many single educated women on urban marriage markets is just a matter of numbers and preference; educated women greatly outnumber educated men because more women than men go to college and because educated women prefer to marry men who are better educated than themselves while educated men do not.

We already know from chapter 1 that women have been attending, and completing, college at much higher rates than men since the late 1980s. We also know that women search for men who will allow them to exercise their comparative advantage and that historically, because of the gender wage gap, men have held a comparative advantage in waged employment and women have held a comparative advantage in home production.

Over time this comparative advantage of men in waged employment has developed into a social norm leading women to expect to find men with higher incomes than themselves. Now that educated men have become scarce relative to educated women, however, at least some of the women who marry will not have that expectation met. Over time expectations are changing, but social norms evolve slowly, leaving many women in the meantime struggling to find a marriage partner they deem suitable.

In the past, when the majority of people were not educated above the high school level, most women married men who were less educated than themselves. This is principally because women have always been more likely to finish high school than have men. My own parents are a good example of this; my U.S.-educated mother has a high school diploma while my South African-born father never had an opportunity to finish high school, having been sent into military training at the age of 14. At the time that they married, there was nothing unusual about a high school-educated woman marrying a man who had left school earlier to join the workforce.

According to Roderick Duncan's paper, in 1940, 45 percent of women who had a high school diploma were married to men who did not complete high school while only 20 percent were married to men who had spent at least some time in college. By 1960, this had changed somewhat. At that time, 33 percent of women with a high school diploma were married to men who had not completed high school, compared with 23 percent who were married to men who had spent at least some time in college. By 1990, more women with a high school diploma were marrying men with at least some college than were marrying men who were educated at below the high school level.

This evidence may run contrary to what I have just said about comparative advantage, but in the earlier decades even men who didn't finish high school still earned more than their high school-educated wives—so women married up in terms of income at the same time that they married down in terms of education.

This information brings to light the following observation: the women who have valued finding a husband who is better educated than themselves have been, for a long time, principally college-educated women. As the wage paid to less-educated workers has fallen in the last thirty years and women's wages have increased relative to men's, however, women with less education have also begun to seek men with more education than themselves. This is because men with less than a high school education no longer earn more than their high school–educated wives.

More women seeking more-educated husbands has meant that educated men have becoming relatively scarce compared with educated women, not only because fewer men go to college, but also because changes in wages are encouraging less-educated and more-educated women to pursue the same men.

Men do not appear to share women's preference for a better-educated spouse, and because social norms dictate that women should be homemakers and men providers, traditionally they are happy to find a spouse who is less educated than themselves, allowing them to specialize in market labor. The evidence on dating sites we looked at in chapter 3 backs up this assertion; men looking for love online seem to care very little about a potential mate's income.

In addition to providing a superior marriage market, educated singles tend to move into cities because the wages paid to well-educated workers are higher in cities than they are in rural areas. While this is true for both men and women, educated female workers have an additional incentive to be in cities; they are significantly more likely to find an educated husband there. Less-educated women also have an incentive to move into cities for the same reason—they may not benefit from higher wages in the city, but they are much more likely to find themselves a well-educated husband than they would had they stayed in the country.

Lena Edlund tests this hypothesis using Swedish data and finds that the higher the income earned by men (ages 25 to 44) in a particular city, the more women there are living in that city relative to the number of men. This is an interesting result since we expect that high male wages would encourage more men to move into a city. This might still be the case, but it appears that high male wages also encourage women to move into the city, in fact more women than men. This has to be true for the ratio of men to women to fall when men's incomes are high.

This leads to me to wonder if women take their marriage market prospects into consideration when they decide how much time to spend in school. Perfect foresight should tell women that the longer they stay in school, the more competition they will have when they search for a husband in the future (if women wait until they finish school before marrying, which many do). Because there are fewer potential partners for women at every education level, and many of those men are perfectly happy to marry women who are less educated than themselves, and because they are older when they start to look for a husband, educated women face competition from women who are both less educated and younger.

New research by Canadian economists Sylvain Dessy and Habiba Djebbari tackles this issue and finds that one of the explanations for why men outnumber women in high-power jobs is that women decide to enter the marriage market when they are younger rather than risk being unsuccessful in that market later in life.

It appears from the evidence that some women, at least, choose to invest less in their education in a competitive marriage market because time in school, if it delays marriage, consumes several years of their fertility. If educated men prefer younger but less-educated women over older but better-educated women, then there is an incentive for women to leave school and try to find a well-educated husband while they are young.

This is especially true for women who feel that even with an education their comparative advantage is in caring for children and a home rather than working in the labor force.

Either way, the current situation that leaves educated women with fewer marriage prospects doesn't sound like equilibrium to me—a market is always out of equilibrium whenever supply exceeds demand. I can think of three things that might happen to bring this particular market back into equilibrium.

EVEN IN HOLLYWOOD MARRIAGES, EDUCATION MATTERS

Using information about the current marital status of the top four hundred movie actors, economist Gustaf Bruze finds that male and female stars are likely to be married to another person who has an education level similar to theirs.

Of the men on the list of the top four hundred movie actors, 52 percent were married at the time the data were collected in 2008. Far fewer of the women were married, only 38 percent, despite the fact that women in the top four hundred actors had an average age of 41. Only about half of married movie stars are with people who are well-known, either because they are also actors or because they are models, singers, musicians, etc. For married stars, the average age at which they entered their current marriage was 38 for men and 35 for women. The vast majority of top actors have either never been married (27 percent) or have been married only once (45 percent), making them slightly less likely than the average U.S. citizen to have been married once and slightly more likely never to have been married at all. While they are slightly more likely than the average person to have been married twice (20 percent) or three times (8 percent), the differences are small enough to be insignificant.

Despite our preconception that marriages in Hollywood are fleeting and frequent, the top stars seem to behave pretty similarly to the rest of us. The interesting thing about movie stars is that, unlike the rest of us, their income is not linked to their level of education but rather to a variety of other skills that are not learned in a classroom. In the Hollywood marriage market, we shouldn't observe couples matching over education but rather other characteristics that increase income—like physical appearance.

The odd thing is that even in Hollywood marriages, the education level of a potential spouse appears to matter; a movie star is almost as likely to be married to someone with the same education level as himself/herself as is any-one from the general public. This is interesting because it suggests that finding someone with a similar education level to yours brings something else to marriage besides an indicator of income. Presumably people who are similarly educated have more in common with each other and, even for celebrities, that commonality is important.

The first is that men will increase their investment in education in the hope of improving their position on the marriage market. It is not likely that teenage boys take their marriage prospects into consideration when making education decisions, but we could reasonably expect that they take into consideration their prospects for getting laid when deciding whether or not to continue in school. For that reason alone, given the evidence we discussed in chapter 2, you would think that there would be more men in college.

The second is that educated women in cities will look in a different market for a mate—the rural marriage market. For the same reason educated women outnumber men in the city, less-educated men must out-number women in rural areas—because women are moving to the cities. In the last decade, technology has advanced in such a way that educated workers have more flexibility about where they spend their workday. If women are prepared to marry men with less education—and in fact, accord-ing to the Pew Research Center the share of women currently married to men with less education (28 percent) is greater than the share who is married

MARRIAGE REINFORCES AN ECONOMIC CLASS SYSTEM

At the end of the marriage market, couples seem to be tidily sorted over characteristics such as income, education, religion, height, beauty, and even body weight. A new paper by Kerwin Kofi Charles, Erik Hurst, and Alexandra Killewald finds an additional element that appears to be important in marital sorting: parental wealth.

If we randomly matched a man whose parents' wealth was less than $1,000 with any woman, there would be only a 16 percent chance that he would end up married to a woman whose parents also had less than $1,000 in wealth. In reality, 35 percent of men with low-wealth parents have wives whose parents' wealth is equally low.

On the other hand, if we randomly matched a man whose parents' wealth was greater than $100,000 with any woman, there would be only a 39 percent chance that he would end up married to a woman whose parents also had more than $100,000 in wealth. Instead, 60 percent of men are married to women whose parents have wealth in the top bracket, and only 7 percent are married to women whose parental wealth is less than $1,000.

It isn't surprising that parental wealth plays a role in marriage market outcomes, for a variety of reasons. It could just be that people meet their future spouses in their parents' social circles, or that they have more common interests with those who have similar wealth backgrounds.

What is interesting, though, is that marital sorting over wealth means that the gains from marriage are not equal among people of different socioeconomic groups; wealthy people have far more to gain from marriage than do those with no wealth. This fact might explain why people with higher incomes are more likely to marry than people with low incomes, given that income (and education level) is correlated with parental wealth.

It also suggests that because of the way people choose their spouses, the divide in wealth levels between the rich and the poor will only expand over time. The children of the wealthy will not only inherit their parent's wealth but also that of their spouse's parents. The children of the poor will inherit their parent's debts and the debts of their spouse's parents. Marital sorting over parental wealth suggests that, over time, wealth will become concentrated in the hands of an increasingly smaller proportion of households.

---

to men with more education (19 percent)—then, for some women, finding a city job that allows them to spend their workdays in rural areas might be the answer.

The final possibility is that, of course, educated women will (and do) choose to remain single rather than marry a man with less education and/or income. In doing so, they won't have the benefits of marriage that we discussed earlier, but the market can provide much of what they need (sperm banks, for example) and, for many, their income is sufficiently high that they can afford to purchase at least some of the goods and services that marriage might have provided. For many women, that is the perfect arrangement.

▰▰▰ A LESSON FROM UNTRADITIONAL MARRIAGE AND THOSE LESS LIKELY TO MARRY

Much of what I have said so far applies not only to heterosexual unions but also to same-sex unions. There is one way in which same-sex unions differ, however; people in same-sex relationships are not subject to the same gender wage gap as are people in heterosexual unions. This means that when choosing how much, or how little, to invest in their careers, lesbians have no reason to expect to be married to a person who earns a higher income than themselves in the same way that heterosexual women might.

There is an interesting observation that lesbians are paid wages that are about 6 to 13 percent higher than the wages paid to heterosexual women. One particular study that seeks to understand this lesbian wage premium gives us some insight into how heterosexual women, who might reasonably plan on being married to men, invest in their careers.

According to the evidence, lesbians are, on average, better educated, more likely to be white, living predominantly in cities, having fewer children, and significantly more likely to be professionals than are other women. Even when researchers control for these differences (essentially comparing women who are in every way similar except in their sexual orientation), the lesbian wage premium persists.

One possible explanation goes back to this story of comparative advantage that we have been discussing—the one that says that because men have historically been paid more to work outside the home, women have been handed the comparative advantage in doing all the laundry.

The gap between women's and men's wages may have narrowed, but if a woman believes that she will eventually be married to a man who earns a higher income than herself, then she has less to gain from investing in skills that will give her an advantage on the labor market. This investment in what economists call "human capital" doesn't include just formal education—researchers can control for that using the data—it also includes a variety of skills that the market rewards with higher wages that we can't observe in the data: for example, the level of effort a woman is prepared to put forward to advance her own career.

Women who have no intention of ever marrying a man and look forward to a future with a female spouse do not have the same incentive to underinvest in their own human capital. They are just as likely to find themselves in a relationship with a woman who earns a higher income as they are with a woman who earns a lower income. With no expectation that they will later benefit from having a comparative advantage in home pro-duction relative to a higher-income-earning husband, it makes sense that lesbian women will invest more in skills that give them an advantage on the labor market.

Nasser Daneshvary, Jeffrey Waddoups, and Bradley Wimmer clev-erly test this theory in a paper that calculates the wage premium paid to lesbians in two distinct groups—those who were once in a heterosexual marriage and those who have never been married. The assumption made is reasonable: lesbian women who were once married to men (about 44 per-cent of lesbian women in the sample) have (presumably) in the past had the expectation that they would have a marriage partner with a higher income. The never-married women might also have had this expectation, but it is much more likely that, on average, women in that group expected to be in a relationship with another woman.

Does the evidence support the theory that the lesbian wage premium can be explained by greater investment in more market-oriented skills by lesbian women? Well, controlling for whether or not a woman was ever in a heterosexual marriage does reduce the lesbian wage premium by about 17 percent, thus providing some evidence to support the theory. At 5.2 per-cent though, the once-married lesbian premium is still high. Why it exists continues to be a mystery to researchers.

There is further evidence that women who expect to eventually be married tend to underinvest in their careers. This time the evidence comes from a group of women who might reasonably expect, if they have looked at the data, that they will never marry—women who are obese.

Health economist Heather Brown observes that single women who are obese earn higher wages than similar women with a lower body mass index (BMI). This result is a bit puzzling given that, as a group that includes both married and single women, obese women generally face a wage penalty for carrying more body weight.

After controlling for all other attributes that contribute to the wages earned (occupation, health, education, age, number of children, etc.),

Brown finds that married men and single women both have a wage rate that is positively related to their BMI—the heavier they are, the higher the wage they are paid.

Among single men and married women, their wage rate and BMI are negatively related; the heavier those men and women are, the lower the wage they are paid.

Brown's argument for why married men are paid more when they are heavier is that being overweight does not disadvantage men in the marriage market in the same way that it disadvantages women (i.e., preventing them from finding a spouse), but it does encourage them to invest more into their careers in order to compensate their wives for their lack of physical fitness.

A paper that uses data from the United States and nine European countries by Pierre-André Chiappori, Sonia Oreffice, and Climent Quintana-Domeque illustrates this point using the trade-offs that we discussed in chapter 3. They find that an average man can compensate his wife for an additional 22 lbs/10 kg of body weight by earning 1 percent more than the average wage. They find that overweight women, however, are seriously disadvantaged on the marriage market. Not only are they less likely to marry, but when they do marry, they are much more likely to be married to low-income-earning men. For every unit a married woman's BMI increases, the lower is the earned income of the man to whom she is married.

According to Heather Brown, single women who are heavy recognize that they are less likely to marry, and if they do, they are likely to be married to men who have lower incomes, and so they invest more in their human capital in order to bring their standard of living closer to the point it might have been had they married.

It is also possible that they invest more in their jobs in an attempt to compensate a potential future spouse for being married to a woman who has a high body weight. There is some evidence they can do that, although not nearly as effectively as men can.

It seems that women who believe they will one day be married to a person with greater earning potential than themselves are underinvesting in their careers as a result of this expectation. Thus, understanding the economics behind the way in which married couples organize production of household goods and services helps explain not only how people choose their partners but also (in part) why the wage gap between men and women persists despite incredible gains by women in the workforce. It is easy to believe that the gender wage gap is entirely the product of discriminatory employers, but it appears that the expectations for marriage of some women is leading to lower workforce productivity and lower wages for women on average.

TIME SPENT IN JAIL IS REDUCING MARRIAGE RATES

According to the Pew Research Center, 62 percent of black women (between the ages of 30 and 44) in 1970 were married, compared with only 33 percent in 2007. The marriage rate has also fallen for black men; in 1970, 74 percent were married, compared with 44 percent in 2007.

Just like other educated women, black women searching for an educated spouse are hard-pressed to find one; 57 percent of black women attend college, compared with only 48 percent of black men. Given that, it is not that surprising that black men with a college degree are far more likely to be married than are black men who did not complete high school: 55 percent of college graduates are married, compared with 27 percent of those with less than a high school education.

This difference in education levels cannot completely explain why the marriage rates for black women are so low. One alternative explanation that has been explored by researchers is that marriage rates are falling because black men are incarcerated at much higher rates than are black women, or anyone else for that matter. If black women have a strong preference to marry black men—and, in fact, 96 percent of married black women are with black men—then high rates of incarceration are disadvantaging black women on the marriage market. This is true not just because

EDUCATION IS GOOD FOR INTERRACIAL MARRIAGE

Here is an interesting question: if people face a trade-off between finding someone of their own education level or finding someone of their own ethnicity, then what do they choose?

Using U.S. Census data, Delia Furtado and Nikolaos Theodoropoulos find that for every additional year of education a man or woman has, the probability that he/she is married to a person who is the same race decreases by 1.2 percent.

This says that the more educated people are, the more likely they are to marry outside of their ethnic group. This result isn't altogether surprising given that people who are better educated are more likely to live and work away from their own community.

What is interesting, however, is that in racial communities where the average level of education is higher, this relationship between education and a willingness to marry a person of a different race disappears. In fact, in racial communities with very high average levels of education relative to the rest of the population, people actually have a greater tendency to marry someone of their own ethnicity.

For example, the average Guatemalan in West Palm Beach has seven fewer years of schooling than the rest of the population. For Guatemalans in that city, a one-year increase in education leads to a more than 5-percentage-point decrease in the probability that they will marry another person of Guatemalan ancestry. So, in that community, more education increases the chance a person will marry outside of his/her ethnic group.

Alternatively, the average Indian in Pittsburgh has four more years of education than the rest of the population. For Indians in that city, a one-year increase in education results in an almost 2-percentage-point increase in the probability that they will marry another person of Indian ancestry. So, in that community, more education decreases the chance a person will marry outside of their ethnic group.

Economists tend to assume that parents choose the education level of their child that maximizes their future earning potential, but it is also possible that parents, if they have a strong preference for intra-ethnic marriage, might choose the education level of their children that gives them the highest probability of marrying within their ethnic group. This could very well be a different level of education than one that will make the child materially better off in the future. Understanding the relationship between interethnic marriage and education might explain why we observe large differences in the level of investment in children's education in different racial communities.

---

black men are absent from their community while incarcerated, but also because a man with a criminal record has a much harder time earning a high-enough income to support a family later in his life.

The "Just Say No" campaign in the late 1980s increased the severity of sentencing for drug offenders in the United States. Since that time, and particularly since the mid-1990s, incarceration rates have been steadily increasing to the point that the United States now has one of the highest incarceration rates in the world. This is not just because there are more convictions, but also because longer sentences are increasing the number of people who are in prison at any one point in time.

Incarceration rates vary greatly by both socioeconomic class and race; in 2004, 12.5 percent of all black males age 25 to 29 were incarcerated compared with only 3.5 percent of all Hispanic males and 1.7 percent of all white males of the same age. If women search for a future husband within their community, then some women are more disadvantaged on the marriage market than others when the men in their community are incarcerated at high rates.

Kerwin Kofi Charles and Ming Ching Luoh's research presents evidence that an increase in the incarceration rate by just 1 percentage point leads to a 2.4-percentage-point decrease in the proportion of women who have ever been married. They argue that 13 percent of the decline in the marriage rate since 1990 can be explained by increased male incarceration alone. Black women have been the most affected by the shortage of men, with increased incarceration explaining about 18 percent of the decline in marriage of black women since 1990.

If incarceration and differential education rates by gender can explain why fewer and fewer black women are marrying, then what explains the fact that educated black men are also marrying at lower rates than they did in the past? We might be tempted to predict that they would marry at higher, not lower, rates as they have become scarce relative to women who are looking for an educated husband. But that clearly hasn't been the case.

Just as educated black men have a higher value on the marriage market when women outnumber them, their relative scarcity also gives them market power on the casual dating and sex market. Educated black men presumably do not worry that by postponing marriage they are hurting their future marriage prospects, and so they can choose, if they wish, to wait until they have tired of the casual sex market before marrying. If they decide to marry later, as a result of the gender imbalance, then of course marriage rates for those men will appear to be low at any particular point in time.

▰▰▰ FINAL WORDS

I don't expect my economic marriage vows to be very popular, but maybe there is something to be said for acknowledging that no one is perfect. I would like to find a man who is almost as well educated as I am, for example, because it would be nice if we had that much in common. But I might change my mind about that if I met a man who had less education than me and was extremely physically fit, for example. I would be willing to make this trade-off not only because physically fit men are easy on the eyes (they are), but because I would like to find a man who has a better chance at living to an older age. Sure, I would like to have a man who is both well educated and physically fit, but if I can't find one (or, perhaps more to the point, I can't find one who wants to be with me), then I have to choose what is more important to me—fitness or education.

I argued earlier that without taking into consideration economic forces, our understanding of the world around us is incomplete. This is particularly true when we seek to understand the way in which people choose life partners. One of the most important concepts in economics is that of *opportunity cost*—the potential benefit that is lost when we choose an alternative option. Being in a committed romantic relationship is all about deciding that the benefits of being in a relationship are greater than the opportunity costs—the benefits to being in an alternative relationship or, even, no relationship at all.

Opportunity costs are subject to economic forces and, as a result, evolve as the economy evolves. Seen within that perspective, it isn't that surprising that as education has become a more-important determinant of how much income we earn, as men's comparative advantage over women in waged employment has dissipated, and as opportunities for skilled employment have drawn workers into urban environments, we have changed how we choose our partners.

All of these economic factors have shaped marriage today and will continue to shape marriages in the future. The importance of accepting that is reinforced when we acknowledge that the relationship between marriage and economic factors goes both ways—men and woman take their marriage-market potential into consideration when making important economic decisions. Looking forward, the evolution of the gender wage and education gaps (just to give two examples of economic outcomes) will be shaped, to some degree, by how individuals behave on marriage markets.

Once people marry, the importance of opportunity cost doesn't disappear; the value that individuals have on the marriage market (or, more to the point, the remarriage market), the greater bargaining power they have within their own marriage. That is the topic for chapter 6, which we will turn to after we take some time to talk about the fine institution of marriage, from a legal and societal perspective.

CHAPTER 5
MARRIAGE IS A FINE INSTITUTION

▰▰▰▰ MARRIAGE IS AN INSTITUTION

Mae West famously said, "Marriage is a fine institution—but I'm not ready for an institution yet." And she was right; marriage is a fine *institution*—in the economic sense of the word. Institutions to an economist are simply the rules and beliefs that govern human social behavior. So while sociologists and anthropologists have spent over fifty years debating the definition of marriage, economists are content to understand that marriage refers to the actions that individuals take that define what it means to be a family in that individual's community.

The usefulness of thinking about marriage as an institution is that what it means to be "married" is not carved in stone; the institution has varied significantly from place to place, from community to community, and, importantly, over time. While individuals within a community cannot choose the form of marriage institution adopted by their community—that is something that is decided by the community as a whole—other factors, *economic* factors, determine how the institution evolves over time.

For example, historically the majority of the world's societies have recognized marriage as the union of one man and several women: heterosexual polygyny. A few have recognized marriage as the union of one man

A BRIEF HISTORY OF MARRIAGE

How marital relationships were organized among our ancient ancestors was very closely related to way they accumulated food.

Early foragers (between 5 million and 1.8 million years ago) lived in a primal horde with no long-term mating. Males and females had sex with many partners, and any food sharing was principally in exchange for sexual favors (which, by the way, went not only in both directions but also between same-gender pairs). Because the diet consisted of fruits, nuts, and insects that could be gathered while still carrying and protecting a baby, males were not needed as protectors or providers, making marriage redundant.

As the climate warmed and the forests receded, humans began to move out into the savanna where their diet consisted of gathered vegetation, scavenged meat left behind by predators, and, eventually, meat killed by hunters using tools. Increased meat in their diet meant that babies were born earlier and required more care from their mothers if they were to survive. Resources were spread evenly among men and, as a result, monogamy was the marriage institution that prevailed in this period (between 1.8 million and 23,000 years ago). Really, though, the best descriptor of marriage in this era is serial monogamy, since couples only stayed together long enough to ensure the survival of their offspring (about four years).

Between 23,000 and 10,000 years ago, people started to become agriculturalists, growing their own food. The invention of the plow over 4,000 years ago led to the division of tasks into those that were done by men and those that were done by women. Agriculture also meant that men could accumulate wealth, bringing an end to the equality among men that had existed in previous eras. Despite this inequality, monogamy prevailed, possibly because field-work made it impossible for a husband to guard more than one wife.

There is another theory, put forward by Brooks Kaiser and me, that humans were biologically hardwired for monogamy because that was the institution that ensured the greatest survival of children, and that certain types of agriculture, particularly dairy farming, encouraged the persistence of that marriage institution despite inequality between men. This was because dairy animals produce pair-bonding hormones, encouraging monogamy even when agriculture encouraged polygyny.

Supporting this theory is the observation that communities in those areas in which cattle farming was prevalent, such as in Europe, mostly practiced monogamy while those in areas that did not, such as in Africa, mostly practiced polygyny.

---

and one woman: heterosexual monogamy. A very small number of societies have recognized alternative arrangements like polyamory (multiple husbands and wives) and polyandry (one wife with multiple husbands).

Most countries today that have monogamy as the legal structure for marriage in reality practice a form of marriage that is better described by the term "serial monogamy"—a marriage system in which one man or one woman can have multiple husbands or wives (so, effectively polygamy)—but are permitted to be married to only one partner at any given point in time.

When we compare the economies of countries with institutionalized serial monogamy to those with institutionalized polygamy, we find that the industrialized nations of the world, without exception, have rejected polygamy as a marriage institution. This observation is a bit of a mystery to economists, for reasons I will describe in a minute, but it illustrates the link between the nature of a country's economy and the form of marriage institution recognized by the government.

A second example of the relationship between economics and marriage institutions is the willingness of the wealthy nations of the world to institutionalize marriage between two men or two women (same-sex monogamy). The individual citizens of countries that have legally recognized same-sex monogamous marriage (or, in some cases, civil unions) may not all feel that same-sex monogamy is "marriage" in their books, but institutional change doesn't require everyone in the community to be on board; a change in the legal framework (i.e., the rules) is all that is required for institutional change to take place.

The relationship between same-sex monogamy and national wealth is less of a mystery than the relationship between serial monogamy and national wealth; one of the reasons nations have been able to accumulate wealth is that their respect for individual rights and freedoms has created an innovative environment in which new technologies flourish. It is this same respect for individual rights and freedoms that have made it possible for advocates of same-sex marriage to fight and win their battles for legal recognition for same-sex monogamous unions. So economic development hasn't made same-sex marriage possible, but rather the same qualities that made it possible for countries to grow rich have also made them more open to institutional change in marriage.

Before talking more about institutions, let me first give you an example of the role economics plays in how individual households choose the way in which their marriages are organized and how those individual choices translate into society-wide adoption of that form of organization.

BILL GATES'S HOUSE HAS ITS OWN WIKIPEDIA PAGE

According to its Wikipedia page, Bill Gates's home is a 66,000-square-foot mansion nicknamed Xanadu after the fictional estate owned by the recluse, Charles Kane, in the movie *Citizen Kane*. Gates lives there with his wife, Melinda, suggesting that he is probably less lonely than the owner of the original (albeit fictitious) Xanadu who lived, and died, alone in his gothic home.

I would like you to consider this entirely fictional scenario: imagine that Bill Gates actually is a little lonely in that big house of his and decides one day that what he really wants is a second wife. The house is certainly large enough for multiple families, so who is made worse off by that decision?

Melinda Gates, presumably, would be psychologically worse off than she would have been had she stayed the only wife, but in terms of economic well-being, it is hard to imagine that the addition of one more wife to the house would in any way reduce the resources available to her and her children below their current level. Also, if Melinda had anticipated that Bill would eventually find a second wife when she decided to marry him, then it has to be true that even if she would rather remain his only wife, she still would be better off as Bill's first wife than if she had pursued other options for marriage, for example, marriage to a man who would never have a second wife.

This argument may sound counterintuitive since most us can't imagine living in a polygynous household, but it has to be true if Melinda had come into the marriage expecting there would be two wives and had acted in her own best interest and that of her children when she made that decision; in choosing hypothetically polygynous Bill, she revealed that she prefers being married to him over being married to another man, despite having to tolerate a second wife.

The second wife Bill finds and marries, let's call her Natalie, is definitely better off than she would have been otherwise. She would be married to one of the wealthiest men in the world, and she and her children would never lack resources. She may not like being the second wife, but again, if she knew that Bill was already married to Melinda before she chose to marry him, as long as she was acting in her own best interest and that of her children, then she must be better off than she would have been otherwise. She could have chosen to be the only wife of another, presumably poorer, man or to have remained single, but the fact that Natalie chose to be Bill's second wife reveals that that is the arrangement that makes her the happiest.

Bill is presumably better off. He can afford a whole harem of wives, so the resources available to him are not diminished, and the fact that he himself made the decision to take the second wife reveals that he prefers the arrangement with two wives to the arrangement with one wife.

It sounds like everyone in the fictitious polygynous household of Xanadu is better off with this marriage arrangement than they would have been without it; they have to be since they all willingly participated. It doesn't mean that polygyny is their ideal marital arrangement, especially for the women, but it does mean that out of their particular set of possible marital arrangements, this one is preferred.

So, here is my second question: if extremely wealthy men, like Bill Gates, could find multiple women to be their wives and if these marriage arrangements made everyone better off, then why do the laws in the United States prevent such arrangements? Or put another way, why do wealthy nations, in which rich men are significantly richer than are poor men, have institutionalized monogamy?

The answer to these questions really boils down to two factors.

The first is that Melinda Gates is an intelligent and educated woman, and in industrialized nations where education and intelligence are highly valued, she has quite a bit of power on the marriage market. She would never have agreed to be the first of two wives because she probably could have found another man who was willing to make her his one and only wife without having to marry a significantly poorer man. Sure, he may not have been one of the wealthiest men in the world, but I suspect that she would be willing to give up a fairly large amount of wealth rather than share her husband with another woman.

This means that if Bill wants a wife who is willing to be the first of two wives, then he has to choose a woman of less intelligence and education than Melinda. That might seem like a fine idea, but if he also wants to have intelligent and educated children, in an economy in which those characteristics are highly valued, he probably wouldn't do that. Sure, some wealthy men are married to less-educated but highly attractive women, but those women also have a great deal of market power and are much more capable of finding a marriage arrangement in which they are the only wife.

So Bill, I suspect, would still have only one wife even if the laws allowed him to have more because wealthy men in industrial nations, just like him, have historically preferred to have one ideal wife rather than several less-than-ideal wives. Wealthy men have revealed that when it comes to wives, quality is more important than quantity.

If this is the case, then the answer to the question "Why do the laws in the United States prevent such arrangements?" is simply that economic factors led to a social norm in which each man had only one wife, and the lawmakers, at the beginning of confederation, simply codified that social norm into law.

As I have already said, there are two factors that can explain why wealthy nations prefer monogamy. In order to understand the second factor, we need to be reminded that there is one other person who has so far been ignored in this fictional story: the man that Natalie would have married had she not married Bill. We are going to call him Charles.

Charles is clearly worse off with Bill's decision to become a polygamist than he would have been if Bill continued to be a monogamist. Charles may find another woman to marry, now that his ideal wife Natalie is married to Bill, but he would have preferred to be married to her rather than any other woman.

Now that Charles has married this less-than-ideal woman, another man is without his ideal wife and now has to marry another less-than-ideal woman. This continues down the line of men—from the richest to the poorest—until somewhere at the end of the line is a man with no prospects of a wife at all.

If there are equal numbers of men and women in a polygynous society, then it is a mathematical reality that some men will be disenfranchised from the market for marriage (and possibly sex) because of that institutional arrangement.

It is odd to think that lawmakers (predominately wealthy and power-ful men) would impose institutionalized monogamy, effectively forcing women to marry poorer men, if they themselves would benefit from polyg-ynous marriage institutions. But in a democracy, and even in other politi-cal systems, it is generally considered disadvantageous for lawmakers to create laws that generate a class of angry, unmarried, and celibate men. A second possible argument for institutionally rejecting polygyny is to placate the masses of poorer men who would suffer as a result of their sexual disenfranchisement.

Before I explain the economic rational that underlies this story, I feel like I would be remiss if I didn't mention that the occupant of the ficti-tious Xanadu, Charles Kane, may have died in that house as a sad and lonely man, but he did marry—twice, in fact. And while he may not have been legally married to both women simultaneously, he, like many other wealthy men, managed for a while to live an essentially polygynous lifestyle with both a wife and a mistress. I think we all know how those stories end—in Hollywood movies at least—badly.

Kane's story illustrates that even without institutionalized polygamy, the existence of both infidelity and serial monogamy belies a social toler-ance of alternative marriage arrangements for the wealthy. We have those topics to look forward to in chapter 8, when we talk about how economics influences infidelity.

MONOGAMY MATH

Economic analysis is based on the logic embedded in mathematics, and I would be remiss if I failed to share any mathematical modeling with you in this book. With that in mind, let me illustrate a model that describes a particular concept that economists use to determine whether or not a current arrangement is the best one possible. That concept is called *Pareto efficiency*, and for an arrangement to be the best in the Pareto sense means that there is no other arrangement that could make some people better off without making others worse off. In a world ruled by economists, the criteria for Pareto efficiency would be used to determine whether or not governments should changes laws, like the ones that impose monogamy or forbid same-sex marriage.

I affectionately call my illustration below "Monogamy Math."

All economic models use symbols that convey specific meaning. Monogamy math is no different, and here we will use four symbols, each representing an individual man or woman.

The first two symbols represent the women in the model who are either married or seeking a husband. They are either happy or unhappy:

The second two symbols represent the men in the model who are either married or seeking a wife, and they are either happy or unhappy:

For simplicity, we will assume that the women are all pretty much identical in the sense that all the men would be happy to be married to any one of them. The men, however, are all different in terms of what they bring to a marriage. This difference could mean income, which is what I will use here, but it could mean other things as well: good genes, a caring disposition—whatever you like to think that women are looking for in a mate.

If there were three men in this economy and we could line them all up according to what they bring to a marriage, then they would be arranged thus:

Everyone in this simple model would like to be married, and the way that men and women meet for the purposes of marriage is by being randomly placed into pairs (think of this as a speed-dating event for stick figures). The men will all be happy with their potential mates, since the women are all effectively the same, and will each make an offer of marriage to their partner. The women, on the other hand, will be either happy or unhappy depending on how much, or how little, their potential partner is able to bring to a marriage. Imagine after the couples are randomly matched they look something like this:

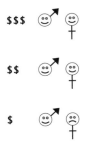

Everyone here is happy with his or her potential spouse, except for the woman who has been matched to the man who has the least to bring to a marriage.

Is there any way that we can make her happier?

If polygamy were permitted, she could be made happier by rejecting her current marriage proposal and pursuing a marriage proposal from the man who has the most to offer a wife. That may not make his first wife happy, but in a society with institutionalized polygyny, she would have anticipated that her wealthy husband would take a second wife if one were available. If she preferred to be married to a poorer man with one wife to being married to a wealthy man with two wives, she would have rejected his offer of marriage. Given that she accepted it, however, she still has to be happier being married to this man than to either of the other two available men.

Societies with institutional polygamy and a very unequal distribution of resources among men often have marriage arrangements that look like this:

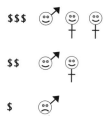

Everyone is happy with his or her mate, if they have one, but the poor man at the bottom of the income distribution is left without a wife.

What is the point of this simple model? Well, the economic criterion for determining if a policy is efficient requires that there is no policy that could make one individual better off without making another individual worse off, given an initial allocation of resources among individuals. This condition does not require that everyone is happy with his or her allocation, nor does it require that everyone be treated equally.

Is the marriage system described in our model Pareto efficient or can it be improved upon by imposing monogamy, for example?

Imposing monogamy would certainly make the man who brings the least to a marriage happier because, with that marriage institution, the woman who was initially matched with him would have to accept his marriage proposal if she wanted to be married. So he would be made better off, but she would be made worse off because that is not the decision that she would have made had she been given the option of marring a richer man. This suggests that the current system of institutionalized polygamy is Pareto efficient. It may not be perfect, someone is still unhappy, but it is as perfect as we can get given the distribution of resources.

I should point out that if in our simple model we started instead with institutionalized monogamy, then that arrangement would also meet the

WHEN PROSTITUTION BECOMES PREFERABLE TO MARRIAGE

In our model, a woman who is matched with a poor man can choose only between being his sole wife and being one of several wives of a wealthy man. There are alternatives, though, including the possibility that she could find more than one poor man (brothers for example) and marry them both. That would both give her more resources and allow all men to marry. For these reasons, it makes sense that societies that allow polygyny should also allow polyandry.

In reality, these institutional arrangements rarely exist.

One possible explanation, proposed by economists Lena Edlund and Evelyn Korn, is that when given the option of being either a wife with multiple husbands or one of many wives, some women would say, "No thanks. I would rather be a prostitute."

As we already know, polygynous marriage leaves many men unmarried. Since unmarried men would still like to have sex, however, unless they are prepared to resort to having sexual relationships with married women (which no doubt happens), the only option available for many unmarried men is to turn to prostitutes for sex.

As a result, polygynous marriage increases the demand for prostitutes where it is prevalent and drives up the price men are willing to pay for sex. That increase in price encourages women to choose prostitution over marriage, leading to high rates of prostitution in polygynous societies and explaining why polyandry rarely exists in conjunction in polygyny.

The idea that women who might otherwise become wives are willing to prostitute themselves when prices are sufficiently high may sound outrageous, but Steven Levitt and Sudhir Alladi Venkatesh observed over the course of their prostitution study in Chicago that when the demand for prostitutes increases over the July Fourth weekend, women who were not prostitutes before the spike in demand begin to enter the market in response to the higher pay.

As an aside, this same logic explains why in China, where single men greatly outnumber single women, many women become prostitutes rather than marry; the excess of men in that market makes entering the sex trades profitable enough that women are willing to forgo the benefits of marriage.

---

criterion of Pareto efficiency. Imposing polygamy on that society may make women who would have otherwise been forced to marry men at the bottom of the resource distribution better off, certainly, but it also would make those men who now will never marry worse off.

In this case, institutionalized monogamy is also Pareto efficient in the sense that if it were replaced with institutionalized polygyny, the criterion would not be met, as some individuals would become better off (the rich men and their wives) but only at the expense of making others worse off (the poor men).

So the first point to be made here is that if a society has institutionalized polygamy, and women are freely permitted to refuse offers of marriage they do not like, then imposing monogamy helps men, but makes women worse off. This is because institutionalized monogamy forces women to marry men they would not have married had they been able to choose an alternative.

The second point is that the more unequal the distribution of resources among men, the more incentive there is for a woman to want to be part of a polygynous household. In a polygynous household, resources have to be shared over more people, not only more wives but their children as well. So if the richest man has 50 percent more resources than the poorest man, that difference in wealth will probably not generate polygyny since the second wife would still be better off being married to the poorer man. The only condition under which a women would choose to become the second wife of the wealthy man would be one in which he has significantly more resources than poor men—at least double but probably more.

I said earlier that the absence of polygyny in wealthy nations is a mystery, and this model illustrates why that is the case. The one characteristic of many modern-day wealthy nations is that they have very high levels of inequality. The wealthiest men in the United States, for example, are not just two or three times wealthier than the poorest men—they are hundreds of times wealthier than even those in the middle of the income distribution.

If all that mattered to wealthy men was the number of wives they themselves had, then wealthy nations should have developed polygyny as the dominant marriage institution at some point in history. The fact that they did not requires a more sophisticated economic explanation than the one described by our model.

IT IS A TRUTH UNIVERSALLY ACKNOWLEDGED, THAT A SINGLE MAN IN POSSESSION OF A GOOD FORTUNE MUST BE IN WANT OF A WIFE . . . OR TWO

One possible reason for why currently wealthy nations have not adopted polygamy is that wealthy men have historically had more sons than did poor men. This is the case not just because wealthy men had more children, they did, but because successful men tended to have more sons on average than did poor men (the ratio of sons to daughters for U.S. presidents used to make a good argument for this claim, but the last three presidents (without a single son among them) have rather made a mess of those numbers). If wealthy men in the past cared about their sons' well-being, they might have supported institutionalized monogamy even if they had preferred polygamy.

Anyone who has read a historic romance novel, such as those written by Jane Austen, knows that in the past the sons of rich men did not all become rich men themselves. Economic historians like Gregory Clark and Gillian Hamilton show that the wealthier landowning class in England prior to the Industrial Revolution had more children that survived to adult-hood, but that many of those children later moved into the lower economic classes; inheritance laws favored the eldest sons, leaving younger children to essentially fend for themselves.

While a wealthy father might have preferred to have more than one wife for himself, and he might lobby for laws that would permit that arrangement, institutionalized polygyny would have reduced the probability that some of his sons, the ones who did not inherit wealth, would marry and have a family. Even if those sons did marry (after all, they did not become the poorest men in society; they just became poorer than their elder brother), polygyny would have certainly reduced the supply of women suitable to be the wife of a nobleman's son. Polygyny would have forced each subsequent generation of men to marry women who were essentially inferior, as all the daughters born into the superior classes would be wed to only the wealthiest men.

Just as inheritance laws that passed the bulk of a man's estate to his oldest son prevented the dilution of the family's assets, laws that enforced monogamy prevented the dilution of the family's genes.

Along the same vein, polygyny increases the demand for wives, which effectively increases the value of wives on the market. I don't doubt that the fathers of middle- and lower-class daughters would have been happy to see their daughters marrying above their station, so to speak, but I wonder how the fathers of upper-class daughters would feel about their daughter being only one of multiple wives. Certainly their daughters would make

IS MONOGAMY DRIVING US TO DRINK?

I will admit this much: if I had to live in a household where my husband had more than one wife, there would have to be alcohol involved. The reality is, though, that most individuals in polygynous relationships in the developed world are part of either Mormon fundamentalist or Muslim traditions, both of which forbid the consumption of alcohol. Is there a relationship between monogamy and alcohol consumption? Is having only one spouse driving us to drink?

Economists Mara Squicciarini and Jo Swinnen pose this question in an American Association of Wine Economists working paper and find that preindustrial societies that had polygyny as the dominant marriage institution consumed less alcohol than those societies in which monogamy was the dominant institution. They also find that as individual societies transitioned from largely polygamous to largely monogamous, alcohol consumption increased.

Both of these facts suggest a relationship between monogamy and drinking alcohol.

Before jumping to conclusions here, I should point out that there is no evidence that monogamy makes us drink more or that drinking makes us more monogamous. The truth is that monogamy and alcohol consumption are merely correlated, and that some third factor, most likely industrialization, is independently driving both the transition to monogamy and the increased alcohol consumption.

We already know why monogamy is more common in industrialized economies, but it turns out that alcohol consumption is also related to industrialization. The technological innovation that goes hand in hand with industrialization makes the production of cheap alcohol possible and gives households a high-enough income to purchase things other than just the food and shelter that are needed to survive— luxuries such as alcohol. And along with industrialization comes urbanization; people who live in cities have more opportunity to consume alcohol, so that cities provided the impetus to develop a drinking culture.

Of course, this doesn't explain why the two dominant religions that permit polygyny also forbid alcohol consumption, but economic inquiry has its limits, and explaining religious doctrine is not a bad place to draw the line.

---

better matches (for example, more women would have a chance to be married to the king), but the political value of a good match for a daughter is eroded when she is forced to compete with multiple wives within the same household.

This is a reasonable argument for why wealthy Western countries did not adopt polygyny in the past, but it isn't the only one. A second is that most European countries have a long history of decentralized power, and monogamy was a gift to the masses that ensured their continued support of the ruling powers.

George Bernard Shaw in his 1903 *Maxims for Revolutionists* presented this argument best when he wrote:

"Any marriage system which condemns a majority of the population to celibacy will be violently wrecked on the pretext that it outrages morality. Polygamy, when tried under modern democratic conditions, as by the Mormons, is wrecked by the revolt of the mass inferior men who are condemned to celibacy by it; for the maternal instinct leads a woman to prefer a tenth share in a first-rate man to the exclusive possession of a third-rate one."

Even without democracy, it might have been smart for an authoritarian ruler to impose monogamy—if he wanted to keep his head. Economist Nils-Petter Lagerlöf developed a model that builds on the idea that an authoritarian ruler will implement laws that forbid polygyny, even at the expense of limiting himself to just one wife, if it pacifies the masses.

As I have already said, with high levels of inequality, wealthy men will be able to have many wives because women will choose to be the second, third, or fourth wife of a rich man over being the only wife of a poor man. Being a poor man in a country in which other men are extremely rich is one thing, but being a poor man who will never be able to marry while other men have many wives is quite another. When inequality is high, both in terms of wealth and access to sex, peasants form rebellions that wreck the rulers of the country. Rulers in this situation may prefer to have multiple wives, but probably not at the expense of being beheaded by an angry mob. And so they impose monogamy on everyone in an attempt to placate poor men.

A ruler will want to be certain that not only his rule will survive, but also the rule of his descendants. Laws can always be changed at the whim of whoever is sitting on the throne. If rulers involved the established church in the imposition of monogamy, however, they are better able to enforce those laws in the future as well as the present. By encouraging the established church to build monogamy into the moral code of a country, the current ruler could win even greater favor with his subjects than by simply passing laws that could be revoked at whim.

All of this is in the past, and yet monogamy persists in industrialized nations today despite the widening gap in incomes between the rich and the poor. The explanation for that phenomenon hinges on the way that we value children in industrial nations and, beyond simply explaining why we do not have polygyny in the West, suggests that even if we did change our laws to permit marriages with multiple partners, the majority of households would never be polygamous even if it were legally permitted.

▰▰▰▰ THE MYSTERY THAT IS MONOGAMY

We have a mystery, the mystery of the persistence of monogamy in the face of a widening income gap between the rich and the poor (not to be confused with the "myth of monogamy," which is a topic for chapter 8, when we discuss infidelity). Thanks to economists Omer Moav, Eric Gould, and Avi Simhon, we have an explanation as to why Western nations have institutionalized monogamy, despite extremely high levels of inequality.

In wealthy nations, women have the right to work and to own assets. Many women don't depend on men to support them the way that they do in countries where women have limited access to education, employment, and property ownership. As a result, a woman in an industrialized nation is free to marry a guy who lives in a cardboard box, if she wants, without starving since she doesn't need to depend on him for survival.

From a modern perspective, our Monogamy Math story probably doesn't make much sense; a woman in modern societies doesn't have to choose between being the only wife of a poor man and being the second wife of a rich man—she can stay single if she likes and still be able to provide for herself and for her children.

Our marriage institutions, however, were determined historically; monogamy was established long before women could go to school, earn income, or own property. So there has to be more to the explanation as to why we don't have polygyny in industrialized countries, with high levels of income inequality among men, other than the unwillingness of modern women to enter into these arrangements.

In the past, when almost all employment was agricultural, how much a worker earned depended more on his/her level of brawn than it did on his/her level of brains. Once countries began to industrialize, however, skills became more important, and workers with higher levels of human capital (a.k.a. education and training) began to be paid more than workers with lower levels of human capital. This change in the way in which skill was rewarded has changed the way households invest in children; industrialization has shifted household preference away from having many children, with little or no education, toward having fewer, better-educated, children.

You will recall that in chapter 1, I mentioned that the decline in U.S. fertility rates began around 1800, at the onset of the Industrial Revolution. That decline was the direct result of the fertility decisions of parents responding to the current labor market conditions (i.e., the increased demand for semiskilled workers) by giving their children the best opportunity to earn an income in the future.

The solution to the puzzle as to why industrialized nations have adopted monogamy lies in this difference between the wages paid to educated workers in industrial and preindustrial nations.

In preindustrial nations, richer men typically have higher incomes than other men purely because they have access to more resources like land, for example. In terms of children, those men prefer to have many children who can work on that land and raise the income of the whole household. If the goal is to produce as many children as possible, then potential wives are not so different from each other; in fact, they are very much like the women in our Monogamy Math example.

In industrial nations, richer men typically have a higher income because they have high levels of human capital (schooling, for example). When it comes to children, those men prefer to have skilled children because they know that in the future it will be the skill level of their children that will determine their income. One way to have highly skilled children is to have a wife who is also highly skilled. Thus, industrialization increases the demand for "high-quality" wives, those who are better educated, and increases in demand have increased the value of these women on the marriage market.

The economic argument here is, essentially, that monogamy has emerged as the dominant marriage institution because the demand for high-quality children has increased the value of high-quality women in the marriage market, making it difficult for even wealthy men to afford more than one wife.

(To clarify this notion of the "value" of a wife, it is helpful to think of a wife's value as determining how much bargaining power a man has to give her in order to encourage her to become his wife. If high-quality wives have high values, that implies that husbands need to give them more say in household decisions—including the decision on how many wives he will have.)

So, while a high level of income inequality for men may encourage a society to adopt polygamy, high educational inequality for women will encourage a society to adopt monogamy. Clearly in most industrial nations the second effect, that of educated wives, has dominated the first effect, that of wealthy husbands.

There are some interesting implications that stem from this story that we have been discussing. The first is that this can explain why wives have more bargaining power in industrialized societies where educated workers earn much higher wages. It also explains why it is that men and women prefer to marry people with similar educational levels to themselves when skilled workers are paid much higher wages than unskilled workers. Finally, it is consistent with the evidence that even in poorer countries, wealthy men with high education levels tend to marry fewer wives and have fewer children, both of which tend to be more educated, than do wealthy men with less education.

In terms of what is the best policy, if we believe that eliminating polygyny in poorer nations would make children better off (there is mixed evidence on whether or not this is the case), then one way to achieve that goal would be to increase education levels. Increased education for all workers should encourage industrialization and increase the wages paid to well-educated workers. Educating women also increases their bargaining power within marriage and should have the effect of reducing the number of wives, and children, in each household.

In my mind, the most important implication from this economic approach to marriage institutions is that even if Western nations did legally allow polygamy, very few people would choose that arrangement. I know I said that legalizing polygamy would not be a Pareto improvement because poor men would be excluded from the marriage market. But if very few people choose to live this way, then that effect would be very, very small. Plus, the reality is that many women prefer to remain single rather than marry a man that they don't desire as a husband. In that respect, economic independence for women is a much bigger contributor to bachelorhood than legalized polygamy ever could be.

▨▨▨ HOW AMERICA CAME TO ACCEPT SAME-SEX MARRIAGE

The biggest change to the institution of marriage in the last decade has been the legal recognition, in many jurisdictions, of the union between people of the same gender.

As I said at the beginning of this chapter, institutions are the rules and beliefs that govern human social behavior. If institutions change, it is often because beliefs change, and that change in beliefs leads to a change in the rules that formally enshrine the institution.

Attitudes toward same-sex marriage have changed in a surprising way over the past two decades. What makes this an interesting story for us here is that it illustrates not only that institutions can evolve, but also that institutional change does not depend on everyone within a particular community changing personal beliefs.

Let me tell you a story that illustrates this evolution.

Several years ago a very close family friend was searching our family name on the Internet and had the good fortune to meet up with the wife of my cousin in South Africa. The two women became friends and eventually fell in love. Divorce (from my cousin) and marriage between them followed (or something legally akin to marriage, since South Africa didn't have equal marriage rights at that time). Immigration laws in Canada allowed my cousin's now former wife to enter the country (with my little second cousins in tow) as the wife of our good friend, and they lived (very) happily ever after.

At the time the big question was this: who was going to tell Dad? I loved my father, but he had not exactly left us with the impression that he was on board with same-sex marriage. But, as it turned out, we underestimated him; he didn't need to be told (while he may not have had liberal views, he certainly wasn't naive), and to our surprise he was thrilled that they had found happiness in each other.

I never would have predicted his radical change in opinion toward same-sex relationships.

The point of the story is that people do change their beliefs, and it is through that evolution of beliefs that institutional change takes place.

As we discussed in chapter 1, public opinion of same-sex relationships has been evolving quickly over the past couple of decades. According to Gallup, in the United States in just fifteen years, there has been an incredible 23-percentage-point decline in opposition to the legal recognition of marriage between people of the same gender.

Part of this trend toward greater acceptance of same-sex marriage has come about because the younger generations are more accepting, and as these generations make up a greater proportion of the population, beliefs, on average, change. This is the "cohort effect." But most of the change in beliefs over the past fifteen years has occurred not because of a cohort effect but because people, like my father, have changed the way they feel about same-sex marriage.

A paper by sociologist Dawn Michelle Baunach analyzes this change and finds that the cohort effect is only responsible for 33 percent of the change in attitudes toward same-sex marriage between 1988 and 2006. This is the last year of available data, but if we were able to look right up until 2011, with the polls showing that a change in opinion is accelerating over time, I suspect that we would find that even more of the trend is attributable to change in beliefs rather than a cohort effect.

So the institutional change has been made possible because many people have changed their beliefs about same-sex marriage and not just because the less-accepting older generation has been replaced with a more-accepting younger generation. As it turns out, though, acceptance is not uniformly distributed over groups of individuals; in fact, nothing could be further from the truth.

SHACKING UP BEFORE MARRIAGE

Two-thirds of recently married Americans lived together before they married and, empirically at least, that seems like a bad idea. On average, couples who live together before marriage have lower-quality marriages that are more likely to end in divorce. They also fare much worse economically, accumulating less wealth over their marriages, than do couples who do not cohabitate before marriage.

New research by Jonathan Vespa and Matthew Painter suggests some hope for couples who want the benefits of living together before they are ready to take a walk down the aisle. It finds that while it may be true that cohabiters as a group fair worse later in their relationships, a subset of cohabiters actually do better over time than couples who didn't live together before they married: couples who have no previous history of cohabiting relationships.

They find that serial cohabiters, even those who had only one prior cohabitation experience, have both lower incomes and lower wealth levels in their marriages. Those who are "spousal cohabiters" (having lived with only their spouse), however, may start their marriages with less wealth (about 5 percent less) than those who did not live together before marrying, but their wealth level grows twice as fast after marriage (about 2 percent per year).

What this means is that over time the wealth levels of people who lived together before marriage, with only their current spouse, eventually converge to the same level as those who married without living together first.

One of the reasons cohabiters look so financially unsuccessful in their marriages, and in their wealth levels, is not that cohabitation is bad for marriage; it is that those who marry without first cohabitating are more confident about the success of their marriages and are therefore willing to invest more heavily into their relationships and their joint portfolio. For example, they are more willing to pool their resources together and buy a house than might someone who has more experience with relationship dissolution, like a serial cohabiter.

A second explanation for why spousal cohabiters do better than serial cohabiters is that they appear to delay marriage for different reasons. While serial cohabiters might consider living together as a trial period to see if the relationship will work, spousal cohabiters are more likely to delay marriage because they want to finish school or because they want to be able to afford a house when they marry. It seems that delaying for these reasons makes the marriage more successful in the long run.

Probably the most important element of this research is that rather than observing that opinions are converging in favor of equal marriage rights, in reality individual communities are diverging in terms of their opinions. So, for example, people who are white have become more accepting of same-sex marriage over time, while the opinion of the black community has remained almost unchanged (71 percent opposed same-sex marriage in 1988, compared with 69 percent in 2006). Democrats have become more accepting relative to Republicans, and non-evangelical Christians have changed their opinions by a greater percentage than have evangelical Protestants.

Baunach argues that the reason for the growing divide is that people in some groups have come to accept that the legalization of same-sex marriage is about equal rights, rather than about morality, while people in other groups have not.

I wonder, though, if the real issue is that the individuals in the more-accepting groups are more likely to have had an opportunity to observe marriages between people of the same gender firsthand. Not only was that the experience in my family, but seemingly the experience of President Barack Obama's family as well. The record shows that it is much harder to be opposed to same-sex marriage when you see your neighbors, your colleagues, or your family members happily united.

Just as an aside, you might try to use the Pareto efficiency test to see if allowing same-sex marriage makes anyone better off at the expense of making others worse off. If they have not, and I would argue that no one is made worse off in any measurable sense when people of the same gender are allowed to marry, then changing those laws has to be a welfare improvement according to that criterion.

▨▨▨ FINAL WORDS

Marriage is a fine institution, and one that is better understood when viewed through an economist's lens. What both these examples, monogamy/polygyny and same-sex marriage, illustrate is that marriage institutions can change over time and that economic factors play an important role in their evolution. Institutions are, by definition, external to the beliefs of the individual whose behavior they govern because, in theory at least, they represent the beliefs of the collective rather than that of a few individuals within the collective. The beliefs of the collective themselves are, in turn, shaped by the nature of the economy in which we live.

Societies in largely industrialized nations have rejected polygamy as a marriage institution because in those economies mental ability is highly valued in the labor force. Thus, men prefer to have fewer, educated, children over having many, less-educated, children. Since monogamy helps them achieve that goal, the collective has come to adopt the view that monogamous marriage is preferred to polygamous marriage.

More recently, in many of those same industrialized countries, the belief in equal marriage rights for same-sex couples has led to a change in marriage institutions. Acknowledging the importance of those rights is currently shaping public opinion, and that change in opinion has made it possible for the institution of marriage to change as well.

The evolution of the institution of marriage, in the legal sense, is not necessarily determined by public opinion in the short run but rather by the opinion of those who have the power to set policy. If the polygyny story teaches us anything, though, it is this: unless policy makers have the power to change public opinion, in the long run, democratic societies (and as we have seen, even authoritarian societies) will ultimately have institutions that reflect the beliefs of the majority, regardless of the personal preferences of those in power.

I said that Bill Gates would probably have only one wife even if the laws permitted him to have two because the economic conditions have given his wife, Melinda, sufficient bargaining power within their marriage that she can insist on a monogamous arrangement. These same conditions that have made the need for anti-polygamy laws irrelevant to most couples in industrialized nations have led to dramatic changes in the way in which couples organize their relationships. Economics has played a big role in shaping the modern family.

CHAPTER 6
BRINGING HOME THE BACON

▰▰▰▰ MARRIAGE IS ALL ABOUT COMPROMISE

Let me start with a story that does a much better job than I might in introducing the material we will discuss in this chapter. It is the continuation of the story of Jane that I promised you earlier, and it tells of the marriage that she entered into in the year after she left her life of post–high school debauchery. You already know how well that marriage worked out, since in the third part of her life she is again unmarried. But while she might not have found her Prince Charming, her not-so-happy-ever-after is an apt description of how marriage is evolving as a result of some powerful economic forces.

Without a university degree or gainful employment, Jane soon discovered that her marriage market deficiencies in terms of her education levels and earning potential were more than compensated for by her youthfulness; at the tender age of 19, she began living with a man who was nine years her senior and well equipped to provide her with much-needed stability. This stability came at a cost, however, as she had to move halfway around the world to live with a relative stranger, having only met him twice before making that decision.

Jane brought youth to the relationship and a willingness to start a new life but was forced to forgo the opportunity to have a husband of similar age who lived in the home country she loved. Her husband, John, brought education and income but was forced to forgo having a wife with similar education and income levels to his own. Neither Jane nor John got what they wanted, but for this particular stage of their lives, they got what they needed.

Now Jane, having moved all the way around the world to live with John, was deeply unhappy. Besides being lonely and isolated, she found herself in a relationship in which, because of both her inability to contribute to the household income and her inferior age, she had no bargaining power. Decisions that other couples would have made together, John made alone and independently of Jane's wishes. Where they lived, whether or not they had children (and how many), who they were friends with, how they divided the household chores, and when they did, and did not, have sex were all decisions made by John alone.

To make matters worse, economic conditions were poor, and, despite his education, John was incapable of keeping a job for more than a year at a time. In five years, John and Jane moved nine times, five times to different cities (including a move back to Jane's home country), all in pursuit of employment opportunities for John. The moves meant Jane was constantly underemployed, continually isolated, and unable to gain any ground on decision making within her relationship. In fact, her say in household decisions eroded over the years as a new baby and John's repeated job losses put the family in a more and more desperate financial situation.

Jane's big break came after one particularly long spell of unemployment in which John had been out of work for more than a year. He announced that he was returning to university to complete a graduate degree in the hope of improving his employability. He decided that in order to pay for the additional education, Jane would find a job and work full time. But twenty months of John's unemployment, and the fact they had been living with Jane's parents, had shifted the balance of power in

WIVES PAY A PRICE FOR TAKING THEIR HUSBAND'S NAME

Taking her husband's name at marriage suggests to potential employers that a woman is less intelligent, less ambitious, inclined to work fewer hours, and more focused on family. And according to experimental research by Marret Noordewier, Femke van Horen, Kirsten Ruys, and Diederik Stapel, women who make the choice to change their name can expect lower wages and fewer job offers as a result.

Women who choose to keep their name upon marriage are far more likely to be educated than women who take their husband's name. According to data collected by Gretchen Gooding, a U.S. woman with a master's degree is 2.8 times more likely not to take her husband's name than a woman who is educated at a lower level. A woman with a professional degree is 5 times more likely, and a woman with a doctorate is 9.8 times more likely not to change her name than a woman with less than a bachelor's degree.

Women who keep their name also have fewer children. In the Netherlands, the source of the experiment I have cited above, a woman who takes her husband's name has 2.2 children on average while a woman who keeps her own has only 1.9. Perhaps because they have more children, or perhaps because they have more traditional values regarding family, name-takers work fewer hours outside of the home per week (22.4) compared with name-keepers (28.3). Even after controlling for education levels and work hours, a woman who took her husband's name earns less—€960 compared with €1,156.

In an experiment, a set of participants was given one of two e-mails from a hypothetical woman applying for a job and asked to assess the woman's prospects for securing the position and to state their expectation of her salary. The participants assessed the applicant who took her husband's name as less intelligent, less ambitious, and more dependent. They expected her to be far less likely to receive a job offer and assessed her salary as being €861 per month less than the woman who kept her name.

Can a woman's name really matter when she applies for a job? If the stereotype of a woman who takes her husband's name is that she is more committed to family and less to the workplace, then we shouldn't be surprised that she is disadvantaged in seeking employment compared with women who are stereotyped as being independent and ambitious.

---

their relationship, and against John's wishes, Jane decided to take a stand. She applied, and was accepted, to earn a bachelor's degree in the same university as John.

In a matter of weeks John, Jane, and baby were living on campus in family housing with John committing all his time to his program and Jane balancing caring for the needs of their young child and studying for her very first degree.

When John found a job in another city two years later, Jane refused to move with him. When he lost that job three months later, she let him come back, but by then the writing was on the wall for their relationship.

For years they had built a relationship in which John had the power to make all the decisions, and the transition to a new equilibrium, in which equal education and employment gave Jane more say, was untenable.

As John said near the end of their relationship, "Marriage has nothing to do with compromise." And, in his defense, for the majority of the time they had been together, that had been absolutely true.

In the past thirty years, woman have, on balance, gained more bargaining power in their marriages as a result of economic forces that have leveled the playing field between men and women in the formal labor market. Those same forces that are closing the gap between the incomes of husbands and wives, however, are causing the gap in incomes of rich and the poor to widen, a factor that some economists argue can explain rising divorce rates. In a surprising turn of events, however, marriage has recently been getting a helping hand from two very unlikely sources—economic uncertainty and increased access to the Internet.

Before we turn to those topics, let me describe a special marriage market that allows men and women to escape their local economic climate, at least temporarily, in search of the perfect romance—the international marriage market.

FREE TRADE DIS-AGREEMENT

Remember in chapter 4 that I told you that one of the reasons why people marry is in order to exploit the gains from trade? Well, there is a group of men who take that approach to marriage literally—importing wives into their county in an attempt to subvert the domestic economic forces that have been working to give women more say in their marriages.

Before I say more on those types of marriages, I want to explain how economists view the way in which couples come to the decision on matters that affect the well-being of everyone in the family.

Anyone who has ever been married knows that negotiation is an important part of how couples make decisions. How resources are allocated between family members, including to children, is a decision most couples negotiate. How individuals divide their time between working for wages and working in the home, and how their nonwork hours are divided between taking care of household chores and playing, is also a decision most couples negotiate. Many couples negotiate over how many children will be born and how much time each parent will contribute to caring for those children. Negotiations don't stop at the bedroom door either; many couples negotiate over how often they have sex and what sex acts they are willing to provide for each other.

Economists use the term "bargaining power" to indicate how effective a person is at negotiating with his or her partner. If two people have equal bargaining power in a relationship, for example, then when there is a disagreement, both have a 50 percent chance that the final decision will be the one they favored. If one person holds more bargaining power than the other, then when there is a disagreement there will be a more than 50 percent chance that the final decision will be the one that person favored. In the extreme case in which one person holds all the bargaining power, then really there is no point negotiating when there is a disagreement since, ultimately, all decisions will be the ones that person favors.

When men had the comparative advantage in market work, women often stayed home and did the work that economists like to call "home production." Over the last half-century, however, the wages paid to women relative to men have increased in a way that has diminished men's comparative advantage in market labor.

At the same time, the tools that we used in our homes, the technology of home production, have become far more efficient in reducing the need for families to have one person engaged full time in household production (discussed in an important paper by Jeremy Greenwood, Ananth Seshadri, and Mehmet Yorukoglu). Likewise the growth of the service sector has meant that many of the services provided in the past by women in their homes can now be purchased and, thanks to the low wages paid to unskilled workers, are affordable to many families.

These technology advances have freed women to invest in their careers and acquire greater levels of human capital—the skills and experience that increase productivity, and earnings, in the labor market.

INDIAN MARRIAGE MARKETS IN A CRISIS

The use of dating websites in India is pervasive, particularly among the well educated and even more so among women who are seeking husbands who live in other countries. Following the recent global recession, however, the income of these particular men appears less predictable than it was in the past.

Are potential Indian brides looking elsewhere for their soul mate/sole provider? If they are, then we can add another collapsed market to the already long list: that of the well-heeled, nonresident Indian groom.

According to reports by Indian-based Internet dating sites, there has been a decisive shift in the search priorities of women away from nonresident Indian men (many of whom have jobs in Internet technology and finance) to resident civil servants. And who can blame them? The life as a wife of a government bureaucrat may not seem as luxurious as that of a wife of a U.S.-based financier, but it is certainly more predictable.

Among the matrimonially hopeful, it isn't only the women who are changing their search priorities. It seems that the beginning of the economic downturn marked an increase in men searching for employed women—an increase of 15 percent in 2008.

This suggests that in the face of increased employment uncertainty, Indian men are more concerned about having wives who can provide them with some insurance should they lose their jobs, and women are more concerned with finding husbands with a stable income.

Higher wages for working women and the ability to invest in their careers have meant that women who grow tired of continually losing in household negotiations have an alternative to being married: they can leave and still support themselves.

This implies that men who don't share decision making, or insist that all disagreements end in their favor, are at much greater risk of divorce than they have been in the past; because women have gained the ability to leave their husbands, both in practice and in law, men have an incentive to split the household bargaining power with their wives more evenly.

There are, of course, considerations other than earning power that influence how bargaining power is divided between spouses. For example, highly attractive women tend to have more bargaining power than less-attractive women because they have the option of finding another husband should they be unhappy with the way decisions are made in their current marriage. Young gay men who are in relationships with much older men tend to have more bargaining power because, just like highly attractive women, they also have a greater opportunity to find new relationships should their current relationship end. Men who are married to women whose legal status in their country is dependent on their marriage remaining intact hold all the bargaining power, assuming those wives prefer being in a marriage where they have no control to being deported to their home countries.

This brings us back to our topic of international marriages.

Not all men embrace the notion of shared decision making with their wives. These men are looking for a "good wife," which, according to at least one website (www.goodwife.com), means a woman who acknowledges that her husband is master of the house and never questions his authority.

One way to circumvent the economic forces that have given married women more bargaining power in industrialized nations is for spouse-seeking men to search for wives on marriage markets dominated by women who are disadvantaged on the labor market—marriage markets in less-developed nations.

Each year hundreds of international marriage brokers extract millions of dollars in revenue from would-be grooms who are willing to go the extra mile to find a good wife. And in response, each year tens of thousands of foreign women (and some gay men) are willing to take the chance that their new life, in a foreign country, will be better than the one they are leaving behind.

International marriage brokers sell the idea of cross-cultural marriages by convincing men that foreign women are more willing to accept an arrangement in which wives are submissive to their husband's wishes.

Don't take my word for it, consider the following quote from the marriage broker website www.goodwife.com:

"We, as men, are more and more wanting to step back from the types of women we meet now. With many women taking on the "me first" feminist agenda and the man continuing to take a back seat to her desire for power and control, many men are turned off by this and look back to having a more traditional woman as our partner."

This website, and hundreds of others like it, promote the notion that women from economically disadvantaged countries will be grateful for the privileges their Western husbands can provide and, as a result, be less likely to ask that household resources be allocated toward their needs or those of their children. What these sites do not mention, but still imply, is that because it is difficult for women who find themselves unhappy with this arrangement to credibly threaten divorce, they will have a hard time insisting on greater say in household decisions.

On the other hand, foreign-born wives who bring with them professional skills and education can reasonably expect that once they are settled, and language barriers have been overcome, to have the same opportunities as domestic women for employment outside of the home. If they do have opportunities to be independent, then there is no reason to believe that the same economic forces that have led to greater bargaining power of domestic wives won't encourage foreign-born wives to insist on more input into household decision making.

It is perhaps this conflict between expectations of domestic husbands and foreign-born wives that has led Jane Kim, and others, to document high levels of domestic abuse and divorce within these types of relationships.

Interestingly, though, economic theory (discussed in chapter 4) predicts that the gains from within household trade are greatest when each partner brings a different set of skills to the marriage. If this theory is correct, then domestic husbands with foreign-born wives should be better off than domestic husbands with domestic wives because their wives have a comparative advantage in home production, leaving them to specialize in labor market employment. It also suggests that foreign-born wives with domestic husbands should be better off than domestic wives with domestic husbands because their husbands have a comparative advantage in labor market employment, which leaves them to specialize in caring for the children and the home.

Fortunately for us, the theory that well-being is greater in marriages where each person brings different skills to the relationship has been tested using data collected from more than eight thousand Australian households. Mathias Sinning and Shane Worner look for evidence that men and women in cross-cultural marriages, those that have the greatest opportunity to exploit the gains from within household trade, are happiest in their marriages. Turns out that this isn't the case.

Happiness in their marriages (measured on a scale of 1 to 10) is highest in couples in which both husband and wife are native-born and in couples in which both husband and wife are foreign-born. The couples who reported the lowest levels of marital happiness, on average, were those in which one spouse was foreign-born and other spouse was native-born.

Contrary to economic theory, the happiest marriages appear to be those in which husbands and wives are more similar to each other, not different. This explains why, in general, we don't tend to seek partners who have vastly different skill sets than our own but rather choose people who are similar to ourselves. This behavior may not maximize the gains from trade in terms of household production—but it does appear to make us happy.

WALKING IN MEN'S SHOES IN THE WORKPLACE

The gender wage gap persists despite economic gains by women and legislation that prevents gender-based discrimination. Economic arguments can explain part of that wage gap (for example, the argument that women experience costly career disruptions when they have children), but is there evidence that the wage gap exists because employers discriminate against women?

There's a unique set of men in the workforce whose experiences just might provide evidence of discrimination. They are the men who partway through their careers stopped being outwardly identified as women and instead became identified as men.

Sociologist Kristen Schilt spoke to female-to-male transsexuals and found that older, white transmen enjoyed greater authority and respect than they had experienced as women. They felt they were perceived to be right more often and encountered much less resistance when they expressed their opinions. Some even reported that employers who had sanctioned them for expressing their ideas as women rewarded the same behavior when they were men. They were given more resources and support at work, improving their job performance, and, as a result, they saw improvements in their income.

Many of the men in the survey observed that, as men, they were more highly rewarded for additional education than they were as women and, as a result, returned to school post-transition in order to take advantage of those additional rewards.

Many of Schilt's participants found that when they "took charge," their behavior was seen in a more positive light than it had been previously. Before their transition, their bosses and coworkers would read that same kind of behavior as excessively assertive.

African American transmen, on the other hand, felt that they couldn't express frustration at work without being sanctioned for being aggressive. Asian transmen faced criticism for being too passive, a stereotype they had not experienced as Asian women. Those transmen who looked young suffered for not fitting a macho stereotype and for appearing inexperienced.

This may not be definitive evidence of wage discrimination based on gender, but it does suggest that employers should think carefully about the way in which they assess the competence of their employees. If female workers are perceived as less competent than male workers, or consistently lack the resources to do their jobs well, then closing the gender wage gap can be achieved only if women can manage to significantly outperform men in their jobs.

THE VALUE OF A UNIVERSITY DEGREE?
A MORE STABLE MARRIAGE

In 1970, only 28 percent of husbands had more education than their wives, but, despite this, only 4 percent of women earned more than their husbands. In 2007, only 19 percent of husbands had more education than their wives, but now 22 percent of women earn more than their husbands.

The big change in last thirty years has been that women are not only more likely to have as much, or more, education than their husbands; they are far more likely to outearn them as well.

Having more education and a higher wage may make it easier for married women to leave an unhappy marriage, but does that imply that higher rates of education for women are responsible for high divorce rates?

LESBIANS ARE BETTER SAVERS

A recent paper by Brighita Negrusa and Sonia Oreffice sets out to test a hypothesis that couples in same-sex relationships plan their finances differently from those in opposite-sex relationships. They find, on average, that women in same-sex relationships are significantly better savers than either men in same-sex relationships or heterosexual married couples.

The authors use the ratio of mortgage payments to the value of a couple's home as a measure of how good they are at saving because couples who are good savers will, on average, repay their mortgages at a faster rate than those who are poor savers.

Compared with heterosexual married couples and gay couples, lesbian couples pay almost 9 percent more on their annual average mortgage even after controlling for age, education, and socioeconomic factors (including the number of children living in the home).

This isn't the only evidence that lesbians are better savers. Looking at the income of seniors, retired women in same-sex relationships have on average $4,715.35 more in Social Security and retirement income than do heterosexual married couples. Gay men also have more income than heterosexual couples, but that result probably stems from that fact that, in general, men retire with higher incomes than do women.

There are two possible reasons why women in same-sex marriages might be better savers, besides having fewer children than heterosexual women. The first is related to life expectancy; women live longer on average and realistically need to save more in preparation for the period of their life when they have no waged income.

The second reason is explained by relationship stability. This data was collected before same-sex marriages were legal in any country; in planning their future, therefore, lesbian women would have had no way to predict that one day they would be offered the same security as heterosexual couples (and of course many are still waiting for that to happen).

If the observed higher savings rate for lesbian woman reflects insecurities around the legal status of their relationships, then when those relationships are given legal recognition, we can reasonably predict that the savings rates of those families will fall.

According to a paper by Philip Oreopoulos and Kjell Salvanes, the answer to this question is "No"; they find that more-educated people are significantly less likely to have ever been divorced.

For example, they find that a person who didn't complete high school has a 16 percent chance of being divorced. A person with a high school diploma, but no more, has a 10 percent chance of being divorced. And a person with a postgraduate degree has less than a 3 percent chance of ever having been divorced.

If you think these numbers look low compared with the 50 percent divorce rate we have all heard before, you are right. That is not only because the 50 percent divorce rate is inaccurately measured (it really is), but also because these numbers are for everyone—not just for people who have been married. But because educated people are more likely to have ever been married than are less-educated people, these results that suggest that educated people are less likely to have been divorced are an even more convincing argument that educated people divorce less frequently.

Why do educated people divorce less frequently? Perhaps they are hotter commodities on the marriage market and end up in higher-quality marriages. Or, maybe, because they are older when they marry, they choose their marriage partner more carefully. Perhaps educated people are more skilled negotiators, making it easier for them to navigate rocky patches in their marriages. Divorce is more expensive for high-income couples, so it would be reasonable for educated people to avoid that expense. Or, as we will discuss shortly, it could be because educated people suffer less job instability, avoiding that additional stressor on marriage.

As an aside, one interesting observation made by Betsey Stevenson and Justin Wolfers is that not only are less-educated people more likely to divorce—they find a 10-percentage-point difference between college graduates and those with less than a college education in the probability that their marriage would still be intact when they are 45 years old—but also that less-educated people are less likely to remarry following a divorce and, if they do remarry, they are more likely to divorce again.

While I have no direct evidence to prove that when women have more say in their marital decisions that their marriages function better, low divorce rates for educated couples suggest that the gains women have made in terms of equality in decision making are not leading to more unhappy marriages.

THE RICH GET RICHER, AND THE POOR GET DIVORCED

According to economists Adam Levine, Robert Frank, and Oege Dijk, the rich are getting richer, and marriage is paying the price.

We already know that the growing divide between the rich and poor has influenced sexual mores, and we will see more evidence of this in chapter 7 when we discuss teen promiscuity, but it also seems to be driving up divorce rates.

Just to give you an example of how wide the divide has become, consider this: The bottom 20 percent of income earners have experienced only a 9 percent increase in income in the years between 1979 and 2003, while those earning in the top 1 percent have seen their incomes increase a remarkable 201 percent.

At the same time, everyone seems to be saving less. The personal savings rate in the United States, for example, has fallen from 10 percent in the mid-1970s to close to zero in recent years, an observation that has led many analysts to suggest that excessive consumption contributed to the severity of the most recent recession.

There are several reasons why personal savings has fallen, but the main reason has to be that we are consuming more than ever before. Not only are we spending all of our current income, but we are also borrowing against our future income so that we can consume more today than we earn. One of the reasons for this is that, as the incomes of wealthy households increase, everyone spends more in an attempt to keep up with their consumption.

To understand how, imagine that you are in a community in which everyone has the same level of income, lives in the same size house, drives the same car, and everyone is good-looking (just for good measure).

Now imagine that one family, let's call them the Joneses, gets a big increase in their income and decides to build a bigger house and buy a nicer car. This increase in consumption encourages the people who live around them to think: "Well, if the Joneses deserve a bigger house and a fancier car, then so do I!"

Other families start to spend more of their income to buy things that compare to those owned by the Jones family. The families in the Joneses' neighborhood can probably manage to pay for this increase in consumption by reducing their savings. But as this effect spreads out into lower and lower income communities, it can lead to an increase in consumption that can cause real economic hardship—especially when people start mortgaging their homes to pay to the bills.

Keeping up with the Joneses' family consumption has encouraged everyone to consume too much and save too little.

So, the rich get richer, and everyone else races to keep up with their consumption. Excess consumption puts stress on families: people start working longer hours, making longer commutes to work so they can own bigger homes, and bankruptcies become more common. Not surprisingly, this race to consume and the financial hardship it causes put a big strain on marriages.

Robert Frank and his coauthors find that in counties where inequality is high, divorce rates are high as well; a 1 percent increase in inequality in a county is associated with a 1.2 percent increase in the proportion of people in that county who are divorced. In just ten years (1990 to 2000), the increase in income inequality caused a 5 percent increase in the number of divorces.

One possible explanation for this relationship between divorce and income inequality, besides the stress created by excess consumption, is that high levels of inequality encourage men and women to seek out new marriage partners whose better income makes it possible for them to buy the things they feel they need to compete in a highly unequal society. If that is the case, it is good news for them that there is a cheap way to look for a new marriage partner—the Internet.

LOVE IN CYBERSPACE FOR THE ALREADY MARRIED

If you have ever searched online for the phrase "why do people divorce," you know it is popular for pundits to blame access to online dating and social networking sites for infidelity and divorce. This conclusion is based on the assumption that because searching online is so easy (and so private), men and women who might otherwise have remained faithful are instead shopping online for a new partner.

A new paper by Todd Kendall presents some compelling evidence that despite the popularity of the claim that access to the Internet is responsible for marriages breaking down, it is simply not true. In fact, the ease with which married people can now find new lovers online might actually be reducing divorce rates, not increasing them.

Remember the model of searching for love that I used to explain why single people migrate to urban centers in search of love? The Internet operates just like a city in that it reduces the cost of searching for new love with the added bonus of allowing married people to search without their partners finding out.

As we already know, when search costs are high, marriages are generally of lower quality since men and women choose to settle on an inferior partner rather than incur the high cost of searching for longer (earlier we referred to this as setting their reservation value at a low level). When search costs are low, however, marriages are generally of higher quality since men and women can continue to search until they find someone closer to their perfect match without paying the high cost (they set their reservation value at a high level).

Inasmuch as access to online dating and social networking sites lowers the cost of searching for a mate, having greater access to the Internet should lead to higher-quality marriages in general.

The implication is that increased access to online dating and social networking will both decrease the probability of divorce (because the quality of marriages increases) and increase the probability of divorce (because married people can continue to search privately for new partners). In order to say which of these two factors has had the greatest influence on divorce, we need to take a look at the data.

Todd Kendall's research uses data collected from 43,552 couples and finds that there is no relationship between access to the Internet and the probability of divorce. He also finds that couples in which the husband uses the Internet daily are actually less likely to divorce than those in which the husband uses the Internet less frequently. There is no relationship between how frequently a wife uses the Internet and the likelihood that the couple will divorce.

We really don't know what these men and women are doing online—they could be shopping or downloading porn for all we know—but even without that information this is pretty conclusive proof that online dating

160 DOLLARS AND SEX

A LUBRICANT LEADING INDICATOR?

Can watching the market for sex toys help economists predict a recession?

Economists at their most playful like to find interesting ways to watch the market for signs of an impending economic downturn. After we get tired of watching inventories and production capacity, we turn to other leading indicators such as hamburger sales and whether or not doughnut shops are moving into downtown cores.

One of the most famous leading indicators of a recession is lipstick sales. Leonard Lauder, who was chief executive of the cosmetics company Estée Lauder until 1999, observed that in the lead up to a recession, lipstick sales tend to increase. It turns out that an inexpensive way to make a woman feel good is a fun way for economists to forecast hard economic times.

Lipstick sales did not predict the economic downturn in 2007 and 2008, though, and sales in that market have been flat over the last few years. Another feel-good market is booming instead: the market for personal lubricants and sex toys.

Market research in 2009 found that sales of lubricants and sexual-enhancement devices were rocketing in the recession. The argument for this surge in sales of sexual aids sounds much like the argument made for lipstick; people need a cheap way to feel good in tough times (or you might say they need a way to get hard in hard times).

The real test as to whether or not this market is a good indicator of economic activity will be revealed in the recovery. If the sales of his-and-her gels and vibrators go limp over the next year, then I think we have a winner.

Maybe then we should ask *The Economist* to start reporting on the sex toy and lubricant markets. After all, they seem to share my perspective when it comes to providing stimulating economic analysis.

---

and social networking sites are not a major cause of divorce. This doesn't imply that no married people are shopping for new mates on the Internet. It just means that those people would still be looking for a new mate even if they didn't have that resource available.

If this does not convince you, there is research from the Netherlands that also examines the relationship between marriage quality and Internet usage and finds that the more frequently an individual uses the Internet, the happier they are in their marriage.

Using data collected from married couples, Peter Kerkhof, Catrin Finkenauer, and Linda Muusses find that frequency of Internet use is associated with happier marriages, marked by partners who keep fewer secrets, feel more attached to each other, and have a greater passion for their relationship.

When they looked only at compulsive Interest users, however, they found that those addicts experienced declining intimacy and passion in their marriages over time, spent less time with their partners, and were more willing keep secrets from them. Overall, the quality of their relationships was lower and appeared to be deteriorating over time. This deterioration wasn't because they spent all their time online but rather because the compulsiveness of their behavior hurt their marriages.

▰▰▰ MARRIAGE AS INSURANCE IN HARD TIMES

There were many problems in Jane's marriage in the story I shared with you at the beginning of this chapter, particularly John's unwillingness to negotiate with Jane on important family decisions, but eventually it was his joblessness that eroded the weak foundation of their marriage.

Besides the toll that living through a period of economic hardship places on a couple, job loss removes one of the reasons for being married

MY HUSBAND THE JUNK BOND

In making financial decisions, women are far less willing to take on risky assets than are men; they appear more risk-averse. Single individuals, in turn, are more risk-averse than married individuals, and so it follows that married women, historically at least, appear to be more willing to take on risky assets than are single women.

If we think of a husband as another asset in a portfolio along with stocks, bonds, and real estate, this behavior of married women makes sense, but only if a husband is a low-risk asset. With the additional safe asset (i.e., the husband) in a married woman's portfolio, it makes sense that she seeks to balance her portfolio by purchasing riskier assets. So married women are not really less cautious than single women, they just look that way because we are ignoring her safe asset that puts his feet on the coffee table at night.

But here's the thing: over the last forty years, the asset that is a husband has evolved from behaving like a risk-free asset to behaving more like a junk bond—a high-yield asset with a high risk of default. Add to that the volatility in the housing market (essentially the returns from which the junk bond pays out in the case of default), and the riskiness of the husband asset has increased over time.

If this is true, and if the husband-as-portfolio item argument explains the lower risk-aversion of married women, then as divorce rates increase, we would expect to see the risk-aversion gap between married and single women shrink.

New research by Italian economists Graziella Bertocchi, Marianna Brunetti, and Costanza Torricelli finds that, starting in the early 1990s, the risk-aversion gap between single and married women actually widened as married women entered the workforce and began behaving more like men in their investment decisions. But that all changed in the beginning of the twenty-first century; since that time, the marriage gap in risk aversion has narrowed considerably and married women have increasingly begun to behave in their investment decisions just like single women—they are acting more risk-averse.

While divorce rates in many countries have been stable for more than a decade, in just three years (2000 to 2002) the divorce rate in Italy has increased by 45 percent. So, in a period of increased risk in marriage, the level of risk-aversion of married women has converged to that of single women. This is consistent with our hypothesis that married women are choosing to rebalance their portfolios with less-risky assets in response to the increase risk associated with their junk-bond husbands.

---

in the first place—to have some additional support when things go wrong. If marriage is a form of insurance in hard times, then when one person in a marriage has already lost his or her job, the insurance, in terms of income for the second person, is essentially gone.

Job loss reduces the motivation that couples have to stay together. This probably doesn't matter for relationships that stand on a solid foundation—after all there is no point in having insurance if the insurer backs out of the arrangement just when you need to make a claim—but not all relationships have a solid foundation, and, for many, the loss of a spouse's job is the straw that breaks the camel's back.

New research by Judith Hellerstein and Melinda Morrill looks for evidence of a relationship between unemployment and divorce, and finds, somewhat surprisingly, that when economic times are good, people are more likely to divorce than they are when economic times are bad. In fact, when the unemployment rate goes up by 1 percentage point, the divorce rate falls by 1 percentage point.

There are two possible reasons for this counterintuitive result.

The first reason is that while in a recession some couples are more likely to divorce (i.e., those who have actually lost their jobs), other couples are more likely to stay married (i.e., those who haven't lost their jobs but fear that they might).

After all, you wouldn't cancel your car insurance just when the risk of an accident is at its highest; even if you no longer wanted it, you would wait until the risk has passed. One reason why divorce rates increase when unemployment rates fall is that improvements in the economy decrease employment uncertainty, reducing the need for the insurance marriage provides.

The second reason that more couples stay together in a recession is that falling house prices make it difficult to part with a family home whose value has fallen well below their expectation, or even fallen below the value of their mortgage.

Imagine you are married and you wish you weren't. If house prices have fallen, then buying a new home—or two, since that is what you now need as a couple—is more affordable than it had been in the past. So falling house prices might increase your willingness to end your relationship since finding a new place to live is now less expensive.

If this is the case, then when house prices fall, divorce rates should increase, and, alternatively, when house prices increase, divorce rates should fall.

According to research by Martin Farnham, Lucie Schmidt, and Purvi Sevak, while it is a good idea to buy new homes when the market is low, couples prefer staying in less-than-satisfying marriages rather than lose equity they had built up in their existing home. These authors contend that an emotional barrier to selling property at a loss encourages people to hang on to their homes, and stay in their marriages, in the hope of reducing that financial loss in the future.

They find that a 10 percent decrease in house prices decreases the divorce rate of college-educated couples (those who are more likely to be home owners) by an incredible 29 percent. When you consider that house prices fell by three times that amount (30 percent) between April

2006 and August 2010, this result translates into a massive decline in divorce rates.

For those who are less likely to own a home, falling house prices had the opposite effect on divorce rates; a 10 percent decrease in house prices increased the divorce rate of those who did not complete high school by an equally incredible 20 percent.

What this tells us is that recessions do have a destructive effect on marriages, but that effect is principally among poorer households. This shouldn't be that surprising given that low-skilled jobs are the hardest hit during recessions; in 2010, a person with less than a high school education was three times more likely to be unemployed than was a person with a college degree.

If the decision to divorce is related to unemployment and house prices, then maybe the decision to marry is also related to the state of the economy. According to the U.S. Census Bureau, the overall marriage rate for individuals between the ages of 25 and 34 fell by 4 percent between 2006 and 2010 (from 49 percent to 44 percent). While it is true that marriage rates have been falling for decades, this downward trend during the recession was different for one reason—while the marriage rate for educated people stayed almost constant, the marriage rate of people with *only* a high school diploma, or less, fell precipitously to 10 percentage points less than it was a decade ago.

Whether or not this decline in marriage among less-educated workers is related to the recession is yet to be proved, but there is some evidence in recent years that marriage as insurance has been replaced with cohabitation as insurance.

According to a report by Rose Kreider, the number of heterosexual couples living together outside of marriage increased by 13 percent between 2009 and 2010. The biggest increase in cohabiting couples in this period was among those in which at least one person was unemployed; only 39 percent of couples who moved in together that year consisted of two employed people compared with 50 percent of couples who were already living together in 2009.

Also, men in these new couples were less likely to be employed than men in previously existing couples as well; 24 percent of the newly created couples were ones in which the man was unemployed compared with only 14 percent of those who were already cohabiting in 2009.

It appears that cohabitation acts as a form of bridging insurance—men and women are prepared to provide temporary insurance (housing for example) to their lovers when times are hard but unprepared to provide full marriage insurance.

Whether or not they will choose to marry when good times return remains to be seen. The one thing that is clear is that recessions and booms can significantly affect the way in which couples approach their relationships.

FINAL WORDS

Interestingly, the usefulness of marriage as insurance in unstable economic times is the reason that Jane ultimately chose a relatively recession-proof occupation for herself—being an academic. At the time that she made that decision, it seemed that if John were going to keep losing his job, then she would need to find stable employment in order to keep the family afloat. Even though she could have chosen an occupation that would have given her a higher income, her choice was the best decision for them as a couple, given the economic environment in which they lived. It turned out she was right to be cautious.

Jane's story, and the other stories that are told here using data and economic theory, remind us that marriage is an economic arrangement. Recognizing that helps us to understand the ways that marriage has changed over the past half century and, just as important, it helps us to see where marriage is heading in the future.

I told you in chapter 1 that a Pew Research Center survey found that young adults, in particular, no longer see the point of marriage, with 44 percent reporting that the institution is outdated. This perception that marriage is obsolete almost certainly stems from the fact that marriage has changed in response to the increased ability for women to be financially independent. Independence of women does not, however, make marriage irrelevant. To the contrary, it increases the value of marriage as a form of insurance in hard times, as families are no longer wholly dependent on a man's ability to earn.

From an economist's perspective, the most surprising way that marriage has changed is in the way that people choose their marriage partners. When economists first started talking about marriage, the best approach was to apply theories of trade that predicted that opposites should attract. As women have become more independent, however, and divorces easier to obtain, men and women are choosing marriage partners who are actually very similar to themselves. One possible explanation for this phenomenon (besides those that we have already discussed) is that the increased need to share decision making is encouraging men and women to choose partners whose objectives are closely aligned with their own.

This sorting over traits, to me at least, signals an increase in the quality of marriages and is a good indicator that, while fewer people are marrying, those who do are happier than married couples in previous generations. That observation, and the fact that marriage gives couples greater financial stability, suggests that marriage as an institution is extremely unlikely to become obsolete in the future. It will be different, but given that the economic environment influences the way in which marriages are organized and given that the economic environment is always changing, that should come as no surprise.

We are going to leave marriage now to return to a discussion that we started in the first section of this book: promiscuity. The promiscuous individuals in this chapter are not the adult men and women we talked about in chapter 1, nor are they the college students we talked about in chapter 2. They are the new generation of sexually active adolescents, and you may be surprised to discover that they are the first generation in a long time that is less sexually active than their parents.

CHAPTER 7
THE NEXT GENERATION
COMES OF AGE

▰▰▰▰ THERE IS A NEW NORMAL WHEN IT COMES TO TEEN SEX

I was talking to a friend's son recently about his love life. He is tall and handsome, so I figured that, at the age of 17, he probably had a girlfriend. He said, "Nope, no girls until I'm 21," to which I responded, "Only boys until then?"

My intention was not to be facetious. In some preindustrial societies, boys were encouraged to have same-sex relationships in adolescence as a way of discouraging premarital childbirth and postponing marriage. To me this illustrates just how what we believe to be "normal" sexual behavior, especially when it comes to adolescents, is really culturally and economically determined; in one society, same-sex relationships between adolescents is perceived as advantageous for the group (for example, by delaying female fertility), and in another, detrimental (for example, by challenging traditional heterosexual marriage).

There is a relationship between the economic environment and what societies believe to be socially acceptable adolescent sexual behavior. Let me give you a few examples of what I mean by that.

The first example is the relationship between the age at which a young person can legally consent to sex and how long people are expected to live. Economic well-being influences individuals' health and, at the societal level, average life expectancy. When life expectancy is low, we find that the age at which a woman can legally consent to sex is also very low. For example, in the United Kingdom in the sixteenth century, the age of consent was 10 years old. At that time, the average life expectancy at birth was thirty-seven years. If people are not going to live very long, then, as a society, you want them to get onto the serious business of reproduction as early as possible. So average life expectancy (an economic outcome) influences societal norms that govern the age at which sexual debut is acceptable.

The next example is the relationship between the age at which people are encouraged to marry and population pressures. Really, the example I just gave, of age of consent in the United Kingdom, is not a particularly good one. At that time, land in the United Kingdom was extremely limited. In a largely agricultural society, with a fixed amount of land, any increase in the size of the population threatens the well-being of everyone. In the absence of reliable contraceptives, a strict prohibition of premarital sex is a good way to limit fertility and prevent population increases from diluting available resources. So limited resources, such as land, increase the age at which society considers it appropriate for a couple to marry. In the United Kingdom in the 1600s, the average age at which women married was 25; societal norms discouraged early marriage as a means to reduce population growth and prevent living standards from falling as a result.

The approval that society feels toward adolescent girls giving birth is related to another economic outcome: the return, in terms of increased future income, to formal education. When having an education does little to increase your income, society takes a favorable view toward adolescent childbearing because becoming a parent early has little influence on future income. When countries industrialize, however, and better-educated workers can earn substantially more than less-educated workers, society begins to take a more disapproving view of teens giving birth—even within marriage—since it limits their productivity in the future.

Economic factors also influence how much sexual knowledge a society feels is appropriate to give children. Our ancestors didn't worry about when it was the right time to have "the talk" with their children.

When homes were small, children grew up with parents who had sex in the same room in which the children were sleeping. Our preoccupation with "protecting" our children from sexual knowledge is directly related to the size of our homes. As we have grown wealthier, we have managed to prolong our children's ignorance in matters of human sexuality and, as a result, open dialogue around sexuality with children has become taboo.

Finally, advances in technology have had a huge influence on society's opinion of same-sex relationships and gender identity. The advancement of Internet technology, for example, has made it significantly easier for gay, lesbian, bisexual, and transgender youths to discover that there are others like them in the world. Thus, technological innovations have encouraged those with sexual tendencies that differ from the mainstream to act on those tendencies and to publically disclose their sexuality. This disclosure has led to a shift in cultural attitudes and, again, economic factors have played a role in that transition.

Before I tell you the economic evidence around evolving norms toward teen sexual behavior, let me tell you another story.

If you remember Sarah from chapter 2, you will recall that, despite her unfortunate pregnancy, she was determined to finish college. Sarah wasn't a virgin when that story started, but you may be surprised to find out that in high school she refrained from sexual relationships altogether. Sarah didn't become sexually active until her college application was accepted, her scholarships were in place, and she had registered for the fall classes that she would later fail as the result of her mistimed pregnancy.

No one had actually ever asked Sarah if she had wanted to go to college. To her family, and her circle of friends, the transition from high school to college was as obvious as the transition from middle school to high school: it wasn't up for debate. But it wasn't those expectations of a college education that had made her sexually cautious in high school (after all, several of her friends were sexually active) but rather a friendship she developed in grade ten with a quiet boy named Troy.

Troy was not Sarah's boyfriend, but she enjoyed spending time with him enough that when he invited her to come and spend the night at his house, she was willing, mostly because she believed their relationship to be platonic. Sarah's mother objected, having observed the behavior of teenage boys for longer than Sarah, but was liberal-minded enough to allow Sarah instead to spend time at Troy's house one day after school.

Troy lived in a part of town that Sarah had never been to before, in a home that belonged to the city's social housing project, an area affectionately known as "the pubs." He lived there with his aunt (who had been given custody of him by social services when he was removed from his mother's care at the age of 9), the aunt's new baby, and an 18-year-old cousin. In addition to these full-time residents, while Sarah was visiting, the cousin's 17-year-old girlfriend also came by to drop off their 10-month-old baby, so that she would be free to head to the mall with her friends.

There were two things about this visit that made a lasting impression on Sarah and later informed her sexual decision making. The first was the condition in which Troy was living; she had never been in a home that was in such a poor state of disrepair. This saddened her on behalf of her friend, but more to the point, she was struck by the unsuitability of these living conditions for raising small children. When she looked forward to her own life as a mother, she wished for so much more than this family was able to provide the two babies who lived here.

The second event that made an impression was prompted by Sarah herself when she asked Troy if he was planning on enrolling in the college stream–level math and English classes in grade eleven. She knew Troy was a good student and so was surprised that, instead of answering her question directly, he tentatively looked to his aunt for guidance. To Sarah's amazement, his aunt quickly dismissed this idea with a wave of her hand responding, "Why would you waste your time taking courses that are only for people who plan to go to college?"

This was the first time that Sarah understood that optimism toward the future is a privilege that not all her friends enjoyed. She later realized that

LEGISLATING THE TEEN SEX AWAY

One possible way to reduce the level of sexual activity among teens is to pass laws that make it impossible for girls and boys below a certain age to consent to having sex.

In 2009 in Canada, the age of consent for sex was changed from age 14 to age 16 under the assumption that younger adolescents (14 to 15) were less capable of making healthful choices about sexuality than were older adolescents (16 to 17). Bonnie Miller, David Cox, and Elizabeth Saewyc took advantage of this change in the laws to test the hypothesis that younger teens make poorer choices about sex than do older teens. Using data from more than 26,000 adolescents, they found that 14- to 15-year-olds seem to be no worse at making sexual decisions than are 16- to 17-year-olds. They also find that the children who are exposed to the most risk and in the most need of protection by the laws are actually those younger than age 12.

Of the 3 percent of students in the sample who had sexual intercourse before the age of 12, more than 40 percent reported that their first sexual partner was an adult over the age of 20. For those who first had sexual intercourse at the age of 14, however, only 1.3 percent reported that their first sexual partner was over the age of 20. For those who had their first sexual experience at age 15, the share with an older partner increased but was still less than 6 percent.

Teens in the age group that lost its ability to consent to sex when the Canadian laws changed were overwhelmingly having sex with people within their own age group; less than 2 percent of boys and 3 to 5 percent of girls had their first sexual experience with an adult who was more than five years older than themselves. They were equally as likely as the older group (16- to 17-year-olds) to have sex under the influence of drugs or alcohol, and they were significantly more likely to report having used a condom in their last intercourse (83 percent, compared with 74 percent). In addition, women in this age group who had their first sexual experience when they were younger were more likely to use a condom together with hormone contraceptives.

The argument behind age-of-consent laws is that young teens cannot protect themselves from the potentially very serious adult consequences of sexual activity. This evidence finds that younger adolescents appear to make equally healthful sexual decisions as older adolescents, regardless of the law.

---

the sexual decisions made by those friends, for example, risking pregnancy and becoming pregnant, were their responses to pessimism about their future, a pessimism that she did not share.

It would be an oversimplification to say that Sarah vowed there and then to be celibate for the remainder of high school; learning often takes time. As it turned out, however, Sarah never found herself in a position of feeling that fulfilling her sexual desires was worth the risks it involved. Over time, she came to believe that hooking up was one more thing she could wait to look forward to in college.

Sarah lost track of Troy at some point in grade eleven, and the truth is he left school early. But she was reminded of him and his family the night that she attended her school prom. Her mother had dropped her and her two best friends off at the door (dates having seemed to be more trouble than they were worth). As they made their way to the "red carpet," she saw that it was flanked on either side, not by paparazzi or even camera-wielding parents, but by teenage women carrying babies on their hips. Many former classmates whose pregnancies had prevented them from staying in school (or at least from going to the prom) had showed up that night to see their friends arrive in their prom finery.

Sarah had, of course, known that quite a few of the girls in her class had become mothers in that final year, and, in fact, one girl was already expecting her second baby, but the stark contrast between shiny prom queens and yoga-pant-wearing moms made clear to her just how different their life paths really were.

You may have judged Sarah when she chose to have an abortion in college and you are free to do that, but you should know that she did not come to that decision lightly. She didn't have to guess how her life would change if she decided to continue with her pregnancy: she already knew.

EVERYONE, IT TURNS OUT, IS NOT DOING IT

Teenagers in the United States today are less sexually active than any other group of teenagers since the mid-1980s. According to the Centers for Disease Control, in 2010 less than half of teenagers had ever had sexual intercourse (42 percent for men and 43 percent for women), compared with 51 percent of teenage women and 60 percent of teenage men just twenty-two years ago. Teens are also not simply substituting sexual intercourse with other sexual behaviors (like oral or anal sex); 46 percent of males and 49 percent of females between the ages of 15 and 17 have had no sexual contact with another person.

More than 92 percent of sexually active teenage men and 86 percent of teenage women reported that in their last act of sexual intercourse they used some form of birth control. Despite this apparent diligence, in the same year 367,752 babies were born to women between the ages of 15 and 19, meaning that almost 3.5 percent of women in this age group gave birth. While this rate has fallen by more than one-third from 1991 to 2010, the United States still has the highest teen birth rate in the developed world— more than double that of its neighbor Canada.

This is not because Canadian teens are significantly less sexually active either; according to Statistics Canada, 43 percent of Canadian teens between the ages of 15 and 19 have had sexual intercourse.

This decrease in teen birth is not the result of an increase in access to abortion. The teen abortion rate in the United States in 2006 was less than half of what it was in 1991 (sixteen per thousand women, compared with thirty-seven per thousand).

Public health researchers John Santelli and Andrea Melnikas have determined that the decline in teen birth rates between 1991 and 2005 was unrelated to the reduction in teen sexual activity or increased access to abortion but rather entirely attributable to teens becoming more careful with their contraceptive usage. This is likely because the type of teens who had reduced their sexual activity would have used contraceptives had they been sexually active. So, when those teens chose not to be sexually active that decision had no effect on pregnancy rates.

Teen sexual behavior, and outcomes, is also very much a race issue in the United States. White sexually active teenage women were more likely to have used the pill the last time they had sex than were black and Hispanic teenagers: 39 percent of white teenage women were on the pill, compared with 14 percent of black teenage women and 17 percent of Hispanic teenage women.

Black and Hispanic teenage women are more than twice as likely to give birth as white teenage women: 2.4 percent of white teenage women aged 15 to 19 gave birth in 2010, compared with 5.2 percent of black teenage women and 5.6 percent of Hispanic teenage women.

Not only are black and Hispanic teenage women more likely to become pregnant, but they are more likely to have several children before they turn 20. For example, black and Hispanic girls, combined, make up about 34 percent of the whole population of teenage women but 58 percent of the teenage women who had their first baby in 2009. We already knew they were overrepresented in that group having a teen pregnancy, but it is worth noting that they made up 66 percent of teenage moms having their second child that year, 73 percent of teenage moms having their third, and 80 percent of teenage moms having four or more children.

Astonishingly, 1,316 women in the United States between the ages of 15 and 19 gave birth to their fourth child or higher in 2009.

Part of the explanation for why birth rates vary between the races is due to differing attitudes toward teen pregnancy. For example, in response to the question: "If you got pregnant now, how would you feel?" only 8 percent of white teenage women said they would be either a little or very pleased, compared with 19 percent of Hispanic teenage women and 20 percent of black teenage women.

Finally, young women are the most likely group to contract a sexually transmitted disease; the Centers for Disease Control estimate that youths between the ages of 15 and 24 represent only 25 percent of the sexually experienced population, and yet nearly half of all new sexually transmitted diseases are acquired by people in that age group. They are four times more likely to have either chlamydia or gonorrhea and twice as likely to have syphilis than the general population.

Again, black teenage women are overrepresented in the group of women who are infected with a sexually transmitted disease. In 2009, they were sixteen times more likely to have contracted chlamydia, seven times more likely to have contracted gonorrhea, and twenty-eight times more likely to have contracted syphilis than white teenage women.

This empirical evidence suggests that while teen sexuality and pregnancy are on the decline, infections with sexually transmitted diseases among teens are not. That seems counterintuitive, but there is an economic explanation as to why that is the case.

And while teen sexuality is changing in positive ways within some socioeconomic groups, there are others in which teenagers are paying a high cost for being sexually active. That suggests that teen sexuality is better understood when we recognize that teenagers are responding to the changing economic environment in which we all live.

▨▨▨ INEQUALITY CREATES A CULTURE OF DESPAIR

One of the things you might have noticed about Sarah's school is that it was attended by youth who came from different socioeconomic backgrounds. In fact, the school drew its students predominantly from two very distinct neighborhoods: a neighborhood where the residents are affluent and well educated and a neighborhood where the residents live in public housing and many live on social assistance: "the pubs."

The second thing you might have noticed was that the teen pregnancy rate was very high. With maybe two hundred students in her graduating class, there should have been no more than eight girls giving birth, and yet judging by how many came to see their friends enter the prom, the rate at that school was actually much higher.

A paper by economists Melissa Schettini Kearney and Phillip Levine provides some interesting evidence as to why the teen pregnancy rate at Sarah's school was so high; they would argue that the diversity of economic backgrounds of the students in the school has played an important role.

One of the interesting features of the United States is that we observe big differences in teen pregnancy rates from one state to the next. These researches take advantage of that state-by-state variation to see what role income inequality has played in promoting teen pregnancy rates. They argue that a "culture of despair" has developed among the less-advantaged residents in states that have very high levels of income inequality. This culture reduces the perceived cost to teenagers of having a baby during high school, since those girls giving birth assume, probably correctly, they will never be able to rise above their current circumstance regardless of whether or not they become a teenage mother.

When we think of culture, we often think that because it is external to us as individuals, that it is somehow external to the world around us as well; it is something we inherit like brown eyes or ugly feet. Economists think of culture as being *endogenous*—determined internally within a given society by the economic environment of that society. Yes, we inherit our

CONDOM AVAILABILITY IN SCHOOLS INCREASES TEEN PREGNANCY

There is a psychological barrier that is crossed the first time a person has sex that, in an economic sense, is akin to paying a fixed cost: a cost that once incurred does not have to be paid again. Adolescents may choose not to have sex initially in order to avoid paying this fixed cost, but once they have lost their virginity, it is more likely that they will have sex again since the fixed cost has already been paid.

If schools make condoms available to teens, and that availability lowers the expected cost of virginity loss, then the availability of condoms could increase promiscuity in teens in both the short run and in the long run. Teens will respond by having sex earlier (the short run) and then continue to have sex in the future (the long run). In the short run, condom use may be high and teen pregnancy low, but the long-run pregnancy rates among teens could increase, since condoms are often used incorrectly.

A policy simulation conducted by economists Peter Arcidiacono, Ahmed Khwaja, and Lijing Ouyang suggests that restricting availability of condoms to 14-year-old students would increase the rate of unprotected sex by 8 percent in the year the policy comes into effect and by 4 percent three years later. But while more students are having unprotected sex, other students will choose not to have sex at all; the rate of sexually active teens falls 3 percent in the year the policy is introduced and by 5 percent three years later.

Despite the increase in unprotected sex, as a result of the reduction in sexual activity, pregnancy rates in the simulation dropped in all three years, suggesting that restricting teen access to contraceptives is a good policy for reducing pregnancy.

The problem with this conclusion is that the teens in this policy simulation are extremely young (14) and are bound to be the most responsive to small changes in availability of condoms. For example, they would probably have a much harder time walking into a store and buying condoms than would an older teen. So, while this policy simulation may say something about their behavior, it probably has less to say about how older teens will respond to the lack of availability of condoms. It also ignores the possibility that early access to condoms will increase both the willingness to use them, and improved skills at doing so, later on in a teen's life.

---

culture, but that is in part because we inherit the economic environment. If that economic environment changes, then the culture of that society will change as well.

So, inequality creates a culture among poorer families that their economic condition is inevitable and unchangeable.

The empirical evidence finds that teenage women from low socioeconomic homes who live in low-income-inequality states are less likely, by 5 percentage points, to give birth by age 20 than are similar women living in high-income-inequality states.

It also suggest that those same women are more likely, by 4 percentage points, to terminate a pregnancy when they live in low-income-inequality states compared with when they live in a high-income-inequality state.

So, the big difference in teen birth rates between low- and high-income-inequality states is not that teenage women are significantly less likely to become pregnant but rather that they are more likely to have an abortion once they have become pregnant.

Troy's aunt's reaction when he was asked about taking the necessary classes for entrance to college is a good example of how culture plays a role in teenage sexual behavior. Troy's family has been economically marginalized for several generations, while over the same period the affluent families in their community have come to hold the majority of wealth. His family's inability to change their fortunes in the past created a culture of despair within the family.

Troy's family believed that he would never rise above their current standard of living and, as a result, never expected him or his cousin to finish high school. While ultimately it was economic hardship that prevented Troy from finishing high school, the fact that no one ever told him that he was capable of furthering his education played a role in that decision. Troy's cousin, on the other hand, finished high school but went no further; instead, he found work to support his girlfriend and their baby. Their choices may not have guaranteed that they stay within their low socioeconomic class, but they did make it significantly more difficult to improve their living standard than it would have been had they not had a baby in high school.

▨▨▨▨ POSTSECONDARY EDUCATION IS A PRIVILEGE

The reality for many students is that they don't need a culture of despair to discourage them from believing that they will go to college. If college were affordable for everyone, then even teens from underprivileged families could dream of one day having a high-paying job that requires a college degree. As education is costly, however, the reality faced by many students is that they will never be able to afford to go to college. If this is the case, then having a baby in high school does not limit their options in terms of furthering their education—because more education never was a viable option.

That suggests that there might be a relationship between teen pregnancy and the price of a college education.

A recent paper by economist Benjamin Cowan uses nationally representative U.S. data to determine if teens in states with lower tuition and fees for public community colleges make better sexual choices in response to increased optimism about future education. He finds that a $1,000 reduction in price of a community college education decreases the number of sexual partners the average 17-year-old high school student has by a remarkable 26 percent.

He also finds that students are less likely to engage in other risky behaviors, such as smoking (down by 14 percent) and marijuana use (down by 23 percent), when college is affordable.

Of course, this argument assumes that teenagers are rational, forward-looking individuals who understand that risky sexual behavior today has the potential to impose costs on them in the future. The idea that teens are rational when it comes to sexual decision making may be a tough sell, but this paper finds that for students in their final year of high school, an increase in college tuition by $1,000 reduces a student's expectations of continuing in school by 5.7 percent, implying that teens do take the cost of education into consideration when setting their expectations about their future.

He also finds that far fewer students continue their education after high school than those who think they will: 83 percent of high school seniors believe they will be enrolled in school in one year's time while only 56 percent actually find themselves in a university or community college. Those, perhaps false, expectations explain why we observe such a big change in teen sexual behavior despite the evidence that not all students continue in school—they don't need to continue; they just need to believe that it is possible.

I said earlier that the teen pregnancy rate in the United States is the highest in the developed world and more than double that of its closest neighbor (thirty-nine births per thousand teenage woman in the United States, compared with fourteen births per thousand teenage women in Canada). This disparity in teen pregnancy rates is even greater when we compare the United States to European nations that provide very inexpensive postsecondary training. The teen pregnancy rate in the United States is three times higher than in Germany and France and four times higher than in the Netherlands. The most obvious, economic, explanation for the differences in teen pregnancy rates between the United States and other developed nations is that teenagers from low-income families in the United States have more reason to be pessimistic about their postsecondary educational opportunities than do similar teenagers in other countries.

▓▓▓▓ LESS SEX IS MORE SEXUALLY TRANSMITTED DISEASES

Promiscuity in U.S. high schools, as I have already said, is at a twenty-year low and teen birth rates have fallen by over one-third from 1991 to 2009. How can it be that teens are sexually active at lower frequencies, and appear to be taking more precautions, and yet 50 percent of new STD infections last year were in people younger than 24?

To understand the answer to this question, imagine a school where there are one hundred students, of which fifty are sexually active with other students in the school. It doesn't matter what their gender is, nor does it matter if they are heterosexual or not; what matters is that they are not in monogamous pairs: they are teenagers after all and so each one can have several sexual partners over the course of a year.

At the beginning of the year, one student arrives infected with an STD. Given that students are not in committed relationships, that student infects his/her partner, who then infects his/her next partner, and so on. By the end of the year, a certain percentage of students in the school are infected—presumably less than half since only 50 percent are sexually active.

Now imagine that the following year, another hundred students arrive at the school, but now only forty students are sexually active. Again, at the beginning of the year, one student arrives with an infection and the whole process starts all over again. Now given that there are fewer sexually active students, we might be tempted to predict that fewer students are infected by the end of the year. But, that prediction would probably be wrong.

Not all students behave in the same way when they are sexually active, and chances are that the students who have chosen to not have sex in this year are the students who, had they been sexually active, would have taken the greatest precautions to prevent infection; they are the students who are the most *risk averse*.

For example, consider the behavior of the following three people. The first person is very risk averse and always insists on proper condom usage. The second person is risk neutral and neither insists nor refuses condom usage. The third person is risk loving and always insists on sex without a condom.

In the past, when more teens were sexually active, the risk-averse person might have ended up in a sexual relationship with the risk-neutral person. If that was the case, then both would be protected from sexually transmitted disease (the risk-averse person would insist on condom usage and the risk-neutral person would comply with that request).

When the costs of sex increased, for example, because college education became more important to future income, teens like the risk-averse person stopped having sex altogether. Now a greater proportion of those having sex on the high school market are just like the second (risk-neutral) and third (risk-loving) people.

The risk-neutral person, who might have been protected in the past from infection by a diligent risk-averse partner, is now having sex with a risk-loving partner. The risk-loving partner insists that no condom is used and the risk-neutral person complies with that request, so both are at a much greater risk of infection.

When the most risk-averse students are removed from the teen sex market, then not only will the infection rate not decrease, but it could very well increase. This is because sexually active teens who might have otherwise found themselves with cautious sex partners are left with partners who are more risk neutral—or even risk loving—when it comes to safe sex.

Economists call this a change on the *extensive margin*—otherwise safe sexual partners have left the market leaving the remaining sexually active teens at greater risk of infection. There is a second change that can explain the rising rates of STDs and that is a change on the *intensive margin*—those people still on the teen sex market have changed their behavior in a way that has increased risk.

A recent paper by economists Peter Arcidiacono, Andrew Beauchamp, and Marjorie McElroy finds that in schools in which teenage women outnumber teenage men, the gender imbalance increases the willingness of women to participate in relationships that involve sex. (This is very similar to the story told earlier that said that in college, girls are more sexually active than they want to be when male college students hold all the "market power.")

They find, for example, that when grade-twelve men outnumber grade-twelve women, the fraction of grade-twelve girls who are in a relationship and having sex is much higher than the fraction who stated that they want to be in a relationship that involves sexual intercourse. They also find that the fraction of grade-twelve boys who are in a relationship and having sex is very similar to the fraction that stated that this is their preference; they want to be in a relationship that involved sexual intercourse.

This says that, in grade twelve, boys have greater bargaining power over sexual activity because they are having as much sex as they want, and the girls have less bargaining power over sexual activity because they are having more sex than they want.

Just as on the college market, this relationship exists because grade-twelve girls have to compete for scarce grade-twelve boys, not only because boys are less likely to finish high school but also because grade-twelve girls have to compete with girls in younger grades who are happy to have relationships with older boys. This market power of older boys not only puts pressure on girls to have relationships that involve sex (even when they would prefer that they didn't), but it also hands bargaining power over to boys when it come to the decision to consistently apply protection against disease (i.e., wearing a condom).

Since women face higher risks of infection from unprotected sex than do men, giving men bargaining power over condom use leads to lower rates of condom usage because those making the decision face a lower cost of unprotected sex and, it could be argued, have a greater benefit from not using a condom.

Add to this the fact that older boys are not only transmitting infections to girls in their own year but also to girls in the cohort below them, and you have the making of an epidemic as diseases are passed through the "generations" of students.

This brings us to the issue of race that I raised earlier in the chapter, particularly the observation that girls who are black have significantly higher rates of STDs than girls who are either white or Hispanic. The authors of this paper observe a strong same-race preference in matching among high school students; specifically they find that over 86 percent of the couples in their sample are ones in which both people are of the same race. Black women were significantly more likely to be in a match with a black man than a man of any other race; 99 percent of black women were having sex with black men. Also, they find that the black teenage men in their sample are more likely to be having a relationship with someone of a different race than are black teenage women; 11 percent of black men were matched with women of a different race.

When we consider the observation that the recent high school completion rates for black men are between 7 and 12 percentage points lower than for black women (according to James Heckman and Paul LaFontaine), all the evidence suggests that black teenage women are competing with each other and with women of other races for far fewer black men on the high school market.

The evidence from the Arcidiacono paper I discussed earlier implies that this gender imbalance will result in black women having sex at much higher rates than would be their preference had there been a more even playing field. It also suggests that the bargaining power handed to black men as a result of their market power will lead to much higher rates of unprotected sex.

ABSTINENCE-ONLY PROGRAMS IN AFRICA INCREASE AIDS RISK TO TEENS

Kenya has an HIV education program that teaches young women moral values, refusal skills, and abstinence until marriage. Despite this call for abstinence, 21 percent of grade-eight girls and 48 percent of grade-eight boys report that they are sexually active. There is no mention of condom use in this program and, perhaps as a result, the HIV prevalence rates for youth in Kenya are high: 3 percent for girls between the ages of 15, 19.9 percent for women between the ages of 20 and 24, and 13 percent for women between 25 and 29.

One of the reasons why HIV is so prevalent among girls in Kenya—four times higher, in fact, than among boys of the same age—is that girls are having sexual relationships with much older men. For example, among girls who have become pregnant within a year of grade eight, 49 percent report the father is more than five years older and 16 percent report that he is more than ten years older.

The economic explanation for this phenomenon is that older men are acting as "sugar daddies," negotiating unprotected sex with young girls in exchange for money and gifts.

Stanford economist Pascaline Dupas recently published the results of a novel experiment in which researchers introduced an educational program into a randomly selected subset of schools in Kenya that gave students one simple piece of information: they informed them of the prevalence of HIV by age and gender in the closest nearby city. They stayed within national guidelines and did not raise the issue of condom use, but they did answer questions that were raised by students.

In the year following the program, the pregnancy rate of girls who were informed that sex with older men exposed them to greater risk of HIV transmission was 28 percent lower than in the control group that had only the standard abstinence-only program. The biggest decline was in girls who were impregnated by men more than five years older than themselves: the number of women who fit that description fell an incredible 61.7 percent. Girls in the treatment group were also 36 percent more likely to report having used a condom in their last act of intercourse relative to the control group.

We don't know if this simple-to-implement program reduced the incidence of HIV—just that it lowered the rate of unprotected vaginal intercourse with older men—but in just one forty-minute presentation in seventy-one different schools, these researchers managed to avert the birth of thirty children born to 15-year-old mothers; it brought about a significant change in student behavior.

Gender imbalances in high school leads to higher rates of risky sex for black teenage women, leading to more pregnancies and more sexually transmitted diseases.

One more thought on this issue. You might remember the evidence on black male incarceration rates we discussed in chapter 4 that showed that high rates of incarceration are reducing marriage rates of black women. In a similar paper, by Stéphane Mechoulan, the evidence suggests that a 1-percentage-point increase in the adult black male incarceration rate leads to an increase in the expected average age at which a black teenage woman gives birth by about seven extra months.

In the face of high incarceration rates for young black males, teenage women are postponing becoming sexually active; they are doing a better job at protecting themselves again pregnancy, presumably in response to concerns that their children's fathers will not be in a position to provide them with support in the future.

▨▨▨ ABSTINENCE MAY MAKE THE HEART GROW FONDER, BUT DOES IT INCREASE GRADES?

U.S. federal guidelines for abstinence-only education have imposed the requirement that students in abstinence-only programs be taught that "sexual activity outside of the context of marriage is likely to have harmful psychological and physical effects." So, even without the unintended consequences of pregnancy and disease, being sexually active in high school is emotionally damaging to teenagers and undermines their chances of academic success, right?

The truth is that if teen sexuality is psychologically harmful, researchers have been unable to find any evidence to substantiate that claim.

A paper by Joseph Sabia and Daniel Rees tackles this issue using a large nationally representative sample of U.S. students taken in three stages: 1995, 1996, and 2001. They find that delaying sexual intercourse by just one year increases a teenage woman's probability of graduating from high school by 4.4 percent. This effect of early loss of virginity on academic success, however, was exclusively among white teenage women. They found no relationship between virginity loss and high school graduation rates for either Hispanic or black teenage women.

If the cause of failing to graduate from high school is psychological harm, then early sexual activity is proven to be harmful only to white teenage women. The problem with this conclusion, however, is that while the authors control for a variety of factors that might influence both sexuality and high school completion, they have left out one thing: teen pregnancy. Given that a girl is likely to get pregnant in a given year only if she is sexually active, then it must be true that becoming sexually active one year earlier increases the chance that she will become pregnant at some point in high school.

We can't use this evidence to decisively say that early entrance to sexuality is psychologically harmful for girls when we already know that the responsibilities of parenting a young child during adolescence makes it very difficult to complete high school.

The same paper finds that delaying having sex by one year has no statistically significant effect on the high school graduation rate of teenage men, regardless of race. You may be tempted to conclude from this evidence that sex is psychologically less damaging for men, but the reality is that it is much easier for a man who has impregnated his girlfriend to finish school than it is for the girlfriend who has experienced childbirth.

Without controlling for childbirth, we can't say for certain whether or not there is any high school completion effect for early entrance to sexuality among girls who can effectively control their own fertility, and the speculation that girls are more psychologically fragile than boys when it comes to sexuality is just that—speculation.

One interesting recommendation made by the authors of this paper is that abstinence-only programs should abandon the claim that premarital sexual activity has psychological effects and replace it with a more "nuanced message." I am sure you share my curiosity as to what that might look like in the classroom, given these empirical results.

For example, perhaps teachers should give a stern warning to their students that sex is psychologically harmful, followed by the clarification that the boys can have sex without fear that it will negatively affect their school performance, but only with either black and Hispanic teenage women who also appear to be unaffected.

That message should, at least, get the kids' attention.

One more question: if teen sex is psychologically harmful, then shouldn't teens who witness the ill effects suffered by their close friends who have become sexually active learn from that friend's mistake and avoid similar consequences?

A recent paper by David Card and Laura Giuliano taps into the unusual feature of the Add Health survey, which allows researchers to identify a

SELLING THEIR MOST VALUABLE ASSET

Teenage women are repeatedly told not to give away their most valuable asset—their virginity. A few years ago, a brothel in Nevada announced it was selling the virginity of Natalie Dylan, a 21-year-old college graduate, for a remarkable $3.8 million. This has made many women wonder if there really is value to this "asset" and, since that time, many have tried to replicate Natalie's success. But market forces are at play, even with this unusual service, and profiting from a virginity sale is unlikely in the future.

A recent paper by Fabio Mariani argues that cross-societal variations in the value of virginity are closely tied to opportunities that women have on the marriage market. His argument goes something like this: If a wealthy man meets a poor woman with whom he falls in love, he might be willing to marry her if she is a virgin despite the fact she is poor. If she is not a virgin, however, he might prefer to marry a wealthy woman who is a virgin even if he doesn't love her.

The return on virginity for a poor girl, therefore, is the probability of marrying a rich man multiplied by his income. Anything that reduces this expected return to virginity in marriage will reduce the compensation a woman will need to receive in order to encourage her to relinquish her virginity outside of marriage. This compensation is her *reservation price* for selling her virginity.

Higher income inequality among men, like that observed in developed nations, should lead to higher-reservation value for virginity as women have more to gain by remaining a virgin when the gap in income between rich and poor men is greater.

At the same time, the virginity market has only one barrier to entry: participants must be chaste up until the point of the sale. This almost-free entry to a market implies competition in the market will be so high that the price will be driven down to a fair market value. I suspect that the price that men are willing to pay on a perfectly competitive virginity market is actually far below the reservation price of most potential sellers.

One final element that almost certainly eliminates the possibility of profitable virginity sales is the competition would-be virginity sellers in the West face from women in markets where virginity has a much lower expected value. The price of a virgin in a U.S.–Mexican border town is only about $400, well below the millions Western women are asking to prostitute themselves in this way.

---

teen's peer group within a high school. They use this evidence to answer the following question: If a student's best friend engages in a risky behavior (sex, smoking, marijuana use, or truancy), then what is the probability that the friend will engage in the same behavior?

Best friends tend to come from similar family situations, for example, be the same race and age, have similar educational goals, and similar attitudes toward risk. The authors are able to control for these factors and still find that if a student's best friend has had sexual intercourse, then she or he is 4.5 percentage points more likely than the average student to have sexual intercourse the following year. If their friend had "intimate contact" (essentially making it to third base), the probability their friend will have intimate contact as well is 4 percentage points higher than the average student.

The best-friend effect is as significant as living in a single-parent household or of having two parents who did not finish high school—both of which increase the probability that a teenager is sexually active.

One possible explanation for the best-friend effect on sex is that teens smoke pot together and that pot smoking leads to a higher rate of sexual activity. Or it is that they drink together and that drinking leads to higher rates of sexual activity. It turns out, though, that pot use doesn't increase entrance to sexual activity in teens, so even though having a best friend who smokes pot increases (to a small degree) the probability that the student also smokes pot, this can't explain the increase in sexual activity. And while alcohol use increases sexual activity (significantly), having a best friend who drinks alcohol does not increase the probably that a student drinks more than the average student.

This leaves us with the perhaps unpalatable explanation that teenagers find sex pleasurable and that at least some teens observe their friends having sex without any of the expected negative consequences, and that encourages them to do the same.

There is one other paper that might explain the best-friend effect. Jesús Fernández-Villaverde, Jeremy Greenwood, and Nezih Guner argue that as contraceptives have become more effective, and the risk associated with premarital sex has fallen, parents have reduced their investment in preventing teens from becoming sexually active.

One way parents prevent their teenage children from becoming sexually active is by teaching them that premarital sex is shameful behavior. Using the same Add Health data we just discussed, these authors find that while teens are more likely to have already had sex if their friends have had sex, they are less likely to have had sex if they believe that sex is a shameful thing to do (with shame measured using the answers to questions like "How would you feel if your mother knew you were having sex?").

This suggests that the reason why teens are more likely to follow in their friends' footsteps—having sex if their friends have sex—is that having a sexually active friend reduces the sense of shame, or stigma, attached to being a sexually active teenager.

▰▰▰ FINAL WORDS

Remember the young man I talked about at the beginning of this chapter, the one who told me he is going to wait until he is 21 to have a girlfriend? The funny part of that story is that his mother is bitterly disappointed that her son is not out there getting some action, just as she was when she was his age (and, in fact, far younger).

Not everyone remembers the sex they had when they were teens as fondly as my friend does, but it is interesting to note that the current generation of parents with teenage children might very well be the first generation in which the parents were more sexually active in high school than their kids.

Personally, I remember realizing in my early 20s that my cohort was on the tail end of the sexual revolution and that subsequent generations wouldn't take the same sexual liberties that my generation had when we were young. At the time, my belief that the sexual revolution was over came from the growing awareness around HIV/AIDS. In hindsight, fear of disease has probably played a role in decreasing teen promiscuity, but the steady persistent decline in teen promiscuity over twenty years suggest that an economic explanation is warranted.

Recent media reports on declining teen promiscuity suggest that fear is playing a major role in that change in behavior and I think they are right. It isn't just fear that life will be hard with a baby; teenagers didn't need reality TV to inform them that trips to the mall aren't the same with a crying baby. It is a fear of being left behind in an economy in which the only workers who have seen real increases in their standard of living over the past thirty years are those who continued their education after high school. It is fear of being at the bottom of the income distribution when those at the top lavishly consume while everyone else races to keep up. It is an understanding that childbirth early in life leads to a permanent decrease in lifetime earning ability that has encouraged both young men and women to be more cautious regarding their sexuality.

Of course, for these economic incentives to bring teen pregnancy rates in the United States to the low levels observed in other countries they would have to be available to everyone. All teenagers, for example, would have to believe that their lifetime earnings would be reduced by a teen pregnancy in order for that incentive to change their risk-taking behavior. But the reality is that the lifetime earning ability of a low-skilled worker is completely unaffected by having a baby as a teenager. And moving from unskilled to skilled worker requires an investment than many low-income families cannot afford for their children, regardless of their sexual behavior.

I started this chapter with a description of the way in which economics has shaped social norms regarding teen sexual behavior. I have one thought to add: Social norms within the socioeconomic groups that have been the most disadvantaged by the modern economy have evolved to take a more permissive view of teen sexuality. This economic perspective is important because without it we are tempted to believe that the causality runs in the opposite direction—that people have become economically marginalized because of their sexual behavior. That skewed perspective conveniently ignores the reality that teenagers in high-income families are not less promiscuous because they have higher moral standards, but because they face an entirely different set of economic incentives that have shaped the way that standards have been set within their communities.

If you read the tabloids, you might be tempted to believe that people who have the most sexual partners belong to an entirely different socioeconomic group—that of extremely wealthy married men. I wouldn't be too quick to jump to that conclusion, though. In fact, as we are about to see, income is a much more important determinant of whether or not women are unfaithful than it is for men.

CHAPTER 8
NAUGHTY BY NATURE

▰▰▰ TILL DEATH DO YOU PART . . . OR AT LEAST UNTIL YOU ARE READY TO SAY "TIME FOR A CHANGE"

Google has a very interesting feature called "predictive queries," which when used for marriage terms reveal a searching history that would convince any casual Web searcher that marriage is an extremely unpleasant state of being.

According to Google, for example, if you are typing the phrase "Why does my wife . . . ?" the most likely question you are phrasing is: "not love me anymore," "cry for no reason," and "not want to be touched."

If you are typing the phrase "Why does my husband . . . ?" Google will kindly offer up the most obvious completions: "hate me," "ignore me," and "cheat."

This chapter is about the people who have reached a stage in their lives where they are searching the term "My marriage is . . . " and the finishing phrase is "over," "failing," and "in trouble."

And while I can't tell you "How do you know when it is time . . ." "to end a relationship," "to break up," or "to divorce," I can give you some economic insight as to why infidelity happens.

Here is a story to get us started.

SWINGERS CLUBS ARE STEALING SEX-TRADE MARKET SHARE

The recent shift in social acceptance of swinging as an activity for married couples has, according to economist Fabio D'Orlando, not only increased participation at swingers events but also encouraged swinging couples to engage in more radical sex acts.

No doubt there have always been couples who would like to be swingers but feared the activity was too costly. I am not talking about entry fees to events, although that might be a consideration, but rather the expected costs of swinging: the risk of humiliation, for example, or the risk that the experience will either be a disappointment or will lead to marital dissolution. Over time though, because the Internet has made it easier to find like-minded couples who are willing to share their experiences, these risks have fallen, reducing the expected cost of swinging.

This fall in costs has encouraged more couples to enter the swinging market and, according to D'Orlando, encouraged couples on that market to move from "softer" sex acts (for example, having sex with each other on a bed in which another couple is doing the same) to "harder" sex acts (for example, involving a single man who has sex with the wife or the husband or both).

The transition to harder sex acts for swingers has drawn single men onto that market at a greater rate, which is what makes the story really interesting from an economic perspective.

Clubs that organize swinging events have a perverse economic incentive (pun intended) to allow as many single men into the club as possible. Many couples don't want them in the club, but since the demand of places for single men exceeds the supply of spaces for single men, the prices they pay to enter are high. Profit-maximizing club owners, therefore, want to sell spaces to single men who are willing to pay a higher fee.

As couples engage in harder sex acts, the demand for single men in the clubs increases. This increase in number of spaces available for single men drives down the price they have to pay to enter the club. And so, more single men are visiting swingers clubs.

For single men, swingers clubs are a substitute for prostitution and, as anyone who has taken an intro-economics class knows, if two goods are substitutes and the price of one good or service falls, then demand for that good increases relative to the other good.

So swingers clubs are cutting into sex market shares by providing similar services to single men at a much lower price.

I am told that a single woman at a swinger event is called a "unicorn," a mythical being that is only rumored to exist. Not surprisingly, these women can enter the clubs for free.

Leonard was a good man. He was committed to social justice and worked to support local politicians who shared his beliefs. He was involved in his church, playing an important role in raising enough money to renovate the building. He was successful in his career, priding himself in the role that he played in his workplace as a strict but caring father figure for those just beginning their careers.

It was fairly well known that Leonard had been married once before he met his current wife, but there were problems in his first marriage that he would rather not discuss publically.

They had married in the early 1970s, while he was still in graduate school and, despite the birth of two children, had maintained a very active sex life. Through the years they had kept their fire burning by frequently acting out their sexual, and often bisexual, fantasies with other like-minded couples they met in swingers clubs.

Over time, though, even those encounters bored Leonard, and he tried to convince his wife to escalate into sexual behaviors that took her farther and farther out of her comfort zone. Eventually she had had enough; he had pushed her too far, and she called a stop to all sex outside of their marriage. Initially he agreed to the new arrangement, of course, but two months later, she heard from a friend that he had tried to enter a swingers event without her.

That betrayal brought an end to their marriage and, ironically, without a partner, it also brought an end to his participation in the swingers club.

Being single was far less sexually exciting than Leonard had imagined. So much so, in fact, that for the five years prior to meeting his second wife, he had depended on the services of sex workers for sexual release. Now in his mid-50s and married again, he was convinced that his need for sexual diversion was behind him. He committed himself to building a more mature relationship with wife number two that involved sex, certainly, but only within the confines of their marriage.

The problem with this arrangement was that over time Leonard began to grow lonely. He loved his second wife, he really did, but he longed for the type of intimacy that comes with new love. More than anything, he wanted to be with a woman who was enthusiastic in her desire for him, extolled his sexual prowess, and would do anything to please him.

In short, he wanted to be adored.

Leonard was just beginning to come to terms with what he had come to consider his externally imposed impotence when something changed. A promotion at work gave him greater authority over, and more one-to-one contact with, some of the younger employees in his firm. He felt

appreciated, if perhaps not adored, by his new charges and that appreciation convinced him that he had something to offer a younger generation
of sexually vibrant women.

A friend of mine once said to me that loneliness when you are alone
is one thing, but loneliness within marriage is loneliness stripped of all
hope. And for that reason, part of me would like to tell you that Leonard
found the fulfilling relationships that he had been seeking. But hope was
all that this new position of authority gave Leonard. Even when he was
younger and single, he didn't appeal to women looking for short-term
relationships. The women he came into contact with now liked him,
maybe even enjoyed flirting with him, but they had no interest in being his
part-time lover.

And so, Leonard was a faithful husband to his second wife, not because
he believed in fidelity but rather because the market on which extramarital
lovers operates did not offer up any alternatives.

No one really knows how prevalent extramarital sexual relationships
really are; a very rough estimate places infidelity at about 50 percent—
half of all men and women will cheat on their spouse at some point in
their marriage.

The problem with that estimate, however, is that what it means to be
"faithful" is often specific to the marriage and, as a result, is very impre-
cisely measured in the data. If you sit at your desk and fantasize about a
coworker, are you being unfaithful? To some people the answer is yes, and
some of the very high estimates of marital infidelity include this behavior
in their measure. If you have had sexual intercourse with someone other
than your spouse at some point over the course of your marriage, are you
being unfaithful? Often yes, but if your spouse condones sex outside of
the marriage, or was with you and having sex with that same person, is it
really infidelity?

A more reliable measure of infidelity is the share of men who have
children whom they mistakenly believe are their own, when they are, in
fact, not related. Evolutionary biologist David Buss reports that in blind

CHEATING AS A PROBLEM OF DYNAMIC INCONSISTENCY

Dynamic (or time) inconsistency tells us that preferences can change over time; what may seem like the optimal choice in period one is not necessarily the optimal choice in period two. It is often used to explain how monetary authorities or governments behave when there is no mechanism forcing them to commit to a specific course of behavior. It can also tell us why as individuals it is difficult to enforce no cheating in marriages.

To give you an example of how dynamic inconsistency applies to cheating, consider a husband who fears that his wife will cheat, so when they marry he tells her that if she cheats he will leave her and provide her with no financial support. At the beginning of their marriage that is his preference—to leave if she cheats—and by telling her this, he hopes that she will chose not to cheat.

Imagine that later she meets a man with whom she would like to have sex. Her husband promised that he would leave her if she cheated, but she knows that he would not fare well on his own and, even if he does, the no-fault divorce laws prevent him from withholding financial support. To her his promise to leave is not credible, and so she chooses to have extramarital sex.

Her husband later finds out that she has cheated and, while very hurt, decides to stay in the marriage because, as she anticipated, he does not wish to leave her. His original preference was to leave if she cheated, but now that she has cheated, his preference is to stay.

The reason why this dynamic inconsistency problem is interesting is that now that we recognize that the problem exists we can find a way to solve it. One solution, for this husband, is to find a way to commit to leave if his wife cheats. For example, he could remain independent and insist on a prenuptial contract that penalizes her financially if she cheats.

Historically, this is not a problem couples have had to contend with on their own because governments imposed laws that harshly punish infidelity—particularly female infidelity. Even without repercussions to infidelity here on Earth, religious faiths have made sex outside of marriage a sin so that cheaters have an eternity of damnation to fear. Social norms that encourage family and friends to disapprove of men and women who choose to forgive a partner who has strayed play a similar role in that they shame people into leaving unfaithful spouses. These mechanisms help solve the dynamic-inconsistency problem couples face by imposing punishment that is external to the individuals involved.

In general, dynamic-inconsistency theory tells us that these mechanisms will be much more effective in preventing infidelity than will unenforceable contracts between two people.

---

paternity studies, approximately 10 percent of children fall into this category. But this measures only female infidelity, and in an era in which approximately 40 percent of births are to unmarried women, even this fails as a measure of extramarital infidelity.

Bruce Elmslie and Edinaldo Tebaldi find that among Americans who are still married to their first husbands or wives, 7 percent of women and 14 percent of men said yes in response to the question "Have you ever had sex with someone other than your husband or wife while you were married?" When they consider only men and women under the age of 35, men and women appear to cheat at similar rates, with 7 percent of women and 9 percent of men admitting to extramarital sex. As we will see, this difference between age groups probably stems from the timing of infidelity rather than a societal shift that has caused a new generation of men to cheat less and a new generation of women to cheat at roughly the same rate.

These numbers seem low and, the fact is, they underestimate the pervasiveness of infidelity because they represent only the behavior of people who are still in their first marriage—anyone ever divorced was excluded from the data set. Donald Cox, using data from a nationally representative survey, finds that people who report that they have cheated on a marriage partner at some point in their lifetime are more likely to be divorced; 49 percent of male and 56 percent of female cheaters are divorced, compared with 29 percent of male and 31 percent of female non-cheaters. So removing divorced people from the data set means that the propensity to cheat in marriage will be predicted as lower than it really is in the general population.

Donald Cox finds that 25 percent of men and 14 percent of women have had an extramarital affair at some point in their lifetime. If we ask only about behavior in the previous twelve months, 8 percent of men admit to having an extramarital affair compared with 3.5 percent of women. When we include people who are cohabitating, as well as those who are married, the share admitting to infidelity increases to 34 percent for men and 23 percent for women. We also know that men who cheat on their partner cheat more frequently than women do; cheating men are twice as likely as cheating women to have had sex with two or more partners in the past year. Men tend to cheat with women who are younger (no big surprise there) and women tend to cheat with men who are better educated. Very young women (less than 26 years old) cheat more than women of any other age, and while men also cheat more when they are young, the relationship between age and infidelity isn't nearly as pronounced for men as it is for women.

You might be wondering how thinking about infidelity from an economic perspective helps our understanding of this behavior. There's no doubt that biology plays a huge role in encouraging married people to seek sex outside of their marriages, but, at some level, the final decision to act on those biological impulses is made by rational people seeking to maximize their well-being. As we will see later, that decision might not always make them happy, but nonetheless the decision to cheat is the optimal one at the time that it is made.

Let me introduce the economic model that can be used to explain infidelity. It will look familiar to you because it is the same approach we used in chapter 1. Rather than explaining how sexuality has changed over time, however, we will use it to explain why it is that some men and women are unfaithful while others are not.

▰▰▰ UNFAITHFUL MATH

Men and women cheat in marriage because they believe at the outset that the benefit of doing so outweighs the expected costs. The expected cost of cheating looks something like this:

PROBABILITY OF
BEING CAUGHT

COST OF BEING
CAUGHT

EXPECTED COST
OF CHEATING

The probability of being caught cheating depends on an individual's circumstances. For example, consider two women who are both considering having an extramarital affair. The first woman works outside of her home, is financially independent, and lives in an urban environment. The second is not employed on the labor force, is financially dependent, and lives in a rural community. Without knowing any more information, it is reasonable to assume that the woman who works at home, and lives in a remote area, has a much higher chance of being caught cheating than the woman who works outside of the home and might even have opportunities to travel for business.

The "cost of being caught" is a little more complicated, but it too is an expected cost—no man or woman really knows what the cost of cheating is until they are caught. If neither the career woman nor the homemaker is paid alimony in the event that her husband divorces her for adultery, the financially dependent woman has far more to lose by being caught cheating. If alimony is paid despite the infidelity, on the other hand, the dependent woman is more likely to be the recipient of alimony payments, and it is the financially independent woman who has more to lose. In fact, she might end up being the alimony payer if her husband earns a lower income.

The final thing we need to know is the probability that each woman's husband will leave if he catches her cheating. In reality we have no idea what those probabilities are as they will vary from woman to woman and from husband to husband. The husband of the financially independent woman might stay if he enjoys the financial stability their marriage gives him, or he might prefer financial insecurity to living with an unfaithful wife. The husband of the homemaker might leave if he is unwilling to support an unfaithful wife or might stay if they have young children whom he wants to protect.

We may not know what these probabilities are, but my guess is that these women already have a pretty good idea what will happen if their husband finds out they have been unfaithful before they make the decision to stray.

Let's say, for argument's sake, that the chance of the homemaker being caught cheating is 30 percent, the probability that her husband will leave her if she is caught is 50 percent, and, in the case of divorce, she loses $100,000 worth of goods and services that her marriage provided her. Her expected cost of cheating is then:

$$0.30 \times 0.50 \times \$100{,}000 = \$15{,}000$$

So the benefit of the extramarital sex would have to be large in order for her to cheat; she would have to value it more than $15,000 in monetary terms.

Now the woman who works outside of the home faces very different risks and costs. Let's say her chance of being caught cheating is only

5 percent, the probability that her husband leaves her if she is caught is 50 percent, and, in the case of divorce, she loses $50,000 worth of goods and services that her marriage provided her. Her expected cost of cheating is:

$$0.05 \times 0.50 \times \$50,000 = \$1,250$$

So the benefit of the extramarital sex is significantly lower for her than for the other woman. She would have to value it as more than $1,250 in monetary terms in order for her to cheat.

Anything that increases the chance a cheater will be caught (for example, if the likelihood of contracting an STD is high) or increases the chance that the partner will divorce him/her (for example, if he/she credibly commits to leaving) increases the expected cost of cheating.

Obviously, financial losses are only a convenient way to explain the costs in this analysis. Other considerations, those harder to measure, are also costs associated with being caught cheating. For example, cheating men and women risk the emotional cost of losing their children and, even if they don't lose their children, imposing hardship on those children in the case of divorce. Many cheaters, both men and women, risk retaliation for their infidelity in the form of physical violence from their partners. They risk losing their spouse's love for them, which is something most married people value. They risk being expelled from their faith communities or being socially isolated by family and friends. Others risk damaging their careers, particularly if the affair is with a colleague or client. Even the risk of living alone for an undetermined period imposes an expected cost on someone contemplating infidelity.

All of these factors, and probably many others, enter into the cost side of this infidelity cost-benefit analysis.

In the years that follow an extramarital relationship, a cheater may not feel that the decision to cheat was as rational as I have portrayed it to be here, especially if the expected costs have become real costs (for example, if the spouse both discovered their infidelity and asked for a

WOULD YOU CONFESS TO VISITING A SEX WORKER?

Many of the men who have had extramarital sex have done so with a sex worker. I have already said that 25 percent of men say they have had sex with another person while married, but if we consider only the subsample of men who have not purchased sex on the market, that number drops to 19 percent. Given that less than 20 percent of men will use a prostitute in their lifetime, this evidence suggests that men who are willing to buy sex are also much more willing to cheat on their wives.

A study conducted by Canadian sociologist Chris Atchison called "A John's Voice" (www.johnsvoice.ca) surveyed a large number of purchasers of sex workers and asked specifically whether or not they had discussed this behavior with their partners. Most of them had spent over a decade of buying sex on the market and had purchased sex on and off the street. Just under half of the men in the sample (371 out of 781) were married or in a common-law relationship at the time of the survey, and 25 percent of those who were not married reported they were in a relationship.

Fewer than 50 percent of these men had ever discussed their prostitute use with anyone. Of those men who had, 23 percent told male friends, 17 percent told other sex sellers, 10 percent told other sex buyers, and 9 percent told female friends.

Roughly 6 percent of the men in the sample had revealed to a spouse or other sex partner that they had used the services of sex workers. Of the men who were in a relationship at the time of the survey, 79 percent reported that they actively hid their sex-buying from their partners, which seems to suggest that 21 percent did not (presumably either because they don't care or they believed there was little chance they would be caught) and 63 percent worried their partner would find out. When asked what they thought would be the repercussions of their partner's discovery that they frequented sex workers, 61 percent thought they would divorce, 11 percent thought it would cause arguments, 10.5 percent thought their partner would be upset, 5 percent thought it would result in "general disaster," and just over 1 percent thought it would result in violence.

The survey also asked about the possible reactions of family members and coworkers. In response to that question, 41 percent thought that if they were outed as johns that they would face "shame, embarrassment, stigma or ridicule," 17 percent thought they would lose friends or family, 13 percent thought there would be more than one form of repercussion, and 13 percent didn't care or felt there would be no repercussions.

---

divorce), but even decisions we later regret, in fact even the worst decisions you have made in your life, can be a rational decision at the time that they were made.

This is because decisions are made based on the likelihood of a bad outcome, not based on the certainty of a bad outcome. If everyone who cheated knew with certainty that they would be caught, knew with certainty that their spouse and community would respond negatively, and knew with certainty the costs they would incur as a result, I think you would agree with me that there would be significantly less marital infidelity than there currently is.

▨▨▨▨ THE MYTH OF MONOGAMY

Humans, like other mammals, are not naturally monogamous; even the overly romanticized female sloth, rumored to be the most monogamous of all the primates, will sneak out for a night of coitus with a nearby sloth if she gets the chance. Understanding the benefit side of the cost-benefit analysis that determines whether or not a man or woman cheats requires an understanding of the biological payoff to giving into the desire to have a sexual relationship outside of marriage.

As we discussed in chapter 2, the males of our species demonstrate a biological desire for multiple sex partners. The best descriptor of this male trait, in my mind, is called the Coolidge Effect. The Coolidge Effect describes how males of any mammalian species, including humans, who are sexually receptive to a sexual partner, will, eventually, lose interest in copulation completely unless a new partner is introduced; males are hardwired not to invest in repeatedly inseminating a female that they have already inseminated.

Psychologists Frank Beach and Lisbeth Jordan tested this effect in laboratories in the 1950s by placing male and female rats in a container and allowing them to copulate until the male was exhausted. At the point of exhaustion, the male lost all interest in copulation, despite persistent attempts by the female rats to encourage him to continue (this scenario may sound familiar to some of you). When the researchers introduced a new female rat into the container, however, the male rat regained his interest in copulation and proceeded to inseminate the new female rat.

Just in case you are either a sexually frustrated women who is tempted to think that introducing another woman to your bed will stimulate your male partner's sexual interest, or a sexually bored man who thinks this is convincing argument to share with your partner, you should know that the introduction of the new female did not renew the male's sexual interest in the original female rat—just the new one that was introduced.

The popular theory for why males behave this way is that, throughout evolutionary history, the men who have had the most sexual partners (we can call him Australo-promiscuous, if you like) were the same men who had the most children. We are descendants of the most promiscuous males, meaning that modern-day men are hardwired to desire multiple sexual partners.

Females are more restricted in the number of children they can produce and having multiple sexual partners does not increase the quantity of children they will bear over their lifetime. It can, however, improve the quality of their children. Children who are taller and healthier are more likely to survive to adulthood and have children of their own. As a result, we are descendants of the women who sought out the tallest and healthiest sexual partners to be the fathers of their children.

Some evidence that women are hardwired to seek high-quality sexual partners for the purpose of fertility can be found in studies that show that women change their preference for sexual partners depending on where they are in their menstrual cycle. For example, evolutionary psychologists Martie Haselton and Geoffrey Miller found that when the participants in their study were ovulating, 93 percent stated that they would prefer a poor yet creative man for a short-term sexual relationship to a financially successful but uncreative man. When this exercise was repeated with participants who were not ovulating, only 58 percent of women preferred the poor yet creative man as a short-term sexual partner.

These effects of ovulation on mate choice were not found when women were asked about long-term relationships. You might be tempted to predict that wealth matters more for long-term relationships than it does for short-term relationships where women are looking for good providers instead of good genes. However, in this particular study when the choice of long-term partner was a poor yet creative artist or a wealthy yet uncreative artist, approximately 84 percent of both ovulating and non-ovulating women expressed a preference for the poor artist.

Another study, by evolutionary psychologists Elizabeth Pillsworth and Martie Haselton, is even more to our point. It finds that women who are married to less-attractive men were more likely to seek extramarital relationships when they are ovulating than are women who are married to more-attractive men. Those same women, who were more inclined to

BIRTH CONTROL CHANGES WOMEN'S PREFERENCE FOR MEN

If ovulation gives women a biological impetus to seek more attractive sexual partners, then a man who wishes to curb his wife's desire to stray might want to encourage her to take an oral contraceptive that eliminates ovulation all together. The question is: what happens to their relationship when they decide to have children?

According to a paper by scientists Alexandra Alvergne and Virpi Lummaa, women who take oral contraceptives lose the stronger preference for a man who is masculine in appearance that occurs in ovulating women when they are most fertile.

This research implies that in societies where large numbers of women are taking oral contraceptives, the ideal of an "attractive" mate is moving away from one who looks like he will provide good genes (that is, more masculine-looking men) toward one who looks like he might be a caretaker (that is, more feminine-looking men). A technological advance, the invention of oral contraceptives, has led to a change in mate preference for women.

I call this the Justin Bieber Effect.

What happens, though, when a woman who has been taking the birth control pill during courtship and early marriage stops taking it because she wishes to become pregnant? I have already said that it is when a woman is young that she is most likely to cheat on her husband. The timing of female cheating is then consistent with the view that women cheat in order to seek better genes for their children. The Bieber Effect might explain why these women didn't seek mates who were more attractive in the first place; oral contraceptives suppressed their biological imperative to finding a more masculine mate.

In reality, good genes are a scarce resource and when resources are scarce, their market price is inflated. The high price of good genes prevents many women from finding a long-term mate with all the qualities she would ideally pass on to her children. It doesn't prevent her, however, from using a different strategy—that of marrying a man with other good qualities, like being a good father to her children, and then finding an extramarital sex partner to be those children's biological father.

Of course, the strategy fails if a woman is caught cheating by her husband and, as a result, he divorces her. This implies that the benefit in terms of increased gene quality must be great in order for women to take that chance.

---

seek an extramarital sexual partner, also reported that their husbands were more attentive and affectionate when they were most fertile; less attractive men seem to realize on some level that they must protect their wives from extramarital relationships by rewarding them for their fidelity through affection.

The point of this evidence on human biology is that it tells us that the benefits of being unfaithful to one's partner are different for women than they are for men.

For example, it implies that when a man cheats, it is because he is desirable enough to persuade a woman, other than his wife, to have extramarital sex with him. He can do this because the benefits to a short-term relationship with a man who has good genes, measured in the quality of her children, is high for the woman he attracts.

It also implies that when a woman cheats, it is not because she is highly desirable but because her husband is less desirable than the men who are willing to have extramarital sex with her. She will do this because there is a benefit, measured in the quality of her children, to having a short-term relationship with a man who has good genes.

IT'S NOT YOU; IT'S ME

This idea that a man's willingness to cheat is a function of his own quality and a woman's willingness to cheat is a function of her husband's quality is a testable hypothesis that was taken on by Bruce Elmslie and Edinaldo Tebaldi, whose research we discussed earlier in this chapter.

The idea that infidelity is related to fertility is supported by their research. Men are fertile for a longer period of their lives; men are more likely to be unfaithful to their wives as they themselves age, but only up to the age of age of 55, after which point the likelihood that they will cheat drops off. The relationship between women's infidelity and age has a similar pattern (increasing and then decreasing), but with a peak in the likelihood of infidelity occurring much earlier—around the age of 45—when a woman's ability to reproduce is in decline. It is at this point that the reproductive benefits to a woman of having extramarital sex end since she is unlikely to have any other children.

Using educational achievement as an indicator of gene quality, they find no evidence that educated men are more likely to have extramarital sex than are less-educated men—in fact they find that men who have only a high school diploma or less are about 3 percent more likely to cheat than are men with a college or graduate degree. This evidence seems to refute the hypothesis that high-quality men are more able to cheat than are low-quality men. The authors attribute this result to the fact that some men are having sex with prostitutes and that gene quality does not determine a sex worker's willingness to have sex with a married man.

If women are seeking short-term sexual partners based on gene quality, however, because they have been hardwired by years of evolutionary forces to select fathers who will give their children the greatest chance of survival, then is a university degree what they are really looking for?

As a woman myself, I have to say that to me the ideal short-term sex partner looks more like someone who would scale a cliff to tackle a tiger on my behalf, rather than a man who can solve systems of equations. I suspect it is their measurement of attractiveness (i.e., education) that has made it difficult to prove their hypothesis that men with high gene quality are more likely to cheat.

Having said that, women whose husbands have a college or graduate degree are 3 percent less likely to cheat than are women whose husbands have only a high school diploma or less. Men don't seem to be more or less likely to cheat dependent on their wives' education. This does lend some evidence to support the hypothesis that for women it is their husband's characteristics that determine whether or not they cheat, but men's decisions are independent of that consideration.

That conclusion leaves something out, however: it assumes that a husband's low educational achievement increases a woman's likelihood of cheating because it increases the benefit of having sex with a superior man through the good-genes effect. This argument ignores the fact that a woman's decision to cheat is determined by the expected cost of cheating as well as the benefit, and we already know that the cost of cheating is partially measured in the income she will forgo if he divorces her.

▰▰▰▰ IF I HAD A RICH MAN

Sometimes it seems that every time I open my Web browser, there is news being reported that a high-ranking politician or high-paid corporate executive or athlete has been caught cheating on his wife. The media never reports on the affairs of married men in lower-paying jobs, of course, since there would then be no time to report other news.

The problem with the imbalance in visibility between the affairs of the wealthy and the poor is that it has left many with the impression that no matter how unfaithful those close to us are, no one is as unfaithful as a wealthy man.

If you think back to when we talked about the mystery of monogamy in chapter 5, this presumption that wealthy men cheat more makes economic sense. Just as it is wealthy men who can afford to have additional

CAN FINANCIAL INCENTIVES REDUCE FEMALE INFIDELITY?

Evidence from an unlikely source suggests that marriage contracts can reduce female infidelity but may actually increase male infidelity.

In Uganda, men's families pay a price to the families of their sons' brides that acts as a security deposit against future bad behavior. Despite laws to prevent the demanding of refunds, a man who suspects that his wife is having sexual relations with another man will return her to her family and ask for his bride price back.

A recent study by David Bishai and Shoshana Grossbard uses a nationally representative Ugandan data set collected in confidential face-to-face interviews with both husbands and wives to determine if these contracts influence sexual behavior. In the whole sample, 5 percent of wives and 19 percent of husbands reported having been unfaithful in the previous twelve months. In the sample that included only couples in which the husband paid a bride price, 2 percent of wives and 21 percent of husbands had been unfaithful. In the sample that includes only couples in which the husband had not paid a bride price, 10 percent of wives and 16 percent of men had been unfaithful.

It appears that refundable bride prices reduce female infidelity and increase male infidelity. However, once the authors control for family characteristics (such as education, polygamy, children, and whether or not the husband is a farmer), the male effect almost disappears, but the female effect persists and is statistically significant.

You may think this system of writing financial contracts to ensure that women comply with their marriage vows is primitive, but prenuptial agreements that include clauses that limit the financial responsibilities of the husband if a wife is unfaithful, or vice versa, serve the same purpose. This is also true in states in which the courts still apply "at fault" rules to the division of marital assets; the spouse who cheats is penalized in the financial settlement.

This all seems fine, but as long as men earn higher incomes and hold a greater proportion of the wealth than do women, or when courts take a harsher view of female infidelity than male infidelity, these systems will only increase male infidelity in the way that refundable bride prices increased male infidelity in Uganda.

The reason is that they prevent couples from forming implicit contracts that looks something like this: if you are faithful, I too will be faithful, but if you cheat, then I will cheat as well. These contracts put women and men in a better position to negotiate fidelity if the threat to reciprocate is credible.

---

wives, it is also wealthy men who can afford to have sex partners on the side. Even if wealthy men do not explicitly pay their extramarital sex partners, or even give them gifts (such as cars, apartments, or clothing), they are bound to have an easier time attracting women who are willing to be the "bit on the side" in the hope that one day they will become the second (or third) wife of a wealthy man.

The thing is, while the observation that monogamy is the marriage institution preferred by wealthy men is a mystery, the fact the wealthy men are less monogamous (in term of fidelity to their one wife) is actually a myth.

There is no evidence that rich men cheat in their marriages any more than do poor men. In fact, after controlling for a variety of different effects, Donald Cox finds very little connection between a man's income and his willingness to cheat on his wife.

The real effect of income on cheating is with women; women in poorer households are significantly more likely to cheat than are women in wealthier households. That evidence is supplied in Cox's paper and also in Robin Baker's well-known book *Sperm Wars: The Science of Sex*. Baker says that while 10 percent of all men on average are raising children they mistakenly believe to be their own (the same figure as found by David Buss), when we look at men who are at the bottom of the income distribution, that share increases to 30 percent. The share of men in the top of the income distribution who are raising children who are not their own, however, is a mere 2 percent. If this is true, it is very compelling evidence that women are more likely to cheat on poor husbands than they are to cheat on wealthy husbands.

The cost-benefit analysis discussed above illustrates why this relationship between income and infidelity for women is what we would expect. Women who are living in poverty have less to lose financially if their husbands leave them as the result of infidelity than do women whose household income provides them with a comfortable life. It might also be the case that poorer women are hoping to use infidelity as a means of finding a mate who not only supplies good genes but also is a better provider.

While a higher income doesn't increase the likelihood of a man's infidelity, and actually decreases woman's likelihood of infidelity, the characteristic that really predicts infidelity isn't income but power. If that's not a completely new revelation, you might be surprised to learn that powerful women are just as likely to be unfaithful as are powerful men.

A study by a group of Dutch researchers (Joris Lammers, Janka Stoker, Jennifer Jordan, Monique Pollmann, and Diederik Stapel) uses data collected from managers, team leaders, and CEOs that report how often these managers had been unfaithful, measured their willingness to cheat again, and probed both the managers' opportunities for cheating and their confidence in their ability to seduce new lovers.

Among their respondents, 26 percent had cheated on their partner at least once. Those who wielded more power in their jobs were not only more likely to be among the cheaters, but the higher up the corporate ladder they had climbed, the more extramarital encounters they reported, and the more likely they were to say that they expected to cheat again in the future.

What explains the link between workplace power and fidelity? Business travel and long hours at the office provide opportunities to cheat (and reduce the probability of being caught), but that is only part of the story. The most convincing statistical explanation has to do with confidence; more powerful business people reported much higher levels of assurance that they could find a sexual partner should they want one.

The women in this study behaved just like the men in indicating a history of cheating; more powerful women cheated more and felt more confident about their ability to seduce new sexual partners.

What I find interesting about these results is that they suggest that one of the reasons why we have observed lower levels of female infidelity in the past is not because women are more inclined to be faithful, but rather because they have traditionally occupied fewer positions of power. If this is true, then the next generation of women might be as promiscuous as men.

CHEATERS NEVER PROSPER

The one piece of evidence that appears repeatedly in the literature is that people who cheat in their marriages are less happy than those who are faithful.

The Elmslie and Tebaldi paper finds that married women who reported being "not too happy" were 10 percentage points more likely to report having cheated on their current husbands than were women who reported being "very happy." Unhappy married men are even more likely to also be unfaithful; they were 12 percentage points more likely to report having cheated on their current wife than were men who reported being "very happy."

That difference between male and female unhappiness when cheating could be related to prostitute use. A different study on happiness by David Blanchflower and Andrew Oswald finds that not only were those who reported having been unfaithful in the previous year less happy, but those who reported prostitute use were unhappier still.

The reason for the relationship between unhappiness and infidelity is unclear. Maybe infidelity itself is making people unhappy. Or maybe unhappy people are more likely to have an extramarital relationship, perhaps using it as a strategy to exit an unhappy relationship. Others may be unhappy for another reason unrelated to marriage and are using extramarital sex as a way to deal with that unhappiness.

Psychologists Denise Previti and Paul Amato used data collected over seventeen years to see if infidelity is a direct cause of divorce or a consequence of an unhappy marriage already on its way to divorce. They find that men and women in couples who are already likely to divorce are more likely to have sex outside of their marriage; infidelity is the consequence, not the direct cause, of an already unhappy marriage. They also find, not surprisingly, that following infidelity, the quality of the marriage deteriorates further, and it is that further deterioration in the quality of a marriage that increases the likelihood of divorce.

Infidelity, it appears, is both a consequence, and a cause, of unhappy marriages.

▰▰▰ FINAL WORDS

You are probably wondering if Leonard's second wife ever found out about his attempts to find sexual relationships outside of their marriage. I honestly don't know, but I suspect she knew when she married him that he was likely to stray if he had the chance. Why would she agree to marry a man who would have a hard time being faithful? Probably because she correctly predicted that he was unlikely to ever get the opportunity. His new job promotion might have given her cause of concern, but she really needn't have worried—the small amount of power he held was not enough to persuade young fertile women that his genes were worth the trouble.

Infidelity is an economic story, but not for the reason you might have expected—that wealthy men are the most likely to be unfaithful to their wives—but because the decision to have, or not have, extramarital sex is the solution to a cost-benefit problem. The costs in this story are a function of several economic factors, including lost income in the case of divorce, while the benefits are, for the most part, biological.

For example, legislation that allows divorce courts to financially penalize adulterers should increase the cost of cheating and decrease its prevalence. In the absence of that legislation, prenuptial agreements that stipulate financial penalties for violations of the contract should serve the same purpose. The movement of women into positions of authority in the workplace appears to be increasing female infidelity not just because powerful people are more likely to cheat, but also because it gives women greater opportunities to be unfaithful without being caught. Increased access to the Internet may not be increasing infidelity, on average (as we saw in chapter 6), but it does reduce the expected cost of cheating by making it easier for those whose impulse it is to cheat to fulfill that desire.

One interesting implication of this argument that the changing economic climate contributes to the propensity to cheat, or not to cheat, is that it suggests that individuals can structure their relationships in a way that decreases the probability of divorce.

For some, that might be writing binding contracts that explicitly forbid infidelity. In the past, that contract was essentially sworn at the marriage altar, but explicit contracts can impose financial penalties in a way that making an oath before family and friends cannot. Betraying marriage vows can be costly, in ways that I have already mentioned, but for some, additional financial penalties can increase the cost just enough to prevent infidelity.

For others, that might mean rethinking traditional marital arrangements in the context of changing economic environment. The current mainstream arrangement was developed in a time in which men depended on marriage to ensure the paternity of their children and women depended on marriage to provide the necessities of life. With increasingly effective contraceptives and the economic independence of women, these two concerns have become irrelevant for many couples. Bargaining over an ability to explore sexual relationships outside of marriage is one possible way for couples to ensure that their marriage stays intact when the probability of cheating is very high. Those arrangements may not be for everyone, but then not everyone wants to have sex outside of marriage. For those who do, and have the opportunity, new ways of thinking about fidelity might be the rational approach.

As you will see in the next chapter, love on the later-in-life market can be very much like during the college years: the scarcity of men ensures their market power. As we are about to find out, though, unlike the women in college, many older women prefer to play the field rather than to find an end-of-life partner.

CHAPTER 9
LOVE IN THE SUNSET (YEARS)

▰▰▰ OH, THE FUTILITY OF IT ALL!

The June 2, 1986, cover of *Newsweek* magazine carried the headline "The Marriage Crunch: If you are a single woman here are your chances of ever getting married." Accompanying this eye-catching headline was a graph that illustrated the bad news for women who had spent their youth in a classroom when they should have been busy finding themselves a husband: their chance of now marrying was shockingly low. The report stunned a generation of college-educated women, warning them that if they were still single when they turned 30, the chance they would ever marry was only 20 percent. If they hadn't married their Prince Charming by the age of 35, the chance they ever would fell to 5 percent. If, heaven forbid, a woman was still single at age 40, she had a better chance of being killed by a terrorist than of ever walking down an aisle clutching a bouquet of flowers.

Honestly. The fact that the article forecast that the probability of a single 25-year-old college-educated woman ever marrying was only 50 percent, in a period in which over 90 percent of women married at some point in their life, should have been everyone's first clue that there was something horribly wrong with these predictions.

LOTTERY WINNING MAKES IT EASIER TO BE ALONE

Does winning the lottery give you a better chance of finding true love, or does it make it easier to say good-bye when the love is gone? A paper by Scott Hankins and Mark Hoekstra asks these questions and finds that money does not buy you love; in fact, for women at least, it buys the freedom to stay solo.

Using data that describe the choices of tens of thousands of lottery winners, the authors compare the relationship outcomes of those people who won the bigger jackpots ($50,000) with those who won less ($1,000). They find that single women who won the larger amounts were much less likely to marry in the three years following the win than were those who won the smaller amounts—40 percent less likely, in fact.

Why are larger-jackpot-winning women less likely to marry? It is possible that their new position of being financially independent gave the women a chance to take their time marrying and to be more discriminating about whom they choose to marry. Or they might not have wanted to share their control of the money with another person and so postponed marriage until the money was all gone.

There is no similar effect for single men—those relationship decisions appear to be completely independent of how much they won.

In terms of divorce rates, the effect is very small; the divorce rate of those who won between $25,000 and $50,000 in the three years following the win was less than 1 percent lower than among those who won $1,000. People are more likely to stay together following a lottery-winning event, though the money ought to make it easier for them to divorce.

This exercise may seem inconsequential, but it has an important implication. It suggests that as societies become wealthier, the coinciding increase in the age at which people marry is the result of marriage decisions that have been made by women and not those made by men. It also says that one of the explanations for the decline in women's eagerness to marry young isn't simply that they are dedicating themselves to their careers instead of the important business of finding a husband. The behavior of single female lottery winners—whose wealth has fallen into their laps—indicates that it is all about the money.

Thanks to the passage of time, and the availability of U.S. Census data, I can tell you now how many of these college-educated women who had dared to postpone marriage into their 30s and (gasp!) their 40s fared on the marriage market in the years following this publication.

By 2010, 75 percent of college-educated women who were exactly 30 years old and single in 1986 had married at some point in the intervening twenty-four years. Sixty-nine percent of women who were exactly 35 and single in 1986 married their Prince Charming. Even the old maids, the women who were 40 at the time that *Newsweek* made these dire predictions, were more likely than not to marry before their 65th birthdays: 68 percent married.

Notwithstanding the bad news media headlines, predicting the demise of the most sacred of institutions at the hands of selfishly educated women, most women and men marry at some point in their lifetimes. The reason why the marriage rate is so low today is that the measure is a snapshot taken at a single point in time. Marriage rates measured over individuals' lifetimes tell a very different story—marriage has not become obsolete.

According to the United Nations *World Fertility Report 2009*, the average share of women, worldwide, who have ever been married by the ages of 45 to 49 has remained fairly constant, and above 90 percent, since 1970.

Between the 1970s and the 1990s, the number of women who had ever married by the time they were in their late 40s had actually increased in all but two of the twenty-five developed nations in their study (Sweden and France were the only exceptions).

This ever-married rate has decreased somewhat in the intervening years in developed nations, but the increasing tendency of women to remain unwed in those countries almost certainly reflects not a rise in spinsterhood, but rather an increase in cohabitation and other nontraditional relationship arrangements.

Not surprisingly, the countries with the lowest ever-married rates for 45- to 49-year-old women currently are those with the most permissive views toward sexual relationships outside of marriage: Sweden (75 percent), Finland (80 percent), Norway and Denmark (82 percent), France (83 percent), and the Netherlands (85 percent).

Marriage rates, those snapshots taken at one point in time, are incredibly low by historic standards—as of this moment, barely 50 percent of the United States adult population is married—but that doesn't mean people do not want to be in committed sexual relationships. It just means that they are having those relationships at a different time of their lives and organizing them in a different way than they have in the past—for example, cohabitating rather than marrying.

What is very new is the incredible size of the late-in-life market for sex and love; many more people now are looking for short-term and long-term sexual partners later in their lives than have ever before.

▰▰▰▰ THE LATE-IN-LIFE DATING MARKET IS BOOMING

Markets, as I have already said, can be described as being thick or thin. When markets are thin, there are few buyers and sellers—it is harder to arrive at price at which both buyers and sellers are willing to engage in trade—and few transactions take place. When the market is thick, however, there are many buyers and sellers, meaning that equilibrium is easier to achieve—buyers and sellers can settle on a market price at which they both want to trade—and more transactions take place.

Over the years, the late-in-life marriage market has become increasingly thick. This market thickness means not only that there are more "transactions" (i.e., single people getting together for sex and love), but also that the quality of relationships formed on this market has improved over what they would have been even ten or twenty years ago.

There are many economic explanations for why the late-in-life market for sex and love is so much thicker than it has been in the past.

The first is that many people are postponing their first marriages until later in life. This trend has been generated, in part, by a desire among men and women to have fewer children. Wanting smaller families has meant that women can marry later in life and still have the number of children they desire. Starting to have children in their 30s with a goal of having one or two is achievable for many women. However, starting to have children in their 30s with a goal of having four or five is achievable for very few.

At the same time, access to fertility treatments and lifestyle choices that make women look younger at older ages has helped promote the expectation, at least, that women can continue to have children into their late 30s and early 40s, removing the pressure for women who want children to marry at younger ages.

Increased access to premarital sex, thanks to the introduction of effective contraceptives and changing social norms (as we discussed in chapter 1), has meant that men and women don't have to choose between being married and being celibate. This freedom to choose has allowed us the opportunity to have multiple sexual partners before making a long-term commitment. That freedom to be both single and sexually active has allowed singles to spend more time searching for a long-term partner.

Improvements in home production technology and the ability to purchase many of the goods and services that historically have been produced by women (like evening meals and clean laundry), have made it easier for everyone to be self-sufficient. Men no longer need women to produce these goods and services, and women can spend their time working for wages instead of performing traditional household tasks. This increased self-reliance of men and women has made it possible for them to remain single for longer periods of time.

These same economic forces have helped to destigmatize childbirth outside of marriage. As more women are able to raise children alone, social norms have evolved in a way that allows unmarried women who accidentally become pregnant to stay that way: unmarried. With shotgun weddings essentially a thing of the past, women who become pregnant as teenagers or young adults are marrying later in their lives.

The second reason why more people are searching for love on the late-in-life market than ever before is that, as we already know, the cost of searching for a mate has fallen with the widespread use of online dating and social networking sites. This fall in search costs has had a bigger effect on older singles than it has on younger singles; older singles tend to be more socially isolated than are younger singles meaning that, in general, their search costs, without Internet technology, are much higher. Because search costs have fallen with the introduction of online dating technology, more older people are entering the market for sex and love.

It is no coincidence that an international study conducted by the Oxford Internet Institute (authored by Bernie Hogan, William Dutton, and Nai Li) found that, among couples who have started dating since 1997, older couples were significantly more likely to have met each other online than were younger couples; only 19 percent of couples in their 20s met online, compared with 23 percent of couples in their 30s, 35 percent of couples in their 40s, 38 percent of couples in their 50s, and 37 percent of couples in their 60s.

The popularity of online dating for older men and women is obvious from the plethora of online services that specifically target that community. (Just as an aside, I have recently noted that with the passing of my most recent birthday, the advertising that appears on my Facebook newsfeeds page has recently changed from "Single dads looking for love!" to "No young women please!" What a delightful daily reminder of where I stand in the market.)

The third reason why more people are searching on the late-in-life dating market than ever before is that people are living longer. For example, according to the 2007 U.S. *National Vital Statistics Report*, a man who was 60 years old in 1960 should have, if he was entirely rational, expected to live for only about fifteen more years. A man of the same age today can expect to live for twenty-one more years. A woman who was 60 years old in 1960 could expect to live only for twenty more years, while a woman of the same today can expect to live for twenty-four more years.

Increasing longevity is important for two reasons. The first, and perhaps most obvious, reason is that new relationships require an investment in terms of searching for a mate and establishing a new relationship (you can think of these as fixed costs to finding new love). The longer both partners are expected to live, the greater the return to that original investment. Thus, increased longevity makes older people more willing to spend the time to find new love.

The second reason is that as the life expectancy of men and women grows more similar, the length of time either partner will have to be widowed decreases. This effect should, on balance, increase older people's willingness to enter new relationships, as women, in particular, may have avoided forming new attachments in the past for fear of being widowed, some for the second time.

Just as an aside, you might have thought that divorce was the main reason for why late-in-life dating markets have become so thick in recent decades, but in reality, divorce probably doesn't explain this phenomenon at all. The reason is that, according to Betsey Stevenson and Justin Wolfers, the divorce rate, measured as the number of divorces per one thousand of the population, is currently at its lowest level since 1970.

This decline in divorce isn't due only to the most recent recession, which as we have already seen has decreased divorce, but is actually part of a much longer trend toward fewer divorces. The divorce rate per thousand married couples has fallen from twenty-three divorces in 1979 to seventeen divorces in 2005.

SHORTER MEN HAVE YOUNGER WIVES

The observation that many women value height in a husband implies that shorter men looking for a wife must settle for a woman who is less attractive. According to economist Nicolas Herpin, however, there is a silver lining to being smaller in stature; a short man who is economically successful could find that later in life he has a younger wife than his taller friends.

Many studies have found a link between a man's height and his income. A study using German data, for example, found that men who are 2¾ in/7 cm taller than average are paid a wage that is about 4 percent more than similar men who are of average height. There are several reasons why this relationship exists beyond simple workplace discrimination, not the least of which being that adult height is related to socioeconomic status in childhood. But it isn't just income that is causing short men to fare worse on the marriage market; even when we control for income, women prefer taller men.

Dan Ariely, Günter Hitsch, and Ali Hortacsu, using the same experiment that we talked about in chapter 2 to determine racial preferences in dating, find that a short man would have to earn just over half a million dollars a year in order for a woman more than 5 in/12 cm taller than him to want to communicate with him on an online dating site.

The same study found that, in online dating, men who were between 6 ft, 3 in and 6 ft, 4 in/190 and 193 cm tall received about 60 percent more messages from interested women than did men who were between 5 ft, 7 in and 5 ft, 8 in/170 and 173 cm tall.

Using data from France, Herpin finds that shorter men are significantly less likely to be either married or in a serious relationship even when controlling for social status; only 60 percent of 30- to 39-year-old men who were less than 5 ft, 7 in/170 cm tall were married, compared with 76 percent of men between 5 ft, 7in and 5 ft, 11 in/170 cm and 180 cm tall.

Shorter men are more likely to still be single when they are a little older, however, putting them in a good position to take advantage of a later-in-life marriage market that is populated with younger women who are less concerned with their husband's physical appearance and more interested in his ability to provide a stable income. Taller men are more likely to be married when they are younger, before they have established themselves as providers and are more likely to be married to women who are closer to their own age.

Certainly many people now find themselves looking for love again, after believing that they would ride off into the sunset with their first (or second or third) husband or wife. Those unrealized expectations, however, are not the reason why this market has grown in size. In fact, the current trends in divorce suggest that this market might shrink over time as fewer people find themselves single at an older age.

▰▰▰▰ A BUYER'S MARKET FOR HORNY OLD MEN?

We have talked several times about casual sex markets—high schools, college campuses—in which women outnumber men and, as a result of that imbalance, men have more control over the sexual behavior of women.

Women often find themselves searching for a partner in markets where men have the advantage, despite the fact that there are roughly equal numbers of reproductive-aged men and women in the population.

This is in part because women are more selective when they choose their sexual partners. But it is also because many women are searching for a single, long-term relationship on the same market in which many men are searching for serial, shorter-term relationships.

Certainly there are biological arguments for the difference in behavior of men and women in terms of the level of commitment they seek, and how selective they are; the behavior that increases the reproductive success of men is to have a series of short-term relationships with fertile women, while the behavior that increases reproductive success of women is to have long-term relationships with high-quality men.

We all know these arguments; in fact, they have become so well accepted that they are part of the lens through which we all have come to view female/male differences in sexual behavior. Is it reasonable, though, to believe that these biological predispositions drive our sexual behavior later in life, when our fertility is in decline?

(And, in case you are wondering, it isn't just women who experience declining fertility later in life. According to medical research conducted in the United Kingdom by Mohamed Hassan and Stephen Killick, couples in which the man is more than 45 years old are five times more likely to have spent more than a year trying to get pregnant, and 12.5 times more likely to have spent more than two years trying to get pregnant, than are couples in which the man is less than 25 years old. They find this result even after controlling for the age of the woman and frequency with which the couple is having sexual intercourse.)

Changes in fertility, for both men and women, should change the choices older adults make in terms of the way they operate on markets for sex and love. Postmenopausal women, for example, lose their biological incentive to find a mate who will produce the highest-quality children at almost the same time that they lose their economic disincentive to having casual sex: namely, the risk that a mistimed pregnancy could reduce both their lifetime earnings and their ability to marry later.

Older men, on the other hand, might initially choose to seek out younger, more fertile, women in order to compensate for their own declining fertility, but beyond a certain age (particularly when fertile women are no longer available to them), the sexual decisions of men should cease to be based on their biological urge to reproduce. Again, this change happens at roughly the same time that a new economic incentive arises for men—the incentive to find a woman who is willing to care for them as they age.

Differential life expectancies between women and men, although decreasing, continue to give women a much overlooked comparative advantage in home production among older couples. The gains from trade within marriage that we discussed in chapter 4, however, depend on both partners bringing something to the table. For an individual woman, if the cost of caregiving is high relative to the benefit a man brings to a relationship, especially when casual sexual relations are less costly, then she will remain single rather than commit to a long-term relationship.

Declining fertility and women's higher life expectancy should, in theory at least, increase the tendency of older women to seek out short-term partners and increase the tendency of older men to seek out long-term sexual partners.

This reminds me of a story. A few years ago, I was at home when an old friend of my father's came to tell us that he was ending a relationship with a woman he had been seeing for a few years. When my father asked why they were splitting, he sadly shook his head and said, "She is only using me for sex." This poor guy had to have been over 80 when he made this observation, but, while he was not my idea of a sex object, he obviously was for her and that just wasn't good enough for him.

I started this section by pointing out the importance that gender ratios have played in the sexual decisions made by men and women. It is tempting to assume that it is a buyer's market for horny older men and that older women are subject to the same sexual pressures as teenage and college-age women. But, personally, I think the underlying assumption that older women want marriage, in the way that younger women might, and that older men want casual sex, in the way that younger men might, is an incorrect assumption to make.

From a purely economic perspective, it makes sense to predict that when sellers are relatively abundant and buyers relatively scarce that the price that "good" is sold for is lower than when there are equal numbers of buyers and sellers. The price that is negotiated on this market is not measured in terms of money; it is measured in terms of the value of the match. If older women who are looking for relationships really are abundant relative to older men who are looking for relationships, then they should be willing to settle for a lower-value match than they might have otherwise.

This is a testable hypothesis: if older women are willing to settle for low-value matches, and older men are not, then we can conclude that older women are relatively abundant on the later-in-life dating market.

This is the hypothesis tested by William McIntosh, Lawrence Locker, Katherine Briley, Rebecca Ryan, and Alison Scott. They find that older men are more selective about their future mates than are younger men because they are more willing continue to look for a high-value match. That result isn't really surprising since the sheer variety of women on the market should make it easier for men to find just the right woman, regardless of their market power. However, they also find that older women are not only more selective than older men about who they will date, they are also more selective than are younger women when it comes to qualities such as race, age, income, and height of a future mate.

It has been estimated that there are three women for every man over the age of 65, evidence that supports my contention that while women may outnumber men on the seniors dating market, that doesn't necessarily mean that men have market power. This is because older women have an acceptable substitute to being in an inferior arrangement; they can always choose to be alone. For women who fear having to care for an aging older man, that just might be the preferred alternative.

I had a conversation recently with a friend of my mother's, a lovely woman in her late 60s, during which she casually remarked that the only way she would consider dating again would be if she found a man willing to provide both a doctor's note and a bank statement. I would have never thought of seeking dating advice from medical experts, but upon reflection it seems to me, at least, that any savvy older woman considering a new partner should not only want a doctor's note, but might consider consulting an actuary as well.

Perhaps it is best to think of an older man as an annuity that provides a steady-income stream of love, affection, and sex. This annuity, rather than providing this income for a predetermined number of periods, has a termination period that is unknown when the asset is purchased. How much a woman is willing to invest then is not just a function of the (love, affection, and sex) income the annuity provides, but also the expected number of periods until termination. Since the number of periods is unknown when the investment in the relationships is made, a woman who is risk averse needs to be compensated for the possibility that her asset will expire, so to speak, before she has seen any profit.

If women are risk averse, the reality that men have lower life expectancies implies that women's reservation values for matches are higher than they would have been otherwise. The reluctance on the part of older women to accept that risk unless match values are very high (i.e., they can find a man who fulfills all of their needs) gives at least some of the market power back to women on the later-in-life dating market.

Back to the comment made by my mother's friend that she would require a medical certificate before having a relationship. I should come clean and tell you that I am, apparently, naive when it comes to the sexual behavior of senior citizens. I originally thought that the reason she needed a doctor's note was that it was important for her to find a partner who would live for many years. I later discovered, after she shared a story about a promiscuous cruise ship captain and a boatload of horny old women, that what she was really seeking was to be assured that her prospective lover was STD-free—not just generally in good health.

That does sound like a good idea, especially since people over the age of 50 have been engaging in increasingly risky sexual behavior over the past decade and paying the cost with rising STD rates.

▨▨▨ HOW TO TEACH MOM THE NO-GLOVE NO-LOVE RULE

The words "young" and "foolish" just naturally seem to go together. An 18-year-old man debating the costs and benefits of condom usage might be excused for mistakenly believing that he will live forever. You would think, though, that by the time that this same man is in his 50s, his primary goal would be to extend his time here on Earth as long as possible or, at a minimum, to avoid painful sexually transmitted diseases.

The young, apparently, do not have a monopoly on being foolhardy; STDs are on the rise in the over-50 population as a consequence of increasing rates of casual sex and extremely low rates of condom usage.

In the United States, among the population with HIV or AIDS, the largest group is people who are between 45 and 49 years old, and between 2007 and 2009, the largest increase in infection rates has been in people between the ages of 60 and 64 years old.

According to the *National Survey of Sexual Health and Behavior*, 23 percent of men over the age of 50 who are sexually active report that their last sex partner was a "casual acquaintance" and only 25 percent of the men who had a new sexual partner, or more than one partner in the previous year, said they had used a condom the last time they had sex.

Whether or not a couple chooses to use condoms during sexual intercourse depends both on how each weighs the expected costs of not using a condom against the benefit and how bargaining power is distributed in the relationship.

The expected cost of unprotected sex depends on both the probability that the person you are having sex with is infected with a disease and the probability that, if they are, the disease will be transmitted during unprotected sex.

Even as STD rates are increasing among older adults, they still have much lower STD rates than do younger adults; the syphilis infection rate of men between the ages of 20 and 24 is ten times higher than it is among men between the ages of 55 and 65, the gonorrhea infection rate is almost forty times higher, and the chlamydia infection rate is one hundred times higher. So unprotected sex between older adults exposes each partner to much less risk of infection than unprotected sex between younger adults.

Having said that, older adult men are more likely than are older women to be infected with any of these diseases, so having unprotected sex with an older man is much more risky than having unprotected sex with an older woman.

The transmission rates, which are the probability that a person will be infected with an STD when they have sex with an infected partner, are much higher for women than they are for men. For example, the likelihood that a man will get HIV from having unprotected vaginal intercourse once with an HIV-infected woman is between 0.01 percent and 0.03 percent while the likelihood that a woman will get HIV from having unprotected vaginal intercourse once with an HIV-infected man is between 0.05 percent and 0.09 percent. These probabilities may seem low, but HIV is just one of several diseases for which women are subject to higher transmission rates than are men.

Infection and transmission rates are two good reasons why older women might want to insist on "no glove, no love," but the declining cost of unprotected sex for men can make it difficult for older women to enforce that rule.

Difficult, but not impossible.

In fact, if older women prefer casual sexual relationships to committed relationships, then it should be easier for them to enforce condom use during casual sexual encounters than it was when they were younger. This is because they are no longer under any pressure to compromise in the hope that doing so will secure them a longer-term commitment from their partner. In this market, the men are the ones under pressure to compromise, that is, if they are looking for an end-of-life commitment.

There is a solution to market imbalance created by differential life expectancies, and that is for older women to have relationships with younger men. The evidence suggests that I am not the only one who thinks that is the best way to resolve this situation.

NO BROTHELS FOR OLDER WOMEN?

It is men's willingness to have sex with strangers—and their love of variety in sexual partners—that fuels the world sex trade, while women's preference for fewer sexual partners and sex within a relationship has made the sex trade for female clients miniscule by comparison. Still, you have to wonder if, given the barriers faced by older women to finding partners for casual sex, there aren't profits to be made in brothels for women that target that specific market.

Sociologist Jacqueline Sánchez Taylor took to the beaches of the Caribbean (literally) to ask female tourists about their sexual interactions with local men and found that even among women who had casual sex with local men, and gave those men cash, none were interested in explicit market exchange of money for sex.

Thirty-one percent of the women Sánchez Taylor interviewed admitted to having had at least one sexual relationship over the course of their holiday, with almost half of those admitting to having had several sexual partners and a few even confessing to having had sex with more than five men.

Sixty percent of women with local sex partners admitted to giving their lovers either cash or in-kind gifts, a measure that underestimates the economic nature of these relationships given that the value of meals and hot showers, even small amounts of cash, is underappreciated by those from more privileged economies. And, because the information was collected partway through their holiday, this ignores the possibility that the men will wait until the holiday is over, or even until the women have returned to their home countries, before asking for money.

When asked to describe their local sexual relationships, only two said they were purely physical, but more
than 20 percent described their relationships as "real love."
Even women who gave men cash after one night of sex
described their relationships as "holiday romances."

There is a sex trade for women, clearly, but would
these women buy sex in a brothel in their home country? Probably not: 25 percent said that over the course
of the holiday they had been explicitly offered sex
in exchange for money, yet not one of those women
accepted that offer.

Female sex tourists are buying a service that can be
cheaply provided only in underdeveloped (and low-wage)
economies: the fantasy of romance. Even if this were a service that brothels in developed nations could provide, and
even if it were affordable, would women really buy it?

COUGARS AS A SOLUTION TO A MARKET PROBLEM

When I was 36, I found myself in an awkward position at a dinner party.
I had been lamenting the fact that no one seemed interested in playing
matchmaker anymore when my hosts realized, to their great delight, that
they knew the perfect man for me. Given their description, he appeared to
be my polar opposite on every measurable dimension. So it wasn't clear
to me what exactly it was about him that made him my ideal mate, but (as
I have already said) I like to keep an open mind when it comes to finding
love. Having said that, I did put the brakes on the whole arrangement when
they told me his age—he was 53 years old.

Why this event was so memorable was not that they wanted to set
me up with a high school–educated rural tradesman who was almost old
enough to be my father; it was the looks that my dinner companions gave
each other when I said that I didn't think I would be interested in someone

who was seventeen years my senior. Those looks clearly communicated, "Which one of us is going to tell this babe that she is never going to do any better?"

I honestly wish I could tell you that this was a one-time experience.

Big differences in age can be problematic in long-term relationships. If you remember Jane's story in chapter 6, you will recall that being the much-younger spouse meant that she had very little say in the decisions that many couples make together and that her lack of bargaining power contributed to how unhappy she was in her marriage. John and Jane's inability to sustain their relationship over the long term was not directly the result of the differences in their ages, but the empirical evidence shows that age differences do matter in how successful marriages are in the long run.

Earlier I argued that household bargaining power within a marriage depends, in theory at least, on the relative opportunities outside of marriage. Relative ages are one factor that determines those outside opportunities. For example, in a market in which younger women are in greater demand than older women, a 25-year-old woman married to a 40-year-old man should have more bargaining power than would a 40-year-old woman married to a 40-year-old man, everything else being equal.

That theory suggests that, since Jane was much younger than John, and therefore had more outside options for remarriage, she should have had more bargaining power and not less. According to research by Sonia Oreffice, however, this is the most common experience in heterosexual marriages—the younger partner has less say in household decisions. What is really interesting about this research, though, is that in same-sex marriages, the relationship between age and bargaining power is entirely consistent with the economic theory.

One of the decisions that households make together is how members allocate their time between working on the labor market and either working on home production or simply not working at all (economists like to call this "consuming leisure"). We assume that the person with the most bargaining power will spend fewer hours on the labor market (after controlling for factors like the number of children at home) and that the person with the least bargaining power will supply more; how much more depends on just how low their bargaining power is relative to their partner's.

Sonia Oreffice finds that if a wife is five years younger than her husband, this one factor will increase her annual labor supply by ten hours and decrease her husband's by almost eleven hours. This says that the older spouse (in this example, the husband, but this is true regardless of gender) holds more bargaining power in that they are able to negotiate fewer hours on the labor market for themselves and more for their spouse because of their superior age.

Within lesbian and gay couples, the dynamic works in the opposite direction and is much larger; the younger spouse holds more bargaining power and, as a result, is able to negotiate less time working on the labor market.

A woman who is five years younger than her (female) partner supplies twenty-one hours less of labor a year and her older partner supplies twenty hours more. A man who is five years younger than his (male) partner supplies twenty-two hours less on the labor market and his relatively old partner supplies twenty-three hours more.

The same relationship is found when we look at income transferred between partners instead of time spent working; in same-sex couples, the bigger the age difference, the more income the older partner transfers to the younger partner ($2,200 in lesbian couples and $1,500 in gay couples when there is a five-year age difference), while in heterosexual couples the income is transferred from the younger spouse to the older spouse ($900 when there is a five-year age difference).

This result for heterosexual couples (that the older spouse has more bargaining power) is counterintuitive if we believe that it will be easier for a younger spouse to remarry in the case of divorce. One possible explanation is that the older spouse is more often than not the husband, and the authority associated with being both older and male, trumps any

BOOB JOBS INDICATE A PERKIER ECONOMY

In chapter 6, I said that watching the market for sex toys could help predict recessions; people spend more on sex toys when they need a cheap way of feeling good in hard economic times. In the same way that lubricants could be a leading indicator of recessions, there is another market that indicates that the economy is improving—the market for boob jobs and other cosmetic surgeries.

According to a 2011 press release by the American Society of Plastic Surgeons (ASPS), demand for perkiness, or perhaps I should say youthfulness, was on the rise with increases in face-lifts (up 9 percent), breast lifts (up 3 percent), lower body lifts (up 9 percent), upper arm lifts (up 5 percent), and thigh lifts (up 8 percent).

The ASPS claims that this increased demand indicates that consumer confidence is on the rise (hence the usefulness of the boob job as a leading indicator of economic booms) and that some of this increase in demand is the result of pent-up demand from the two preceding years of economic turmoil.

There is an alternative explanation though. It is possible that a portion of the aging workforce took a long, sad look at the state of their retirement funds and decided that they had a few more years left to spend in what has become, and will no doubt continue to be, a very competitive labor market. And so, they have invested in taking up the slack, so to speak, in order to maintain their position in a market that, as we know, rewards the appearance of youth and virility.

> If that is the case, it isn't consumer confidence that is driving up demand for plastic surgery. In fact, it seems more likely that plastic surgery is the direct result of a lack of confidence, rather than the other way around.

advantage had by a younger wife. A second possibility is that for legally married couples, exercising their outside option is very costly and, as a result, the influence of those outside options on bargaining power is significantly diminished.

Among same-sex couples, there are fewer barriers to dissolving a relationship (the data used here was collected in 2000, before there was any legal recognition for same-sex marriage) and neither partner has a socially determined authority over the other based on gender. In this respect, same-sex couples operate far more like a free-market economy, allowing us to observe the outcome that economic theory predicts; younger partners hold the balance of power.

A second issue around age differences in marriage is whether big age differences between marriage partners lead to happier marriages. Rebecca Kippen, Bruce Chapman, and Peng Yu answer this question using Australian data. They find that the greater the age difference in married couples, the more likely it is that their marriage will end in divorce.

For example, they find that a marriage in which the man is as little as two years younger than his wife is 53 percent more likely to end in divorce than a marriage in which the man is between one year younger than his wife and three years older. This increase in the probability of divorce when there is an age difference isn't just an issue in marriages in which the wife is older; a marriage in which the man is nine or more years older than his wife has double the chance of ending in divorce than a marriage in which he is between one year younger and three years older than his wife.

A GENUINELY HAPPY ENDING

A few years ago, a truly creative (and brave) researcher by the name of Hugo Mialon collected data from sixteen thousand men and women so that he could tell an economic story about their orgasms. He didn't want to talk about the dopamine-induced euphoria of genuine orgasms, however; Mialon wanted to know what causes women and men (I'm surprised, too!) to regularly fake ecstasy.

Approximately 26 percent of men have faked an orgasm in their current relationship compared with 72 percent of women. Men fake orgasms relatively infrequently because they overwhelmingly feel that they wouldn't get away with it if they did. No one likes to get caught deceiving his or her partner and, since the expected cost of deception is a function of the probability of being caught, the cost of faking an orgasm is higher for men than it is for women.

One question this research raises is this: When a woman fakes an orgasm, who exactly is being deceived? Is it the man, because she has fooled him? Or the woman, because she only thinks she has?

The majority of men in the survey (55 percent) claim that they are not fooled into thinking that their partner is ecstatic when she is not. Statistically, at least half of these men must be in a relationship with women who are faking orgasms. At the same time, only 24 percent of women say they believe their partner can tell when they are faking (a percentage that includes women who said they did not fake). The only explanation for these statistical discrepancies is that either the men believe that the women are not faking, when they really are, or the women believe the men cannot tell they are faking, when they really can.

Do men not let on when they know their partner has tried to fool them? Maybe, but according to the Center for Sexual Health Promotion, 85 percent of men reported that their partner had an orgasm the last time they had sex compared with only 64 percent of women who reported that their most recent sexual experience had that particularly happy ending.

By the way, want to know who fakes the most? Older men fake more frequently than do younger men, perhaps because they experience the real deal less often, and better-educated men and women fake more frequently than less-educated men and women.

Hugo Mialon postulates that educated people are either better liars or better actors, and so can fake without being caught. My students think that educated people don't have enough time for the real deal, which makes me wonder why they are investing in an education if the cost is a life so busy that they won't have time for twenty seconds of ecstasy.

Regardless of how well marriages function when one partner is much older, if it were true that only significantly older men are interested in me at this stage of my life, then my dinner hosts that night would probably be right in thinking that if I want to be in a relationship, then I have to accept that I can't get what I want—which is a man who is closer to my own age.

The problem is that the preconception that older men are looking only for younger women is actually false. Don't get me wrong, older men want younger wives, but remember the wise words of the one-time economics student Mick Jagger: you can't always get what you want. When it comes to dating, older men may want younger women, but what they often get is a woman closer to their own age.

Psychologists Sheyna Sears-Roberts Alterovitz and Gerald Mendelsohn found, using data collected from Yahoo! Personals, that as men age, they seek women who are increasingly younger than themselves. For example, between the ages of 20 and 34, men seek women who are on average younger by only one year; between the ages of 40 and 54, they seek women who are on average five years younger; between the ages of 60 and 74, they seek women who are on average eight years younger; and men 75 and over seek women ten years younger than themselves.

As women age, they also seek increasingly younger men; very young women seek men who are about three years older than themselves, but as they age they tend to seek men who are increasingly closer to their own age. By the time women are between 60 and 75, they are mostly looking for men who are their age. By the time they are over 75, they are mostly looking for men who are, on average, three years younger.

I took a look at the U.S. Census to see what the market looked like when it closed and found that in many of the marriages that took place between 2008 and 2010, the husband was, in fact, much older than his wife; about 50 percent of newly married men between the ages of 40 and 65 married women who were five or more years younger.

On the flipside, however, many women also married younger men.

About 17 percent of newly married women ages 40 to 65 married men who were more than five years their junior. This is a big change from not that long ago; at the end of the 1970s, only 3 percent of marriages involving women under the age of 60 were between a woman and a man who was more than five years her junior. Thirty years later, the share of these "toy-boy" marriages had risen to 8 percent. More recent evidence suggests that in the ten years since this data was collected, the rate of toy-boy marriages has grown much larger still.

A recent economics paper by Melvyn Coles and Marco Francesconi argues that this trend in women marrying younger men is the direct result of women becoming better educated—not just better educated than they were thirty years ago but also better educated than the group of men from which they are choosing their marriage partners.

It appears that when given the choice, some men, at least, would prefer to have a wife who is perhaps older but more economically successful over a wife who is younger and less able to provide financial stability. According to the evidence, a woman who is better educated and in a higher occupational class than her husband has a 45 percent better chance of being married to a man more than five years her junior than does the average woman.

FINAL WORDS

We started this chapter talking about the *Newsweek* article that warned that women who spent time in school when they should have been looking for a man now had next to no chance of ever finding a husband. I have wondered over the years how many women gave up hope at that point and just didn't bother looking for love; sure, 68 percent of women who were single and age 40 in the year the article was written eventually did marry, but was there another 5 or 10 percent who would have married had they not been discouraged? Or rushed into bad marriages for fear of being left on the shelf? Or underinvested in their education for fear that the cost of a college degree was the lost opportunity to have a family?

As an economist, I know that the numbers do not look good for older women. When we add the assumption that older men will date only significantly younger women, I am not surprised that many older women believe they are destined for lives of lonely social exile. But just as the *Newsweek* predictions gave educated women a false sense that they would never marry, these statistics that report the skewed ratio of men to women in the seniors market give older women a false sense that they have no market power. And perhaps, just as dangerously, give older men exactly the same impression.

Personally, I keep a postcard-size picture of the *Newsweek* cover pinned above my desk as a constant reminder of the power of statistical evidence to distort public perceptions in a way that is potentially damaging to people's lives.

Economic markets only function properly if all the players have all the information. If men overstate their market power, then some are bound to be disappointed in the long run. This probably isn't an issue for men who are both wealthy and healthy; those types of men will always be in demand on a market where women (like my mother's friend whom I mentioned previously) are apprehensive about dating men who may end up being a physical or financial burden. But wealthy and healthy men represent only a small fraction of men available on the later-in-life market.

Let me give you an example of how this perception of market power by men can prevent the market from clearing properly. I have a friend who is in her mid-70s and is single and searching online for a relationship. She is, on every dimension, a catch—she has a good income, multiple recreational homes, she is healthy, very attractive, and knows how to have a good time. She told me recently that she had responded to an expression of interest she had received from a man through an online dating site with a standard "Hello, it's nice to meet you" message. His response to her simple note was to send an angry diatribe in which he rebuked her for her lack of effort and informed her she should have considered herself lucky that he had messaged her at all. (Incidentally, it later turned out that he was, in fact, ten years older than he had claimed to be in his profile, making him ten years older than her.)

In this case, two people continue to be single because one mistakenly believes that he holds all the market power and the other, who mistakenly believes that she holds none of the market power, would rather stay single than lower their relationship standards.

I want to finish off with a little piece of evidence that I think speaks to the difference between what men and women get from their relationships later in life. In a study undertaken on sexual behavior of people over the age of 50, researchers found that the last time they had sex, men found the experience more pleasurable if their partner was a man or woman with whom they were having a committed relationship; 91 percent of men who had sex with a relationship partner had an orgasm compared with only 80 percent of men who had sex with a friend or casual acquaintance.

Women, on the other hand, had a far more pleasurable sexual experience if their partner the last time they had sex was a man or woman with whom they were not having a committed relationship; 58 percent of women who had sex with a relationship partner had an orgasm, compared with 80 percent of women who had sex with a friend or casual acquaintance.

This may not look like economic evidence to you, but it is—the markets for sex and love are far more complex than simple supply and demand.

FINAL THOUGHTS

Economics, as you probably already know, has two fields of general interest: microeconomics and macroeconomics. Microeconomics seeks to understand the behavior of individuals, and so an economic appreciation of the markets for sex and love, essentially, leads us to apply theories that have been developed by microeconomists.

Having said that, as we have worked our way through the various markets for sex and love, I have been struck by the profound influence that macroeconomic variables have had on the players in these markets. Macroeconomics seeks to understand the behavior of everyone in the economy, collectively, using variables like education, technology, national income (gross domestic product), unemployment, income inequality, consumption, and saving as part of the analysis. Whether we realize it or not, each one these variables has been influencing the way we approach our own love lives.

Let me give you a few examples.

We talked about how the ever-increasing importance of education in employment has helped shaped social norms around premarital sex in the twentieth century. Higher education rates of women are increasing promiscuity on college campuses and encouraging educated women to marry less-educated men. We saw that the expansion of Internet technology has contributed to the formation of couples who are more similar in terms of education and income than they were in the past and is improving the quality of marriages in a way that reduces divorce. Industrialization has played an important role in how we structure our marriages, and those same influences have made it easier for those of us living in industrialized nations to accept same-sex marriage. We learned that married partners are finding new ways to make household decisions as women's earning abilities are becoming comparable to men's. The growing divide in incomes between the rich and poor is not only making divorce rates higher than they might have been otherwise but also encouraging high school students from low-income families to engage in riskier sexual behaviors.

It seems to me that if we want to predict where we are going as a society in terms of sex and marriage, we cannot ignore the effect that these constantly evolving macroeconomic conditions are having on very personal decisions.

If I were to predict two trends that I think will be among the most important when trying to envisage intimate relationships in the future, I would choose technological change and the growing educational divide between men and women. Both have had significant impact over the past twenty years, and there is no reason to believe that they won't continue to have a bearing on these markets in the future.

And so, while acknowledging that economists have poor track records when it comes to making predictions, I would like to conclude with some of my thoughts on how these markets might change as we go forward.

TECHNOLOGICAL INNOVATIONS

As we have already seen, improvements in birth control technology in the middle of the twentieth century significantly decreased the risks associated with premarital sex. That change in expected costs, made possible by new technologies, helped to bring down social barriers that had been discouraging men and women from having casual sexual relationships. The result has been higher rates of promiscuity, increases in both unintended pregnancies and sexually transmitted diseases, and an increase in the average age at which people marry.

So, we already know that new technologies can have a profound effect on sexual decision making.

Two new technologies that are on the very near horizon are unlikely to have such a large effect, but, nonetheless, I believe that STD testing technology and male birth control technology will change the markets for casual sex.

Let's start with an example of STD testing technology.

British firms are sinking millions into a new technology that will enable people to test themselves for STDs using a chip purchased for less than $2 and their mobile phone. They argue that the technology could help reduce the high STD rates in the young adult population. But just as improvements in birth control technology have increased births outside of marriage, so might improvements in STD testing technology increase STD rates.

This is how investors envisage this product being used: A young man becomes concerned that he has an STD but is nervous about going to a clinic to be tested. So instead, he buys a chip that he will either pee or spit on and then insert into his mobile phone. In a matter of moments, the nanotechnology in his phone will let him know if he has an STD. If infected, he will go immediately to a clinic (yes, the same clinic he was too nervous to go to just moments before) to receive treatment for the infection. He will then choose to use safe sexual practices until he is certain the infection is gone, presumably buying another chip to determine at what point he can return to using unsafe sexual practices.

Before you know it, the nation's STD rate has been cut in half—at least, that is the prediction made by those who are investing in this new technology.

Here is how I envisage this product being used. A young woman has met someone in a nightclub with whom she would like to have unprotected sex. She buys the chip at a vending machine in the club (which is exactly where investors intend to sell them) and administers a self-test in the bathroom.

At this point one of two things happens.

The first possible outcome is that the device tells her that she is not infected with either of the two diseases the phone can identify (chlamydia or gonorrhea). She then uses this information to negotiate unprotected sex with her new partner. In fact, this is the real commercial value of the technology—to make it easier to negotiate for sex without a condom. That has to be true since the transmission of both these diseases can be effectively prevented by proper condom use.

The second possible outcome is that the device tells her that she does have an STD—late at night, in a nightclub bathroom, under the influence of alcohol—while a willing member of the opposite sex is waiting keenly outside the door clutching his/her negative test results. This isn't really an economic issue, but to me this seems like a terrible setting in which to discover an STD infection.

If this technology encourages more young people to engage in unsafe sexual practices, then—even when used properly 100 percent of the time—the impact of this innovation will be higher rates of infection from the diseases the phone does not detect (for example, syphilis and HIV) and higher rates of accidental pregnancy. If not used properly, it could actually increase chlamydia and gonorrhea infections as well.

In chapter 1, I predicted that access to male birth control technology (MBC) would erode women's ability to negotiate condom usage and lead to a higher increase in STD rates. While I don't think that MBC will increase promiscuity the way that female oral contraceptives did in the 1960s and '70s (that horse has already left the stable, so to speak), there is one market in which people will likely change their behavior as a result of access to MBC technology: the teen sex market.

This is best explained in a way that anyone who can imagine having a teenage daughter understands.

Imagine your teenage daughter has a boyfriend who has been pressuring her to have sex with him for some time. She is not ready to take that step, however, and so far has been able to stall his attempts to take their relationship further by reminding him that an accidental pregnancy will make life difficult for both of them. One night he tells her that he has had treatment that will make him 100 percent sterile for at least the next six months.

What is her bargaining position now?

Making male birth control available to teenage men has the potential to decrease the age at which teens have their first sexual experience. I have said that there is no evidence that early virginity loss, without pregnancy, is harmful in a measurable way. However, having sex earlier is strongly correlated with having more sexual "events" in high school. If every additional sexual event brings with it an increased risk of infection and pregnancy, then MBC has the potential to increase both STD rates and accidental pregnancy in a population that is already at risk, even if condom use does not change.

Of course, that assumption, that condom use will not change, depends on the willingness of teenage men to wear condoms even when they know there is almost no chance of pregnancy. I'll let you make your own approximation of the percentage of young men who will make that decision.

I am not advocating against these technologies, in any way. I just believe that before we embrace new technologies that promise to reduce either STD or accidental pregnancy rates, we need to recognize that, when new technologies become available, people change their behavior. If that behavioral response works against the primary goal of the new technologies, then they can't begin to solve the problems they were designed to address.

If you doubt me, just look at how much pregnancy outside of marriage has increased in the decades following the availability of safe contraceptives.

▰▰▰ THE GROWING EDUCATIONAL DIVIDE
BETWEEN MEN AND WOMEN

As you are already aware, female students started to outnumber male students on college campuses at the end of the 1980s. This trend toward higher university enrollment of women, at all levels of education, has shown no signs of diminishing in the near future.

Since we have already talked about the role this gender imbalance has had on sexual behavior on college campuses—increasing promiscuity and decreasing traditional dating—I thought we might talk about how this imbalance will affect a different group of women: those who have no education beyond high school.

Most women and men postpone marriage and family until they have completed their education and so, on average, less-educated people marry earlier than do more-educated people. With more women than men enrolled in university, women who complete their education at the end of high school have an initial advantage on the marriage market. This is not only because they have access to the much larger pool of less-educated men, but also because the gender imbalance on the not-in-college market hands market power to women and, in theory at least, should increase the level of traditional dating on that market.

In the long run, however, less-educated women are significantly more likely to divorce and, more important, less likely to remarry if their first marriage ends. That says that by the time university-educated women enter the marriage market, their market consists of both educated men and those less educated who are unmarried either because they remained single or are already divorced. And, as we have seen, educated women are not limiting their search to men who are older.

With the number of educated women marrying younger, less-educated men on the rise, young women who did not go to college are now competing on the same marriage market as older, better-educated women.

If it is true that, in this economy, families care more about having well-educated children than they care about having many children and that educated mothers tend to produce better-educated children, then the value on the marriage market of less-educated women will fall even further. This is because educated men will change their preference away from having younger, more-fertile wives to having educated, slightly more-mature wives.

Women outnumbering men in higher education programs will make it increasingly difficult for less-educated women to compete on the marriage market and force them to either choose between setting a reservation value for a mate at a low level (i.e., entering a low-quality marriage) or remaining single. With the marriage rates of these women already in decline, it seems that many are remaining single rather that entering less-than-satisfying marriages—even if that means they are raising children on their own.

As we have seen, women who have little reason to believe that they will eventually marry are more likely to engage in riskier sexual behavior. This response to poor marriage prospects explains, in part, the high teen pregnancy and STD rates among economically marginalized women.

None of this really is news, but rather it is a lead-up to a prediction I would like to make as to how social norms will evolve in the future as an indirect result of the growing educational divide.

The very recent increase in the willingness of well-educated women to marry men who are less educated, younger, and/or have lower incomes than themselves is encouraging social norms to rapidly evolve along the same lines that social norms changed during the sexual revolution. This change in social norms, which has resulted directly from the changes in university enrollment, has the potential to revolutionize male/female relationships and will challenge traditional societal views of masculinity and femininity.

But while educated women are becoming liberated to marry whomever they please, those same forces will essentially disenfranchise less-educated women from the marriage market and, potentially, push more children into poverty.

One of the solutions is, of course, to allow wealthy men to take more than one wife—that is, institutionalize polygamy.

I have argued that male income inequality encourages polygamy while female educational inequality encourages monogamy, so this suggestion that polygamy is the solution to growing female educational inequality is counterintuitive. But the claim that female inequality encourages monogamy depends on the assumption that educated women are a relatively scarce resource, which is no longer true. That suggests that, over time, having multiple educated wives will become "affordable" by wealthy men.

Educating women in underindustrialized nations should discourage polygamy, but educating women at much higher rates than men just might encourage a movement in support of institutionalization of polygamy in industrialized nations.

One final implication of this story is that the growing educational divide will contribute to the growing divide in household incomes of the rich and the poor. This is because while women may be better educated, men tend to be better paid than women at higher levels of education. As a result, households in which the wife is better educated than her husband will generally have a significantly higher income than households in which the wife is less educated than her husband because the former household will have two high-income earners.

As more and more households are of the first variety—those in which the wife is better educated than her husband—the already wide gap between the rich and the poor households will widen even further.

▰▰▰ FINAL, FINAL WORDS

I have argued that almost every option, every decision, and every outcome in matters of sex and love is better understood by thinking within an economic framework. Whether or not you have been convinced of that, I hope that the stories that I have told here—fictional, empirical, and theoretical—have persuaded you that we are all, throughout our lives, playing on our own markets for sex and love. When all is said and done, though, I hope that when your market clears, you have found a buyer who greatly exceeds your reservation value for a mate. After all, I'm nothing if not a romantic at heart.

Since we have been talking about macroeconomic variables, I thought I'd conclude with an idea that was suggested to me by a group of enthusiastic students in my Economics of Sex and Love class. This idea is not about how macroeconomic variables can influence sexual behavior but rather how sexual behavior can help us better understand macroeconomic variables.

You may have heard of the Big Mac Index that is produced annually by *The Economist* magazine. The point of that index is to make exchange rate theory more palatable to readers by giving a real-world example of how well *purchasing power parity*—the theory that exchange rates adjust to make the level of goods and services that can be purchased with a unit of currency equal between countries—holds around the world. *The Economist* does this by comparing the price of a uniform, tradable good—a Big Mac—in about 120 different countries. The idea is that by converting the foreign price of a Big Mac into U.S. dollars, we should be able to determine if a country's currency is either over- or undervalued relative to the U.S. dollar.

Okay, so here is the big idea: the Blow Job Index.

Blow jobs are, I assume, a fairly uniform service, and they have to be at least as tradable as a Big Mac. After all, I am certain that sex workers cross borders looking for higher wages more frequently than do McDonald's workers. And, while tourists may eat at McDonald's when visiting a foreign country, they don't exactly flock to the countries where they can find the cheapest Big Mac; sex tourists vastly outnumber Big Mac tourists. These two factors, one supply and the other demand, should make the price of a blow job at least as internationally competitive as the price of a Big Mac.

I have no evidence as of yet, but I think that if we created this index, we would find that the prices charged for this uniform service do not converge between countries. There may be only one input in the production of a blow job, the sex worker, but numerous other factors contribute to how expensive a blow job is in one country relative to another.

For example, social norms around casual sex should influence the market price of a blow job, so we would need to correct for prices in cities where casual sex is freely available. Marriage institutions also play a role, so we would need to correct for prices in a polygamous societies. And when women outnumber men. And when foreign wives can be easily imported. And when Internet technology reduces blow-job search costs.

You get the idea. Many of the economic conditions that influence the informal markets for sex and love we have been discussing all along also influence another market for sex—one in which value is more easily measured—the sex trades.

Perhaps this is a discussion we can have another day.

BIBLIOGRAPHY

Abma, Joyce C., Gladys M. Martinez, and Casey E. Copen. "Teenagers in the United States: Sexual Activity, Contraceptive Use, and Childbearing, National Survey of Family Growth 2006–2008." *Vital and Health Statistics* 23, no. 30 (2010): 1–47.

Adshade, Marina E., and Brooks A. Kaiser. "The Origins of the Institutions of Marriage." Queen's University, Department of Economics, Working Paper no. 1180, 2012.

Alan Guttmacher Institute. "U.S. Teenage Pregnancies, Births and Abortions: National and State Trends and Trends by Race and Ethnicity." www.guttmacher.org, (January 2010).

Alterovitz, Sheyna Sears-Roberts, and Gerald A. Mendelsohn. "Partner Preferences across the Life Span: Online Dating by Older Adults." *Psychology and Aging* 24, no. 2 (2009): 513.

Alvergne, Alexandra, and Virpi Lummaa. "Does the Contraceptive Pill Alter Mate Choice in Humans?" *Trends in Ecology & Evolution* 25, no. 3 (2010): 171–179.

American Society of Plastic Surgeons. "Plastic Surgery Rebounds Along with Recovering Economy." www.plasticsurgery.org, 2011.

Anik, Lalin, and Michael I. Norton. "The Happiness of Matchmaking." Unpublished manuscript, 2011.

Arcidiacono, Peter, Ahmed Khwaja, and Lijing Ouyang. "Habit Persistence and Teen Sex: Could Increased Access to Contraception Have Unintended Consequences for Teen Pregnancies?" Unpublished manuscript, 2007.

Arcidiacono, Peter, Andrew W. Beauchamp, and Marjorie B. McElroy. "Terms of Endearment: An Equilibrium Model of Sex and Matching." National Bureau of Economic Research Working Paper no. 16517, 2010.

Ariely, Dan, and George Loewenstein. "The Heat of the Moment: The Effect of Sexual Arousal on Sexual Decision Making." *Journal of Behavioral Decision Making* 19, no. 2 (2006): 87–98.

Banerjee, Abhijit, Esther Duflo, Maitreesh Ghatak, and Jeanne Lafortune. "Marry for What? Caste and Mate Selection in Modern India." National Bureau of Economic Research Working Paper no. 14958, 2009.

Baumeister, Roy F., and Juan P. Mendoza. "Cultural Variations in the Sexual Marketplace: Gender Equality Correlates with More Sexual Activity." *The Journal of Social Psychology* 151, no. 3 (2011): 350–360.

Baunach, Dawn Michelle. "Decomposing Trends in Attitudes Toward Gay Marriage, 1988–2006." *Social Science Quarterly*, 92, no. 2 (2011): 346–363.

Beach, Frank A., and Lisbeth Jordan. "Sexual Exhaustion and Recovery in the Male Rat." *Quarterly Journal of Experimental Psychology* 8, no. 3 (1956): 121–133.

Becker, Gary S. *A Treatise on the Family.* Cambridge, MA: Harvard University Press, 1991.

Belot, Michèle, and Jan Fidrmuc. "Anthropometry of Love: Height and Gender Asymmetries in Interethnic Marriages." *Economics & Human Biology* 8, no. 3 (2010): 361–372.

Bertocchi, Graziella, Marianna Brunetti, and Costanza Torricelli. "Marriage and Other Risky Assets: A Portfolio Approach." *Journal of Banking & Finance* 35, no. 11 (2011): 2902–2915.

Blanchflower, David G., and Andrew J. Oswald. "Money, Sex, and Happiness: An Empirical Study." *Scandinavian Journal of Economics* 106, no. 3 (2004): 393–415.

Brooks, Taggert J. "In Da Club: An Econometric Analysis of Strip Club Patrons." Unpublished manuscript, 2007.

Brown, Heather. "Marriage, BMI and Wages: A Double Selection Approach." *Scottish Journal of Political Economy* 58, no. 3 (2011): 347–377.

Bruze, Gustaf. "Marriage Choices of Movie Stars: Does Spouse's Education Matter?" *Journal of Human Capital* 5, no. 1 (2011): 1–28.

Buss, David M. *The Dangerous Passion: Why Jealousy Is as Necessary as Love and Sex.* New York: The Free Press, 2000.

Cameron, Samuel. "The Economic Model of Divorce: The Neglected Role of Search and Specific Capital Formation." *Journal of Socio-economics* 32, no. 3 (2003): 303–316.

———. "The Economics of Partner Out Trading in Sexual Markets." *Journal of Bioeconomics* 4, no. 3 (2002): 195–222.

Card, David, and Laura Giuliano. "Peer Effects and Multiple Equilibria in the Risky Behavior of Friends." National Bureau of Economic Research Working Paper no. 17088, 2011.

Center for Sexual Health Promotion. *National Survey of Sexual Health and Behavior (NSSHB)*, www.nationalsexstudy.indiana.edu, 2012.

Central Intelligence Agency. *CIA World Factbook*, www.cia.gov/library/publications/the-world-factbook. Washington: Central Intelligence Agency, 2012.

Charles, Kerwin K., Erik Hurst, and Alexandra Killewald. "Marital Sorting and Parental Wealth." National Bureau of Economic Research Working Paper no. 16748, 2011.

Charles, Kerwin K., and Ming Ching Luoh. "Male Incarceration, the Marriage Market, and Female Outcomes." *The Review of Economics and Statistics* 92, no. 3 (2010): 614–627.

Chesson, Harrell, Paul Harrison, and William Kassler. "Sex under the Influence: The Effect of Alcohol Policy on Sexually Transmitted Disease Rates in the United States." *Journal of Law and Economics* 43, no. 1 (2000): 215–238.

Chu, Simon, Danielle Farr, John E. Lycett, and Luna Muñoz. "Interpersonal Trust and Market Value Moderates the Bias in Women's Preferences Away from Attractive High-Status Men." *Personality and Individual Differences* 51, no. 2 (2011): 143–147.

Coleman, Martin D. "Sunk Cost and Commitment to Dates Arranged Online." *Current Psychology* 28, no. 1 (2009): 45–54.

Coles, Martin G., and Marco Francesconi. "On the Emergence of Toyboys: The Timing of Marriage with Aging and Uncertain Careers." *International Economic Review* 52, no. 3 (2011): 825–853.

Cowan, Benjamin W. "Forward-Thinking Teens: The Effects of College Costs on Adolescent Risky Behavior." *Economics of Education Review* 23 (2011): 133–141.

Cox, Donald. "The Evolutionary Biology and Economics of Sexual Behavior and Infidelity." Unpublished manuscript, 2009.

Daneshvary, Nasser, Jeffrey Waddoups, and Bradley S. Wimmer. "Previous Marriage and the Lesbian Wage Premium." *Industrial Relations: A Journal of Economy and Society* 48, no. 3 (2009): 432–453.

DeSimone, Jeffrey S. "Binge Drinking and Risky Sex among College Students." National Bureau of Economic Research Working Paper no. 15953, 2010.

Dessy, Sylvain, and Habiba Djebbari. "High-Powered Careers and Marriage: Can Women Have It All?" *The B.E. Journal of Economic Analysis & Policy* 10, no. 1 (2010).

D'Orlando, Fabio. "Swinger Economics." *Journal of Socio-economics* 39, no. 2 (2010): 295–305.

Dupas, Pascaline. "Do Teenagers Respond to HIV Risk Information? Evidence from a Field Experiment in Kenya." National Bureau of Economic Research Working Paper no. 14707, 2009.

Edlund, Lena. "Sex and the City." *The Scandinavian Journal of Economics* 107, no. 1 (2005): 25–44.

Edlund, Lena, and Evelyn Korn. "A Theory of Prostitution." *Journal of Political Economy* 110, no. 1 (2002): 181–214.

Elmslie, Bruce, and Edinaldo Tebaldi. "So, What Did You Do Last Night? The Economics of Infidelity." *Kyklos* 61, no. 3 (2008): 391–410.

Farnham, Martin, Lucie Schmidt, and Purvi Sevak. "House Prices and Marital Stability." *American Economic Review* 101, no. 3 (2011): 615–619.

Fernández-Villaverde, Jesús, Jeremy Greenwood, and Nezih Guner. "From Shame to Game in One Hundred Years: An Economic Model of the Rise in Premarital Sex and Its De-stigmatization." National Bureau of Economic Research Working Paper no. 15677, 2010.

Fiore, Andrew, Lindsay Shaw Taylor, Gerald Mendelsohn, and Marti Hearst. "Assessing Attractiveness in Online Dating Profiles." Paper presented at Proceeding of the Twenty-Sixth Annual SIGCHI Conference on Human Factors in Computing Systems, 2008.

Fiore, Andrew, Lindsay Shaw Taylor, X. Zhong, Gerald Mendelsohn, and Coye Cheshire. "Whom We (Say We) Want: Stated and Actual Preferences in Online Dating." Poster presented at the Eleventh Annual Meeting of the Society for Personality and Social Psychology, Las Vegas, NV, 2010.

Fisman, Raymond, Sheena S. Iyengar, Emir Kamenica, and Itamar Simonson. "Racial Preferences in Dating." *Review of Economic Studies* 75, no. 1 (2008): 117–132.

Francis, Andrew M., and Hugo M. Mialon. "Tolerance and HIV." *Journal of Health Economics* 29, no. 2 (2010): 250–267.

Fry, Richard, and D'Vera Cohn. "New Economics of Marriage: The Rise of Wives." *Pew Research Center Publications*, 2010.

———. "Women, Men, and the New Economics of Marriage." *Pew Research Center Publications*, 2010.

Furtado, Delia, and Nikolaos Theodoropoulos. "Interethnic Marriage: A Choice between Ethnic and Educational Similarities." *Journal of Population Economics* 24, no. 4 (2011): 1257–1279.

Gooding, Gretchen E., and Rose M. Kreider. "Women's Marital Naming Choices in a Nationally Representative Sample." *Journal of Family Issues* 31, no. 5 (2010): 681–701.

Gould, Eric D., Omer Moav, and Avi Simhon. "The Mystery of Monogamy." *American Economic Review* 98, no. 1 (2008): 333–357.

Greenwood, Jeremy, Ananth Seshadri, and Mehmet Yorukoglu. "Engines of Liberation." *Review of Economic Studies* 72, no. 1 (2005): 109–133.

Greenwood, Jeremy, and Nezih Guner. "Social Change: The Sexual Revolution." *International Economic Review* 51, no. 4 (2010): 893–923.

Hankins, Scott, and Mark Hoekstra. "Lucky in Life, Unlucky in Love? The Effect of Random Income Shocks on Marriage and Divorce." *Journal of Human Resources* 46, no. 2 (2011): 403–426.

Haselton, Martie G., and Geoffrey F. Miller. "Women's Fertility across the Cycle Increases the Short-Term Attractiveness of Creative Intelligence." *Human Nature* 17, no. 1 (2006): 50–73.

Hassan, Mohamed A. M., and Stephen R. Killick. "Effect of Male Age on Fertility: Evidence for the Decline in Male Fertility with Increasing Age." *Fertility & Sterility* 79 (2003): 1520–1527.

Hazan, Moshe, and Hosny Zoabi. "Do Highly Educated Women Choose Smaller Families?" Centre for Economic Policy Research Discussion Paper no. 8590, 2011.

Heckman, James J., and Paul A. LaFontaine. "The American High School Graduation Rate: Trends and Levels. " National Bureau of Economic Research Working Paper no. 13670, 2007.

Hellerstein, Judith K., and Melinda S. Morrill. "Booms, Busts, and Divorce." *The B.E. Journal of Economic Analysis & Policy* 11, no. 1 (2011): 54.

Herpin, Nicolas. "Love, Careers, and Heights in France, 2001." *Economics & Human Biology* 3, no. 3 (2005): 420–449.

Hersch, Joni. "Compensating Differentials for Sexual Harassment." *American Economic Review* 101, no. 3 (2011): 630–634.

Hitsch, Günter J., Ali Hortaçsu, and Dan Ariely. "Matching and Sorting in Online Dating." *American Economic Review* 100, no. 1(2010): 130–163.

———. "What Makes You Click? Mate Preferences in Online Dating." *Quantitative Marketing and Economics* 8, no. 4 (2010): 393–427.

Hogan, Bernie, Nai Li, and William H. Dutton. "A Global Shift in the Social Relationships of Networked Individuals: Meeting and Dating Online Comes of Age." *Feedback* 287 (2011): 211.

Janssens, Kim, Mario Pandelaere, Bram Van den Bergh, Kobe Millet, Inge Lens, and Keith Roe. "Can Buy Me Love: Mate Attraction Goals Lead to Perceptual Readiness for Status Products." *Journal of Experimental Social Psychology* 47, no. 1 (2011): 254–258.

Kanazawa, Satoshi, and Mary C. Still. 1999. "Why Monogamy?" *Social Forces* 78 (1999): 25–50.

———. "The Emergence of Marriage Norms: An Evolutionary Psychological Perspective." In *Social Norms*, ed. Michael Hechter and Karl-Dieter Opp, 274–304: New York: Russell Sage Foundation, 2001.

Kearney, Melissa Schettini, and Phillip B. Levine. "Early Non-marital Childbearing and the 'Culture of Despair.'" National Bureau of Economic Research Working Paper no. 17157, 2011.

Kendall, Todd D. "Pornography, Rape, and the Internet." Paper presented at Law and Economics Seminar Fall Term, 2006.

———. "The Relationship between Internet Access and Divorce Rate." *Journal of Family and Economic Issues* 32, no. 3 (2011): 449–460.

Kerkhof, Peter, Catrin Finkenauer, and Linda D. Muusses. "Relational Consequences of Compulsive Internet Use: A Longitudinal Study among Newlyweds." *Human Communication Research* 37, no. 2 (2011): 147–173.

Kim, Jane. "Trafficked: Domestic Violence, Exploitation in Marriage, and the Foreign-Bride Industry." *Virginia Journal of International Law* 51, no. 2 (2010): 443–506.

Kippen, Rebecca, Bruce Chapman, and Peng Yu. "What's Love Got to Do with It? Homogamy and Dyadic Approaches to Understanding Marital Instability." Paper presented at the Biennial HILDA Survey Research Conference, 2009.

Klofstad, Casey A., Rose McDermott, and Peter K. Hatemi. "Do Bedroom Eyes Wear Political Glasses? The Role of Politics in Human Mate Attraction." *Evolution and Human Behavior* 33. no. 2 (2012): 100–108.

Kopp, Marie E. *Birth Control in Practice: Analysis of Ten Thousand Case Histories of the Birth Control Clinical Research Bureau.* New York: Arno Press, 1972.

Kreider, Rose M. "Increase in Opposite-Sex Cohabiting Couples from 2009 to 2010." *Annual Social and Economic Supplement (ASEC) to the Current Population Survey (CPS)*, 2010.

Lagerlöf, Nils-Petter. "Pacifying Monogamy." *Journal of Economic Growth* 15, no. 3 (2010): 235–262.

Lee, Leonard, George Loewenstein, Dan Ariely, James Hong, and Jim Young. "If I'm Not Hot, Are You Hot or Not?" *Psychological Science* 19, no. 7 (2008): 669–677.

Lee, Soohyung, Muriel Niederle, Hye-Rim Kim, and Woo-Keum Kim. "Propose with a Rose? Signaling in Internet Dating Markets." National Bureau of Economic Research Working Paper no. 17340, 2011.

Levine, Adam, Robert Frank, and Oege Dijk. "Expenditure Cascades." Unpublished manuscript, 2010.

Logan, John A., Peter D. Hoff, and Michael A. Newton. "Two-Sided Estimation of Mate Preferences for Similarities in Age, Education, and Religion." *Journal of the American Statistical Association* 103, no. 482 (2008): 559–569.

Luci, Angela, and Olivier Thévenon. "La Fécondité Remonte dans les Pays de l'OCDE: Est-ce dû au Progrès Économique?" *Bulletin Mensuel d'Information de l'Institut National d'Études Démographiques* 481 (2011).

Mather, Mark, and Diana Lavery. "In U.S., Proportion Married at Lowest Recorded Levels." Washington: Population Reference Bureau, 2010.

McIntosh, William D., Lawrence Locker, Katherine Briley, Rebecca Ryan, and Alison J. Scott. "What Do Older Adults Seek in Their Potential Romantic Partners? Evidence from Online Personal Ads." *The International Journal of Aging and Human Development* 72, no. 1 (2011): 67–82.

Mechoulan, Stéphane. "The External Effects of Black-Male Incarceration on Black Females." *Journal of Labor Economics* 29, no. 1 (2011): 1–35.

Mialon, Hugo M. "The Economics of Faking Ecstasy." *Economic Inquiry* 50, no. 1 (2012): 277–285.

Miller, Bonnie B., David N. Cox, and Elizabeth M. Saewyc. "Age of Sexual Consent Law in Canada: Population-Based Evidence for Law and Policy." *The Canadian Journal of Human Sexuality* 19, no. 3 (2010).

Negrusa, Brighita, and Sonia Oreffice. "Sexual Orientation and Household Financial Decisions: Evidence from Couples in the United States." *Review of Economics of the Household* 9, no. 4 (2011): 445–463.

Noordewier, Marret K., Femke van Horen, Kirsten I. Ruys, and Diederik A. Stapel. "What's in a Name? 361.708 Euros: The Effects of Marital Name Change." *Basic and Applied Social Psychology* 32, no. 1 (2010): 17–25.

Oreffice, Sonia. "Sexual Orientation and Household Decision Making: Same-Sex Couples' Balance of Power and Labor Supply Choices." *Labour Economics* 18, no. 2 (2011): 145–158.

Oreopoulos, Philip, and Kjell G. Salvanes. "Priceless: The Nonpecuniary Benefits of Schooling." *Journal of Economic Perspectives* 25, no. 1 (2011): 159–184.

Padian, Nancy S., Stephen C. Shiboski, Sarah O. Glass, and Eric Vittinghoff. "Heterosexual Transmission of Human Immunodeficiency Virus (HIV) in Northern California: Results from a Ten-Year Study." *American Journal of Epidemiology* 146, no. 4 (1997): 350–357.

Pillsworth, Elizabeth G., and Martie G. Haselton. "Male Sexual Attractiveness Predicts Differential Ovulatory Shifts in Female Extra-Pair Attraction and Male Mate Retention." *Evolution and Human Behavior* 27, no. 4 (2006): 247–258.

Previti, Denise, and Paul R. Amato. "Is Infidelity a Cause or a Consequence of Poor Marital Quality?" *Journal of Social and Personal Relationships* 21, no. 2 (2004): 217–230.

Puts, David A., Lisa L. M. Welling, Robert P. Burriss, and Khytam Dawood. "Men's Masculinity and Attractiveness Predict Their Female Partners' Reported Orgasm Frequency and Timing." *Evolution and Human Behavior*, 33, no. 1 (2011): 1–9.

Regnerus, Mark, and Jeremy Uecker. *Premarital Sex in America: How Young Americans Meet, Mate, and Think about Marrying.* Oxford: Oxford University Press, 2011.

Rotermann, Michelle "Trends in Teen Sexual Behaviour and Condom Use." *Health Reports* 19, no. 3 (2008): 53–58.

Sabia, Joseph J., and Daniel I. Rees. "Boys Will Be Boys: Are There Gender Differences in the Effect of Sexual Abstinence on Schooling?" *Health Economics* 20, no. 3 (2011): 287–305.

Santelli, John S., and Andrea J. Melnikas. "Teen Fertility in Transition: Recent and Historic Trends in the United States." *Annual Review of Public Health* 31 (2010): 371–383.

Schick, Vanessa, Debra Herbenick, Michael Reece, Stephanie A. Sanders, Brian Dodge, Susan E. Middlestadt, and J. Dennis Fortenberry. "Sexual Behaviors, Condom Use, and Sexual Health of Americans over 50: Implications for Sexual Health Promotion for Older Adults." *Journal of Sexual Medicine* 7 (2010): 315–329.

Schilt, Kristen. "Just One of the Guys? How Transmen Make Gender Visible at Work." *Gender & Society* 20, no. 4 (2006): 465–490.

Schmitt, David P. "Sociosexuality from Argentina to Zimbabwe: A Forty-Eight-Nation Study of Sex, Culture, and Strategies of Human Mating." *Behavioral and Brain Sciences* 28, no. 2 (2005): 247–275.

Sen, Anindya, and May Luong. "Estimating the Impact of Beer Prices on the Incidence of Sexually Transmitted Diseases: Cross-Province and Time Series Evidence from Canada." *Contemporary Economic Policy* 26, no. 4 (2008): 505–517.

Sen, Anindya, Marcel Voia, and Frances Woolley. "The Effect of Hotness on Pay and Productivity." Carleton University, Dept. of Economics Working Paper no. 10–07, 2010.

Shaw, George Bernard. *Man and Superman; a Comedy and a Philosophy.* Cambridge, MA: The University Press, 1903.

Singh, Susheela, Gilda Sedgh, and Rubina Hussain. "Unintended Pregnancy: Worldwide Levels, Trends, and Outcomes." *Studies in Family Planning* 41, no. 4 (2010): 241–250.

Sinning, Mathias, and Shane M. Worner. "Inter-Ethnic Marriage and Partner Satisfaction." Ruhr Economic Working Paper no. 221, 2010.

Skopek, Jan, Florian Schulz, and Hans-Peter Blossfeld. 2011. "Who Contacts Whom? Educational Homophily in Online Mate Selection." *European Sociological Review* 27, no. 2 (2011): 180–195.

Stevenson, Betsey, and Justin Wolfers. "Marriage and Divorce: Changes and Their Driving Forces." National Bureau of Economic Research Working Paper no. 12944, 2007.

———. "Bargaining in the Shadow of the Law: Divorce Laws and Family Distress." *Quarterly Journal of Economics* 121, no. 1 (2006): 267–288.

Stoker, Janka I., Jennifer Jordan, Monique Pollmann, Joris Lammers, and Diederik A. Stapel. "Power Increases Infidelity among Men and Women." *Psychological Science* 22, no. 9 (2011): 1191–1197.

Taylor, Jacqueline Sánchez. "Dollars Are a Girl's Best Friend? Female Tourists' Sexual Behaviour in the Caribbean." *Sociology* 35, no. 3 (2001): 749–764.

Toma, Catalina L., and Jeffrey T. Hancock. "Looks and Lies: The Role of Physical Attractiveness in Online Dating Self-Presentation and Deception." *Communication Research* 37, no. 3 (2010): 335–351.

Uecker, Jeremy E., and Mark D. Regnerus. 2010. "Bare Market: Campus Sex Ratios, Romantic Relationships, and Sexual Behavior." *Sociological Quarterly* 51, no. 3 (2010): 408–435.

United Nations. *World Fertility Report 2009.* New York: United Nations Department of Economic and Social Affairs, Population Division, 2011.

Van den Bergh, Bram, Siegfried Dewitte, and Luk Warlop. "Bikinis Instigate Generalized Impatience in Intertemporal Choice." *Journal of Consumer Research* 35, no. 1 (2008): 85–97.

Vernon, Victoria. "Marriage: For Love, for Money . . . and for Time?" *Review of Economics of the Household* 8, no. 4 (2010): 433–457.

Vespa, Jonathan, and Matthew A. Painter. "Cohabitation History, Marriage, and Wealth Accumulation." *Demography* 48, no. 3 (2011): 983–1004.

Westling, Tatu. "Male Organ and Economic Growth: Does Size Matter?" Helsinki Center of Economic Research Discussion Paper no. 335, 2011.

INDEX